The
LIGHTHOUSE
ENCYCLOPEDIA

The
LIGHTHOUSE
ENCYCLOPEDIA

The Definitive Reference

SECOND EDITION

Ray Jones

Guilford, Connecticut

Project editors: David Legere and Meredith Dias
Design/layout: Lisa Reneson

Library of Congress Cataloging-in-Publication Data is available on file.

ISBN 978-0-7627-8670-1

Printed in the United States of America

10 9 8 7 6 5 4 3 2

For Allison, Abby, and all those who bring light to the world

CONTENTS

Shutterstock.com

Bodrum/Turgutreis Marina Lighthouse, Turkey
Ufuk Zivana/Shutterstock

ACKNOWLEDGMENTS

Years ago in my first lighthouse article, I quoted the great English poet John Donne, who reminds us that "No man is an island." It is evident to me now that no author is an island, since this book, which I would like to see as my own proudest achievement, has been brought to life in such large measure through the efforts of others. My sincere thanks to all those extraordinarily talented and dedicated people who lent a hand. Among them:

The Photographers

How does one thank his longest and best friend? Who knows, but I must attempt it for any number of reasons, not the least of which is that more than half the beautiful photographs in this book are his. Bruce Roberts has earned the right to be acknowledged as one of our era's most important photojournalists, and although he seldom displays them, he has a roomful of awards to prove it. His early work on the civil rights movement and poverty program was groundbreaking, his documentation of the emerging "New South," eye-opening. Today he is recognized as America's most prolific and accomplished photographer of lighthouses. The images he has offered us of beautiful and endangered light towers have convinced Americans that our maritime heritage must be saved. For me personally Bruce has been a mentor, frequent traveling companion, and—how else to say it—a brother. It may be that the photographs of Jean Guichard are influenced by the French impressionists. Years ago, as a mighty storm swept over the French coast, the young Monsieur Guichard hung precariously in a helicopter above La Jument Lighthouse snapping pictures. The haunting images he captured that

Munising Rear Range Light on the Michigan Upper Peninsula

Bruce Roberts

day of the awesome power of nature unleashed against the unyielding stone of a man-made structure helped make him one of the world's most celebrated photographers. Jean has given us a new way to see lighthouses and, perhaps, to understand ourselves. In *The Lighthouse Encyclopedia* Jean shares some of his more inspiring work with us. Have Bob and Sandra Shanklin, also known as "The Lighthouse People," photographed every lighthouse on the planet? No, but the fact that the question is asked suggests the enormous scope of their efforts. If you need a picture of a lighthouse no one else has ever heard of, let alone photographed, Bob and Sandra are the folks to see. They made indispensable contributions to *The Lighthouse Encyclopedia,* as did Henry Gonzales, who, like them, wields a camera largely for love of his subject. Henry provided a number of captivating images of lights along the coasts of Spain and Brittany. Egbert Koch, cofounder of the World Lighthouse Society, also helped out with pictures of European towers, including some truly amazing images of Cordouan. When it comes to a visual topic such as lighthouses, word pictures count for a lot, and for helping make my language vivid and real, I owe an enormous debt to educator, author, and my lifelong friend Grace McEntee.

The Preservationists

No one has worked harder and with greater effect to save lighthouses than Tim Harrison, editor of *The Lighthouse Digest.* Without Tim's support and encouragement, I would never have attempted

Tévennec Light in France
Copyright Jean Guichard

this daunting project. A notable quantity of the information and photography invested in *The Lighthouse Encyclopedia* came courtesy of Tim and the *Digest*. Marv Theut is one of those people you are eternally glad you've met. Marv founded the Great Lakes Lighthouse Festival in little Alpena, Michigan. Thanks to Marv I made more valuable contacts and received more inspiration at Alpena than anywhere else. Without the tireless efforts of Cheryl Sheldon-Roberts, the Cape Hatteras Lighthouse might never have been moved and might even today be lying in a tumbled heap on the sands of the Outer Banks. Author of several of her own books and publications, Cheryl was generous with insights and research materials that made my work possible. Incidentally, Cheryl is the spouse of another dear friend, Bruce Roberts, and I'm not embarrassed to say that I introduced them.

Lighthouse Folks

It would be wrong not to thank all those other hardworking lighthouse lovers and preservation activists who were not directly involved in this project but without whom there might have been little left for me to write about. One such person who comes to mind is Wayne Wheeler, founder of the United States Lighthouse Society. Another is Dick Moehl, longtime president of the Great Lakes Lighthouse Keepers Association. Still others are retired keepers or their children whose memories are helping us keep alive an age-old tradition. And finally, there is you. If you're reading this, that's a vote for saving the old lights. In fact, anyone who visits a lighthouse or makes a small contribution to its upkeep is a preservationist. If you're not one of us yet, then please join us.

Cape Lookout Light in North Carolina
Bruce Roberts

Hania Lighthouse; Crete, Greece.
axyse/Shutterstock

Egbert Koch

INTRODUCTION
A LIGHT ON THE HORIZON

Lighthouses call to us, not just from across the water but also from across time. Their primary purpose—to guide mariners—and their basic form—a structure with a light at the top—have changed little in more than 2,000 years. Another characteristic of lighthouses that has barely changed at all is their very powerful emotional appeal. Ancient light towers such as the Pharos in Egypt and the Colossus of Rhodes must have astounded everyone who saw them whether from land or sea. Over the centuries lighthouses have never lost their capacity to impress. The fact is, nearly everyone, whether child or adult, male or female, seaman or landlubber, is fascinated by these bold and romantic structures.

Radar and satellites now make pinpoint navigation possible in all weather and along any coastline, so lighthouses are no longer as important to mariners as they once were. However, even though their usefulness to navigation has declined, lighthouses are more popular today than ever before. In recent years they have been the subject of dozens of books, films, and video documentaries. While real light stations are used as settings for novels, movies, and daytime television dramas, photographs and sketches of light towers emblazon business cards, stationery, cereal boxes, and the mastheads of major newspapers. Lighthouses can be seen on road signs, automobile license plates, placemats, shower curtains, and the walls of churches and public buildings. Miniature granite lighthouses serve as

Point Sur Light in California
Bruce Roberts

tombstones, while neon light towers brighten the façades of Skid Row missions. Widely recognized as icons of our outward-reaching concern for others, lighthouses are a comforting, deeply human symbol.

Light towers also serve as symbols of strength. Generally recognized as the first true lighthouse, the mighty Pharos tower of ancient Alexandria was far more than a mere signpost for mariners. It proclaimed the city's wealth and power while announcing to one and all that Alexandria considered itself a light to the world. Today, the Statue of Liberty—which, interestingly enough, once served as lighthouse—performs a similar function not only for the city of New York but also for the entire United States.

Lighthouses also have served as sources of inspiration. While fires built atop ancient Sumerian ziggurats may have guided mariners, their primary purpose was religious. The flames reaching toward the sky were meant to carry sacred messages into the heavens. Worshippers in many Islamic countries have long been called to prayers by criers in tall minarets, a word derived from the Arabic word *minara,* which means "place of fire." This suggests that some early Arabic towers may have been lit, and it demonstrates a clear link between the construction of soaring towers and the human search for spiritual meaning.

The same link can be found in the West, where many of the earliest light towers were built or maintained by the clergy. A saintly monk named Dubhan is said to have established Ireland's first navigational beacon in the sixth century at Hook Head. During the Hundred Years War, Edward the Black Prince of England erected a light tower at Cordouan near Bordeaux, placing its beacon in the care of a local convent. As penitence for an act of theft, English nobleman Walter de Godeton built St. Catherine's Light, completing it in 1323. A priest was paid to tend the light and, of course, to pray for de Godeton's soul. The famous medieval church on St. Michael's Mount in Cornwall doubled as a lighthouse, displaying a spiritual light and a maritime beacon simultaneously.

Lighthouses continue to awe, inspire, and uplift us today. By reminding us of heroic deeds and of a rich worldwide maritime heritage, they guide our hearts, minds, and imaginations. They educate, entertain, and, increasingly nowadays, attract curious visitors. Perhaps that is why many local communities seem almost as eager to preserve old, abandoned lighthouses as they were to see them built in the first place.

If you are interested in lighthouses, plan to visit one of the many lighthouse monuments, museums, or bed-and-breakfast inns that now dot the coasts of the United States, Canada, the United Kingdom, France, and many other countries. Before you go or after you return, spend some pleasant hours with *The Lighthouse Encyclopedia.* This easy-to-use, thoroughly researched, and colorfully illustrated resource will answer most of your questions about navigational lights in general as well as about many individual lighthouses in America and throughout the world.

The Lighthouse Encyclopedia is organized into three sections to help you get the most out of the information it has to offer. Part I offers a concise look at the history of lighthouses. Here you'll learn about the Roman light tower built by the mad emperor Caligula, the wave-swept Eddystone lighthouse that took the lives of its builder and several keepers but saved the lives of countless mariners, the Boston Harbor lighthouse that was blown up by British regulars during America's Revolutionary War, the spindly legged, screw-pile lighthouses of the Chesapeake that were often crushed by winter ice, the mighty Cape Hatteras tower, which was moved in 1999 to save it from the sea, and more.

Part II is a detailed alphabetical reference guide to a host of lighthouse topics, ranging from acetylene lamps to George Worthylake, who was America's first lighthouse keeper; from the US Coast Guard to the venerable Trinity House, which administers English lighthouses; from the nineteenth-century inventor Augustin Fresnel to the famed Scottish lighthouse engineer Robert Stevenson—the grandfather of author Robert Louis Stevenson.

Also arranged alphabetically in Part Three are the more than 160 individual lighthouses described and colorfully pictured. This section of

The Lighthouse Encyclopedia offers a globe-trotting tour of major lighthouses in the United States, Canada, England, Scotland, Ireland, France, Spain, Greece, Norway, Australia, Argentina, South Africa, and several other countries. Here you'll learn how nations around the world have attempted to solve their own unique navigational problems and how they manage and maintain their lighthouses.

A considerable number of the lush color photographs in *The Lighthouse Encyclopedia* have been contributed by well-known photographers. Bruce Roberts, an award-winning photojournalist and author or coauthor of nearly two dozen beautifully illustrated lighthouse books, supplied more than 150 of the magnificent color pictures reproduced on these pages. Many other *Encyclopedia* photographs come courtesy of Jean Guichard, renowned not just in Europe but all over the world for his unforgettable images of French light towers caught in the grip of powerful gales.

We sincerely hope you enjoy *The Lighthouse Encyclopedia* and find it useful in your effort to learn more about lighthouses and maritime history. As you read, you may come to the conclusion that a knowledge and appreciation of these topics is indispensable to a well-rounded education. Learning about lighthouses may help you or your children learn about yourselves and what it means to explore the light, the dark, and the unknown.

LIGHTHOUSES
THROUGH HISTORY

Imagine a world in which there are no lighthouses and never have been any. Such a place would have few mariners or explorers, for the greater part of the joy in travel lies in the possibility of reaching home again. The ancients understood this even better than modern folk, and all their adventures, no matter how far-flung, were meant to be round-trips. That's why they built fires on hills overlooking the sea.

The earliest mariners sailed close to the shore, but as they grew bolder, they ventured far enough from land that they needed help finding their way back. Being lost at sea, especially in the dark, was then and remains today very simply a matter of life and death. Friends and loved ones called those ancient mariners home with beacons using the one light source available to them—fire. Since an elevated light can be seen from a much greater distance than one shining from sea level, they built their fires on prominent headlands.

No one knows for sure who first thought of using a tall structure as an artificial hill and placing a navigational light on top. As far back as 5,000 years ago, mariners in the Persian Gulf may have used the sacrificial fires burning on top of Sumerian ziggurats for guidance, but this is only speculation. We do know, however, that the ancient Greeks and Romans made extensive use of lighted towers for navigation.

Fires of the Pharos

The first true light tower known to history was the Pharos, an immense marble and sandstone edifice built about 280 BC on an island near the harbor entrance of the Greco-Egyptian city of Alexandria. Located on the flat Nile Delta, this bustling port had no bluffs or other lofty natural features to serve as seamarks for mariners, so the city built one—the Pharos. As with so many Egyptian structures, the scale of the tower was truly colossal. Likely, its 360-foot-wide base and 100-foot-wide walls contained

Point Arena Light, California
Bruce Roberts

Alexandria. Apparently, the builder assumed the plaster would eventually crumble away along with the name of Ptolemy, leaving no doubt in minds of later generations as to who should get final credit—Sostratus.

Mariners likely cared little about who had built the Pharos, but they surely considered it a wonder. Even when far from sight of land, they could see the Pharos in daylight and follow it all the way into the harbor. At night the tower was even more effective as an aid to navigation. Soldiers or slaves—the first lighthouse keepers—built huge fires in a great cauldron on the tower's top level, filling the skies above the city with bright flames and luminous smoke. The precise range of the fiery Pharos beacon is, of course, unknown, but depending on weather conditions, it might have been seen from as far as 30 miles at sea.

Ancient Alexandria had another famous building, one that was not included among the Seven Wonders of the World, although it certainly might have been. It was the Alexandria Library, once the repository for much of civilization's literature and wisdom. Vessels arriving at the Alexandria wharves were required to pay a toll of two books, and in time, the city's library came to own copies of nearly every book on the planet.

The Pharos communicated a visual invitation to merchant ships, helping to make Alexandria the most prosperous city on the Mediterranean. All the many thousands of lighthouses built after the Pharos have been similar to it in this way: They dispense information, usually in its very simplest form—light. Their messages can be interpreted in a variety of ways depending on the situation: "Attention! Attention! Find safe harbor here!" or "Attention! Come trade with us!" or "Warning! Save yourselves! Avoid these rocks and shoals!"

Lighthouses of the Roman Empire

The importance of the Pharos to Alexandria's economy certainly was not lost on the Romans,

enough stone to build a city, and estimates of its height range up to 450 feet. Even at half that height, the Pharos would still have been, after the Pyramids of Egypt, the tallest building on the planet. The ancients were so impressed with the tower that they included it, along with the Pyramids, on their list of the Seven Wonders of the World.

Not surprisingly, Alexandria took great pride in the Pharos. So, too, did Sostratus, the man thought to have designed the tower. To make sure his achievement was remembered, Sostratus carved his name on the tower walls. It is said he then plastered over the inscription so that he could carve a second name on top—that of his employer and patron, Ptolemy, the Macedonian ruler of whose freighters made regular trips to Alexandria to fill their holds with Egyptian wheat. After AD 50, Roman grain ships returning from Egypt had a beacon of their own to guide them into Ostia, the primary port of Rome. The emperor Claudius ordered the tower built atop the sunken hulk of an enormous barge that had been used to transport an obelisk from Egypt. Workers filled the vessel's hull with rock, and on this crude but effective foundation they erected a stone tower with four levels, each smaller than the one below. The top level supported a platform on which signal fires were lit each evening. For several hundred years, the Ostia tower marked the maritime gateway to Rome. Then it vanished from the historical record, leaving behind only its image on ancient coins and artwork.

Erected shortly before the Ostia tower was the Tour d'Ordre, a lighted monument to Caligula, a Roman emperor whose madness was legendary even during his own short lifetime (AD 12–41). The tower commemorated a bizarre conflict between the wildly delusional Caligula and his imaginary nemesis, the sea god Neptune. Unable to cross the stormy English Channel with his legions to engage the Britons, Caligula made war on Neptune instead, ordering his soldiers to walk along the shore collecting seashells. When Neptune failed to respond to this supposed insult, Caligula declared himself the victor by default and had the lighthouse built at Boulogne-sur-Mer in honor of his triumph. A few years later, Caligula's Praetorian guards assassinated him, much to the relief of saner heads in Rome, but his lighthouse would far outlive him. The 125-foot-tall octagonal brick and stone structure stood for nearly 1,600 years, the tower finally collapsing along with the cliff on which it stood in 1644.

It is believed the Romans maintained navigational beacons at ports and on promontories throughout their empire, but nearly all of these have been lost in the mists of time. However, a

Michigan City Pier Light
Bruce Roberts

Roman lighthouse that still stands and, amazingly enough, continues to serve mariners can be seen today near the city of La Coruña on the Galician coast of Spain. The hulking stone tower, designed by Gaius Sevius Lupus, is believed to have been built in the second century AD during the reign of Trajan. Although it had been renovated or repaired many times over the centuries, the tower remains essentially the same structure. Known today as the Tower of Hercules, the lighthouse is fitted with a revolving prismatic lens that is considered somewhat old-fashioned today, but no doubt would have astounded the Romans.

A fanciful eighteenth-century engraving (above) depicts Alexandria's 450-foot Pharos, one of the vanished Wonders of the Ancient World. Although not as grand in scale, modern-day navigational towers, such as the Michigan City Pier Light (preceding page) on the Great Lakes or the Needles Light in England, are no less wondrous. Like the ancient Pharos, they both guide and inspire.

Courtesy William R. Perkins Library, Duke University

Lighthouses in the Dark Ages

The fall of the Roman Empire toward the end of the fifth century plunged much of Europe and its coastline into an era of darkness. A general cultural and commercial malaise fell over the continent, dramatically reducing sea trade and with it the need for mighty beacons such as those at Alexandria and Ostia. Anyone who dared sail at night was forced to rely on minor beacons shining from coastal monasteries or from the watchtowers of castles overlooking the sea.

Large navigational towers continued to be built during this period, although not in the West. While European ports languished in twilight, the Chinese were erecting tall, narrow pagodas to help seamen find key harbors. In 874, Buddhist monks built a five-story pagoda in the middle of the Moa River near the entrance to the harbor of Shanghai. A lantern hung from its highest level served as a beacon. Employed as a lighthouse until near the end of the thirteenth century, the old pagoda still stands and is considered a Chinese national historical treasure. South of Shanghai, vessels entering Wenzhou Harbor used a pair of tenth-century pagodas as range beacons. Mariners seeing the pagodas lined up one behind the other could be confident they were sailing in safe waters. The Wenzhou pagodas still serve this function.

Of course, the lights in Europe would not stay out forever. As early as the beginning of the ninth century, Charlemagne is believed to have repaired the Tour d'Ordre and put it back to work guiding mariners. Charlemagne's son and successor as emperor of the Holy Roman Empire, Louis the Pious, is said to have established a key light on the island of Cordouan near the mouth of the Gironde on France's western coast. Rebuilt several times over the last 1,100 years, most notably by England's Black Prince Edward in the second half of the fourteenth century and by architect Louis de Foix during the sixteenth century, the Phare de Cordouan (Cordouan Light) remains in operation to this day.

As maritime commerce increased, new lights and lighthouses began to appear in Italy. For ages, vessels approaching Porto Pisano off the coast of Tuscany had torn their hulls open on a vicious shoal near Meloria, but after 1157, a tower built on a wave-swept islet warned mariners away from this hazard. Beginning in 1194, a lighted tower at Messina guided ships through the narrow straits separating the boot of Italy from Sicily. Venice built its first lighthouse in 1312, and Genoa followed in 1321. Genoa's lighthouse, known as La Laterna, had a profound if accidental impact on the course of world history. The keeper of this light during the mid-fifteenth century was a man named Antonio Colombo. Very likely Colombo passed his fascination with the sea and knowledge of navigation along to his nephew, Christopher Columbus, who would forever change the way mariners and landlubbers alike look upon the oceans of the Earth.

Egbert Koch

Built in 1932, Michigan's Frankfort Breakwater Light is of relatively recent construction, but its form and function are much the same as those of ancient beacons. Nearly 2,000 years ago, scenes similar to this one probably greeted mariners approaching the Imperial Roman port of Ostia, where an offshore tower held aloft a bright, guiding light. Geometric details (top) decorate the ceiling of the medieval Cordouan Lighthouse in southwestern France.

Bruce Roberts

Egbert Koch

A CLOSER LOOK

Light of Lights

Cordouan. Is it the world's greatest lighthouse? Although there are older, taller, more powerful, and perhaps even more architecturally interesting lighthouses, none can match Cordouan's remarkable history or its almost ethereal beauty.

Marking the entrance to the Gironde River and the approaches to the famous old wine port of Bordeaux, the Cordouan Light dates far back into the Middle Ages. The family of Charlemagne maintained a beacon here in the ninth century, as did Edward, the warrior "Black Prince" of England, some 500 years later. During the sixteenth century, Henry III of France ordered an impressive tower built at Cordouan, and it is essentially the same lighthouse we see today. Its designer was court architect Louis de Foix, who made it a lighthouse fit for a king. He included sumptuous apartments and an ornate chapel just in case a king or church bishop should pay a visit—though none ever did.

However, a bishop of science and technology did stop at Cordouan during the 1820s to try out his world-changing optical invention: Augustin Fresnel tested his chandelier-like lens in the Cordouan lantern and found that it worked even better than he had hoped. It has been said that Fresnel lenses were 200 years ahead of their time. Yet those 200 years represent a scant fraction of the time the Cordouan beacon has served France and guided mariners.

The photographs on these pages lovingly examine the old Cordouan Lighthouse in all its magnificence and fine detailing. Have a close look and see if you, too, believe this is the "greatest lighthouse in the world."

Egbert Koch

Sunshine brightens the ornate arch of a marble doorway (opposite page) at Cordouan, where an early maritime beacon brought welcome light to Europe's Dark Ages. Maintained mostly by monks, medieval lighthouses were few, but as the modern era dawned, navigational towers began to be built everywhere.

Beacons in the Age of Light

As the modern world that Columbus helped create emerged, ships began to link not just one port to another but also nations to their destinies. As a consequence, lighthouses and the safe navigation they made possible became matters of vital concern to governments throughout the world.

Not surprisingly, England, with its long and rich maritime tradition, was among the first European countries to recognize the importance of a stable system of navigational lights. The Romans built the first lighthouses in the British Isles, but only one of these structures—a crumbling stone building at Dover—has survived into modern times. Medieval beacons were displayed in the British Isles at forts, monasteries, and even nunneries along the coast.

During the fifteenth and sixteenth centuries, a number of local mariners' guilds, known as trinity houses, were formed in various British port cities. Originally intended as charitable organizations committed to the care of aged seamen or widows and orphans of sailors lost at sea, the trinity houses became increasingly involved in the placement and maintenance of navigational markers. The London guild, which called itself the Brethren of Trinity House of Deptford Strand, eventually received a royal commission to build and operate lighthouses in England, Wales, and the Channel Islands. The London Trinity House also was granted the right to collect tolls from ships to pay for the maintenance of beacons and channel markers.

To this day, Trinity House continues as a semi-autonomous corporation that functions much like a government agency. It now oversees more than seventy major light towers. The most famous of these, and for good reason, is the wave-swept Eddystone Lighthouse, located in open water about thirteen miles southwest of Plymouth off England's southern coast. Rising just above the surface of the English Channel at high tide, the jagged Eddystone Rocks are all but invisible even in fair weather,

and they have been the ruin of innumerable ships and lives. For the last three centuries, these losses have been held to a minimum by the presence of a lighthouse at Eddystone, a fact that illustrates the extraordinary skills of British engineers and the determination of Trinity House to mark all obstacles no matter how difficult the task.

In 1696, Trinity House approved a plan submitted by a remarkable British designer and builder named Henry Winstanley to build a lighthouse directly on top of the Eddystone Rocks. No project like this one had ever been attempted, and many scoffed at Winstanley for undertaking it. The work progressed slowly, and storms frequently forced Winstanley and his crew to flee the rocks and head for shore. The project was further delayed when French privateers attacked the construction site and carried Winstanley off in chains to be held for ransom. Released in exchange for French prisoners being held in England, Winstanley returned to his task and completed an 80-foot stone tower late in 1698.

The first Eddystone Lighthouse had served for little more than a year before storm damage forced Winstanley to completely rebuild the structure, this time with a much taller and supposedly stronger tower. Winstanley visited the station in 1703 to make repairs; while he was there, a furious storm struck Plymouth. When the weather cleared, no sign of the tower or its builder could be found.

The next Eddystone Lighthouse proved considerably more durable—remarkably so given that it was made in part of wood. Built in 1709 by John Rudyard, a silk merchant and part-time engineer, it survived the Channel's fierce winter storms for more than forty-six years before finally succumbing to fire. The blaze that consumed the tower in 1755 took the life of the station's eighty-four-year-old keeper, and in a particularly gruesome manner. While he stood on the rocks gazing up at the flames, a piece of hot lead fell from the gallery into his mouth.

The quality of lighthouse engineering steadily improved. The fourth Eddystone Tower, built in 1759 by John Smeaton, lasted more than a century. Built with interlocking granite blocks and flared at the bottom for added stability, it stood up to even the most ferocious gales. It served mariners until the early 1880s, by which time subsurface settling had undermined its foundation. Trinity House hurried to replace the crippled structure, opting for a design similar to that used by Smeaton. With a solid stone base and walls of massive, interlocking granite blocks, the fifth—and current—Eddystone Lighthouse was ready for duty in 1882. Able to resist giant, storm-driven waves—even those that sweep nearly to the top of the 150-foot tower—it has become an icon for those who see lighthouses as bold, romantic structures poised between the wild forces of nature and the ordered intentions of men.

Eddystone Light in the distance

Shutterstock.com

Brighter Lights on the Horizon

No matter how well placed or skillfully engineered, a navigational tower serves little purpose if mariners cannot see its light. Early maritime beacons made from simple wood or coal fires usually had a range of only a few miles; if sea breezes blew the flames back toward shore, they became all but invisible. Later on, keepers guided vessels with brightly burning oil lamps, sometimes employing spherical or parabolic reflectors to concentrate the light. Such innovations provided only incremental improvement in the performance of beacons.

During the late eighteenth and early nineteenth centuries, engineers in Europe and the United States were building taller and stronger navigational towers, but weak lights limited their effectiveness. However, a profound breakthrough in lighthouse technology lay just over the horizon. To make it, a young French inventor named Augustin Fresnel would rely both on his training as an engineer and on the world of pure science.

While growing up during the 1790s, Fresnel had been fascinated by light streaming through the windows of his home in Normandy. After studying engineering in Paris, he built roads for Napoleon but continued to work on mathematical formulas related to light. Newton had incorrectly assumed that light was a stream of particles, but Fresnel came to the conclusion that light was pure energy moving in waves, much like those on the surface of the ocean. The movement of light through transparent solids such as glass particularly interested Fresnel, and he discovered that prisms could be used to bend and channel the waves. In 1819, Fresnel's study of light won him a coveted award from the French Academy of Science, and shortly thereafter he put his

discoveries to a practical purpose—the invention of an extraordinarily efficient lighthouse optic.

Ironically, Fresnel tested his revolutionary device at one of the world's oldest navigational stations—Cordouan. In this place where monks once guided ships with wood fires, Fresnel now arranged his glittering prisms. Little more than the light of a candle was needed to demonstrate the brilliance of his concept.

Fresnel's optic consisted of a barrel-shaped array of highly polished glass prisms that funneled light into a concentrated band many times brighter than the source. Powered by a relatively simple lamp, these Fresnel lenses could produce a light beam visible from a distance of 20 miles or more. Such a lens in a tall tower could alert mariners who were still beyond the horizon. Now, vessels far from land could receive the call of a welcoming port or be warned to turn away long before they approached a destructive hazard.

No one can say how many seamen owed their lives to Fresnel, but the number is large. Fresnel himself had little time to enjoy any profit from his labors; he died of tuberculosis in 1827 at the age of thirty-nine.

Of course, others profited mightily, and not just maritime interests. Before long French companies such as François Soleil and Henri LaPaute were producing the new lenses and selling them to government lighthouse services in France and around the world for what even today might seem astronomical prices. Never content to be left behind by the French, British manufacturers also pitched in with their own Fresnel-type lenses. They soon had an abundance of customers because the lenses were quickly adopted as the standard optic for lighthouses throughout the British Empire. This had less to do with politics, economics, or the brilliance of the optics themselves than with the engineering savvy of a family of sturdy Scotsmen.

Eddystone Light
Courtesy Library of Congress

Scotland's "Lighthouse" Stevensons

The author of *Treasure Island* and many other classics, Robert Louis Stevenson ranks among the best known and loved writers of the nineteenth century. Strangely enough, he was considered something of a failure and a black sheep by his relations, a tight-knit clan of Scotsmen who had something other than literary lights on their minds. Among them were several of the most innovative and highly skilled lighthouse engineers who ever lived.

In Scotland, the Northern Lighthouse Board plays a role similar to that of Trinity House in England, and for a century or more, it was dominated by members of the Stevenson family. The close identification of the Stevensons with the board and with Scottish lighthouses in general began even before family patriarch Robert Stevenson (1772–1850) undertook construction of the famed open-water Bell Rock Light off the Isle of May. Robert Stevenson's stepfather, Thomas Smith, had preceded him as a respected Lighthouse Board engineer and had designed one of the first parabolic reflectors for lighthouse lanterns. But it was Stevenson's successful completion of the challenging Bell Rock project that cemented the family's reputation.

The granite Bell Rock tower took 110 men more than three years to build and cost more than £60,000. When it was completed and its beacon first lit on February 1, 1811, those who saw it, whether from land or sea, were likely to agree that it had been worth every shilling of its cost. A pillar of stone rising 116 feet from the North Sea waters, it had a fine rotating light that flashed red and white signals. Consisting of 2,835 massive stones weighing more than 2,000 tons in all, it was a solid piece of work, as its nearly two centuries of continuous service testify.

Robert Stevenson went on to build seventeen additional lighthouses in Scotland, while his sons David (Robert Louis Stevenson's father), Thomas, and Alan built many others. The most prominent engineer and prolific builder among the three sons was Alan, who was responsible for Scotland's remarkable Skerryvore Lighthouse. Said by some to be the world's most nearly perfect lighthouse, the flared Skerryvore tower balances like an inverted golf tee on a platform of rock barely exposed at low tide.

Perhaps even more remarkable than his skills as a builder were Alan Stevenson's contributions to the field of lighthouse optics. As a young man, he had taken an interest in the theories and designs of Augustin Fresnel. After visiting the Fresnel offices in Paris during the early 1830s, Alan returned to Scotland with a firm grasp of the concept and workings of a Fresnel lens. Convinced that none of the more conventional optical systems could match the performance of this new technology, Stevenson persuaded the Northern Lighthouse Board to install a Fresnel lens at Skerryvore. This ensured the widespread use of Fresnel lenses throughout the British Empire and the world. Stevenson added a few innovations of his own to the original Fresnel design, including additional upper and lower prisms that significantly increased the light-concentrating efficiency of the lens.

Although Robert Louis Stevenson did not follow in the footsteps of his father, grandfather, and uncles, he eventually wrote a history called *Records of*

Fascinated by light, a young French scientist named Augustin Fresnel launched a nineteenth-century revolution in navigational technology. His efficient prismatic lenses produced beacons so bright they could be seen from distances of 20 miles or more—even from over the horizon. As this sparkling first-order giant (opposite page) on display at the Ponce de Leon Inlet Lighthouse Museum in Florida makes clear, these extraordinary devices were not just effective but also quite beautiful.

Bruce Roberts

Scotland's Robert Stevenson (above) founded an engineering dynasty responsible for scores of major lighthouses, many built on exposed offshore rocks. His son Alan Stevenson designed the granite Skerryvore tower (opposite page), said to be a "nearly perfect" structure. Among Robert Stevenson's descendants were several other prominent lighthouse engineers and one of history's greatest storytellers—grandson Robert Louis Stevenson, author of Treasure Island.

a Family of Engineers. Not surprisingly, he remained interested in lighthouses and the sea all his life. He traveled widely, and in addition to his better known works of fiction, Stevenson wrote a number of travelogues describing his personal adventures and, on occasion, mentioning the lighthouses he had seen along the way. One of his trips took him to the United States, a place where advanced lighthouse technology was slow to take root.

Lighthouses in Colonial America

Like ancient Rome and modern Europe, America relies on maritime trade to boost and support its economy, and this was the case from the very beginning. Early colonists were reluctant to break their ties with Europe. They imported metalwork, clothing, and whatever small luxuries they could afford while shipping out tobacco, grain, and other produce to pay for them. The brave merchant seamen who made this bustling trade possible ran an obstacle course of shoals and shallows when they entered American waters. Most captains would not even consider approaching the shore at night, but even during the day, the dangers could be extreme. Thousands of large vessels and countless lives were lost due to a lack of adequate charts and seamarks.

In time, this rather bleak situation improved as the colonies and their key port cities began to build lighthouses. Urged on by businessmen and the owners of New England's own sizable merchant fleet, the colony of Massachusetts built a lighthouse at Boston in 1716. Believed to have been the first lighthouse in North America, it stood on Little Brewster Island near the entrance to Boston Harbor. The stone tower, about 70 feet tall, displayed a light first produced by tallow candles, and, later, by whale-oil lamps.

To pay for building and maintaining the Boston Harbor Lighthouse, colonial officials imposed a duty of one penny per ton on ships entering the harbor. This lighthouse levy defrayed a number of expenses, including the keeper's modest salary of £50 a year. The station's first keeper, a shepherd and harbor pilot named George Worthylake, found it difficult to support his family on such a pittance, but he faithfully tended the light. After less than two years on the job, the nearly penniless keeper drowned in a boating accident.

His replacement, Robert Saunders, lasted only a few weeks on Little Brewster before drowning in a similar mishap. In America, the profession of lighthouse keeper had gotten off to a dismal start. Most later keepers would prove more fortunate than Worthylake and Saunders, however. A small room at Boston Harbor Light lists the names of more than sixty keepers who served during the station's almost three centuries of operation.

Although Boston was the site of America's first true lighthouse—it had guided mariners for more than a half century by the time the Declaration of Independence was signed in 1776—the tower seen today is not the nation's oldest. While retreating from Boston during the Revolutionary War, British troops stacked barrels of gunpowder in the original tower and blew it to pieces. The existing lighthouse dates to 1783, the last year of the war and the year American independence finally was recognized by Great Britain.

The oldest light tower still standing and operating in the United States is an octagonal stone structure located on New Jersey's Sandy Hook near the entrance to the Hudson River estuary. Funded by New York City businessmen who had grown jealous of the prosperity the Boston Harbor Light had brought to Massachusetts, the 85-foot Sandy Hook Light was completed in 1764. Although it also came under attack during the Revolution, Sandy Hook Light survived and serves mariners to this day.

When European mariners first approached North America, they found its shores strewn with dangerous obstacles and lit only by the campfires of native tribes. Not until the 1700s did trade-conscious settlers build lighthouses, first at Boston (opposite page), then at a dozen other key locations along the colonial coast. By 1769 a twin-light beacon (above) marked Plymouth Bay, where the Pilgrims had found shelter nearly 150 years earlier.

Courtesy *Lighthouse Digest*

A number of other lighthouses were established during colonial times. Among these were Brant Point Light, built in 1746 to guide whaling ships to Nantucket; Beavertail Light, built in 1749 to point the way to Rhode Island's Narragansett Bay; and New London Harbor Light, built off the Connecticut coast in 1760 with the proceeds of a public lottery. Colonial light stations also were established at Delaware's Cape Henlopen in 1765 to guide ships into Delaware Bay, at Charleston in 1767 to mark the gracious South Carolina city founded by French Huguenots, at Plymouth in 1769 to serve the old bayside community founded by the Pilgrims, at Cape Ann in 1771 to guard the northern approaches to Massachusetts Bay, and at Portsmouth in 1771 to mark New Hampshire's main seaport.

During the colonial period, the individual colonies took responsibility for construction and maintenance of their own lighthouses. Since funding for these light stations varied greatly and there was no central authority to govern their operations, the service they provided was, at best, unreliable. This continued to be the case in the years immediately following the Revolution, when the states handled their affairs more or less as if they were independent countries. But George Washington and other early American leaders could see that greater unity was needed, both for the nation as a whole and for its system of navigational lights.

Early Federal Lighthouses (1789–1820)

Although not a seafaring man himself, George Washington understood the importance of maritime commerce and was a great believer in lighthouses. When traveling along the coast, he often took note of strategic points as likely locations for navigational lights. While touring Long Island in 1756, the then twenty-five-year-old Washington visited Montauk Point and told his companions that he could

Established in 1716, the Boston Harbor Light has served mariners for nearly three centuries. A window in the keeper's residence frames the tower rebuilt in 1783, after retreating British troops destroyed the original during the Revolutionary War.
Bruce Roberts

envision a lighthouse standing there. Many years later, when he became president, Washington would help make that vision a reality.

In 1789, the failed Articles of Confederation gave way to the US Constitution and a federal government strong enough to take charge of important national concerns, including maritime safety. Among the very first acts of Congress was a bill authorizing the federal government to take responsibility for all navigational lights and creating what eventually would be called the US

Nantucket's Brant Point Light as it appeared during the nineteenth century. Still in operation today, this light station dates all the way back to 1746.

Courtesy *Lighthouse Digest*

Lighthouse Service. Signed into law by President George Washington on August 7, 1789, the bill gave the job of overseeing the new system to the Secretary of the Treasury, who at that time was Alexander Hamilton. At first Hamilton personally ran the system, appointing keepers and reviewing contracts before sending them to the president for his signature. Later he delegated these tasks to the Commissioner of Revenue.

Soon after, the fledgling federal government shouldered its first major construction project—a lighthouse on Portland Head in what would later become the state of Maine. Able to pry a stingy appropriation of only $1,500 out of Congress, Hamilton instructed his contractors to build the tower with stone gathered from nearby fields. This they did, and despite the meager funding, a

surprisingly solid structure was standing and ready for duty by early 1791. No less a figure than General Marie Joseph Lafayette, the French nobleman and Revolutionary War officer, was on hand for the dedication.

Impressed with these results, Congress soon became more generous, and the construction of new towers began in earnest. Later in 1791 contractors completed light towers on Virginia's Cape Henry and on Tybee Island near Savannah, Georgia. Rugged Seguin Island, northeast of Portland, received a tower in 1795. Then in 1796, the last full year of Washington's presidency, work began on a lighthouse at New York's Montauk Point. The contractor chosen for the project was John McComb, who had built the Cape Henry lighthouse and would later build several other important American light towers. Within a year, McComb had completed a fine stone tower, placing it atop a sandy bluff—in fact, the very one on which George Washington himself had stood some forty-one years earlier and envisioned a lighthouse.

The Pleasonton Era: 1820–1852

Begun in colonial times and greatly expanded by the federal government, the US lighthouse system eventually would become the finest and most extensive in the world, but this would take generations. Until the middle of the nineteenth century, the United States was considered a navigational backwater. Compared with their European counterparts, lighthouses in the United States were, in general, poorly built and equipped with outmoded optics. Without uniform standards for either their construction or operation, American light stations were at best unreliable and sometimes worse than useless.

Many of the failings of early US navigational lights can be traced to the tightfisted policies of a single Washington bureaucrat—Stephen J. Pleasonton.

Few government officials ever left such a mark, for better or worse, on the United States than Stephen Pleasonton. For more than thirty years, Pleasonton presided over the US lighthouse system, not so much like an efficient public servant as a parsimonious tycoon, unable to part with a nickel. When he finally stepped down as General Superintendent of Lighthouses—his informal title—practically everyone was glad to see him go, but none so much as the nation's mariners.

Pleasonton's career started out on a promising note. As a young government bookkeeper working in Washington during the War of 1812, Pleasonton had been among the last to leave the city when British troops captured and burned the capital. Commandeering a wagon, he piled it high with documents he had managed to rescue from the flames—among them the original, signed copies of the Declaration of Independence and the US Constitution. Perhaps unaware of just how important a load his wagon was carrying, Pleasonton hitched it to a team and drove it into the Virginia countryside, where the documents were stored in a farmhouse until the danger had passed.

His presence of mind and determination earned Pleasonton the admiration of his superiors, and he soon worked his way up to the position of Fifth Auditor of the US Treasury. In 1820 his office was given administrative authority over the

Completed under federal authority in 1791, the Portland Head Light in Maine signaled US determination to build and maintain a first-rate system of coastal beacons. Scenic as well as historic, the old light station has been the subject of poems, paintings, and literally millions of photographs.
Bruce Roberts

nation's lighthouses, which at the time numbered about seventy. Over the next thirty years, that number grew nearly fivefold to more than 330, not including a fleet of forty lightships that marked obstacles and key turning points beyond the reach of shore beacons.

Pleasonton excelled at getting things done, but it is fair to say that, all too frequently, they were

Bruce Roberts

not done well. Facing constant budget pressures in what then was still a relatively poor country, Pleasonton focused his concerns on cost rather than the effectiveness of light stations. Neither a seaman nor an engineer, he had no experience in maritime matters and relied heavily on the advice of cronies.

Among the so-called experts who deeply influenced Pleasonton's administration of US lighthouses was Winslow Lewis, a former New England sea captain and self-styled inventor. Lewis had sold the government on the merits of a lamp and reflector system he claimed would greatly improve the range and effectiveness of the nation's navigational beacons. Apparently based on an outmoded design developed and later discarded by Scotland's Stevenson family, Lewis's patented system employed an oil-burning Argand lamp, a large, rounded mirror to concentrate the light, and a green-tinted convex lens to focus the rays. The mirror proved only modestly effective and the lens completely useless; nonetheless, the government adopted the system for all its lighthouses. Pleasonton likely saw the device as a cheap way to produce navigational beacons and its inventor as a kindred spirit. Lewis represented the old way of doing things, the make-do-with-what-you-have approach of a frontier America that even during the 1820s was rapidly disappearing. He epitomized the era of wooden sailing ships, log roads, stone forts, and naturally enough—stone lighthouses.

Having been hired to outfit lighthouses with his questionable optics, Lewis started seeking contracts to build the towers as well. Pleasonton, for his part, saw no reason to deny mariners the benefit of Lewis's lighthouse "expertise." As with all large government construction projects, lighthouse contractors were chosen on the basis of competitive bids, but this did not deter Lewis. The old seaman submitted bids so low that he nearly always got the jobs. Then, working within unrealistic budgets, he produced structures that met all or most of the required specifications but were generally poor in quality. Many of Lewis's towers crumbled, collapsed, or were bowled over by storms after only a few years. In 1830 at St. Marks, Florida, Lewis and a subcontractor produced a tower that was little more than a worthless pile of bricks. The following year

George Washington himself chose a site for the Montauk Point Light (opposite page) on Long Island. Having guided mariners since 1796—more than two centuries—it still functions as an active maritime beacon. Unfortunately, only a few such early federal lighthouses have survived to the present day. The octagonal St. Simons Light tower (above) stood from 1810 until 1862, when it was blown up by Civil War combatants.

National Archives

The tightfisted policies of bureaucrat Stephen Pleasonton, who administered the federal lighthouse system from 1820 to 1852, encouraged poor construction standards. The ramshackle, 1830s-era Cedar Point Range Lighthouse on Lake Erie (above) served for only a few years. Some such rough-hewn structures lasted longer, however. New York's 1838 Selkirk Point Lighthouse on Lake Ontario (opposite page) has been restored for use as a hostelry and private aid to navigation.

Courtesy *Lighthouse Digest*

the useless structure was torn down and rebuilt—not surprisingly, by a different contractor. In fairness to Lewis, some of his lighthouses were solid enough, and a few, such as the all-brick Sapelo Island tower near Darien, Georgia, still stand.

The most damaging effect of Pleasonton's deference to Lewis sprang from the auditor's dogged preference for lamp-and-reflector optics. Some of Lewis's optics were so weak that mariners might run aground within shouting distance of a lighthouse without ever having seen its beacon. During the 1820s, European light stations began to use Fresnel's advanced prismatic lenses, but Pleasonton turned a deaf ear to mariners and port officials who suggested that these expensive glass instruments be imported by the United States. Although their shiny prisms were hand-polished by Parisian street

waifs who might be paid no more than a penny a day, finished Fresnel lenses could cost thousands if not tens of thousands of dollars. Such sums were not lightly spent by a nation still largely agricultural, and Pleasonton saw himself, above all, as a guardian of the US Treasury purse strings.

Pleasonton stubbornly refused to adopt Fresnel technology or even give it a hearing. During the late 1830s, however, Congress finally ordered Pleasonton to test Fresnel optics and dispatched Commodore Matthew Perry to Paris to purchase sample lenses. Perry returned with a pair of giant Fresnels, which were installed in the twin towers of the Navesink lighthouse in Highlands, New Jersey. Smaller lenses later found their way to the Sankaty Head tower on Nantucket Island and the Brandywine Shoal lighthouse in Delaware.

Bruce Roberts

The dour expression of US Treasury auditor Stephen Pleasonton matched his attitude toward costly advances such as Fresnel's efficient prismatic lens. Pleasonton's resistance to expensive but much needed improvements kept US coasts in twilight for decades. Ironically, his demise as the nation's chief lighthouse administrator was hastened by the collapse of an experimental light tower at Minot's Ledge in New England. The more traditional stone tower (opposite page) that replaced it still stands.

National Archives

The new optics brightened these beacons to such an extent that mariners picturesquely described them as "rocket lights" or "blazing stars," but when comments like these made it to Pleasonton, they ended up buried in his Washington files. The Fifth Auditor remained firmly against the acquisition of costly French lenses—and in firm control of his far-flung lighthouse domain—up to the early 1850s, but by then a sea change was in the air.

Tragedy at Minot's Ledge

Pleasonton had resisted change and innovation throughout a government career spanning more

than three decades and nearly a dozen presidential administrations. How ironic that he should finally be toppled from his position by one of the most ambitious and visionary projects ever undertaken by American engineers—the Minot's Ledge lighthouse.

It is not clear whether Pleasonton initially favored or opposed construction of an open-water steel-skeleton light tower on the infamously hazardous ledge off Cohasset, Massachusetts, southeast of Boston. What is known is that the project began with great promise in 1848 and ended three years later—in tragedy.

On October 6, 1849, a sizable brig known as the *Saint John* struck Minot's Ledge near the southeastern lip of Boston Bay. Loaded to capacity with Irish immigrants and their belongings, the shattered vessel quickly disintegrated in heavy seas. For days afterward the bloated bodies of victims washed up on the beaches near Cohasset. This appalling incident emphasized the need for a lighthouse on Minot's Ledge.

In fact, one was already under construction. Maritime authorities were only too familiar with this ship-killing obstacle and the danger it represented to mariners. During the thirty years prior to the ruin of the *Saint John,* the blade-like ledge had ripped apart no fewer than forty vessels, with great destruction of life and property. The mounting losses in ships and cargoes led to a bold and unprecedented attempt to place a light directly over the ledge.

At that time, many believed it impossible to build a lighthouse in such an exposed place, but a young engineer named Isaiah (I. W. P.) Lewis argued that it must be done. Lewis was the nephew of Winslow Lewis, but he did not share his uncle's old-fashioned approach to lighthouse construction. Armed with a long list of shipwrecks, Isaiah Lewis managed to convince federal officials—apparently Pleasonton among them—to endorse an innovative plan put forward by Captain William Smith of the

US Topographical Department. Most light towers of the time were stone or brick cylinders, but the lighthouse Smith envisioned for Minot's Ledge would consist of an elevated dwelling and lantern supported by eight stiltlike cast-iron legs. In effect, the skeletal tower would have open walls, allowing fierce storm winds and high waves to pass through without damaging the structure.

Construction of the lighthouse began in 1848 and proceeded slowly. To anchor the tower's spidery legs securely, iron piles had to be driven into holes drilled deep into hard rock. The drilling and driving could be done only for a few hours each day—at low tide, when the ledge was above water. It took nearly three years to build the lighthouse; finally, on January 1, 1850, twelve weeks and a day after the wreck of the *Saint John,* its light was displayed. Had it been in service only a few months earlier, Minot's Ledge Light might have saved the unfortunate brig and its passengers.

Described as a monument to "modern" construction techniques, the tall iron sea tower was thought to be indestructible—many would believe the same of the *Titanic* more than sixty years later. As it turned out, however, the Minot's Ledge tower would prove all too vulnerable.

For a little more than a year, all went well. Each night, the station's crew lit the lamps inside the glassed-in lantern room, and mariners passing the ledge were pleased to see its brilliant warning beacon. Ship captains had nothing but praise for the light, calling it "the brightest star in the west."

But while mariners off Cohasset might have felt secure, the keepers who lived and worked in the Minot's Ledge lighthouse did not. There had been signs of trouble almost from the first. Whenever storms swept in from the Atlantic, the crew noticed an uncomfortable swaying motion as large waves slammed into the structure. The station's first head keeper resigned rather than ride out another gale in a building he considered a deathtrap. His replacement, a local man named John Bennett, also

Minot's Ledge
Courtesy *Lighthouse Digest*

reported problems with the tower. "She sways and rattles when the sea comes up," he said. Bennett was told the shaking was normal and that he should not be concerned.

In mid-March of 1851, Bennett went ashore on leave to enjoy a day or two away from his duties. He also hoped to purchase a new dory for the station, since the old one had been smashed by a recent storm. He left the station in the care of Joseph Wilson and Joseph Antoine, his two assistants. Bennett knew he could trust the two to keep the light burning regardless of the conditions. What he could not have known was that he would never see them alive again.

On the evening of March 16, a powerful storm swept down on the coast of Massachusetts. With high waves overturning boats even in the usually calm harbor at Cohasset, Bennett had no way of getting back to the station. He could only watch from shore and with increasing anxiety as the gale grew stronger. Bennett feared for the safety of his assistants in the lighthouse—and with good reason.

Enormous waves rolled in off the Atlantic and pounded the tower throughout the morning of March 17. By the afternoon, the steel skeleton began to give way. With each passing wave, the tower leaned closer to the churning water. Finally, it could take no more and, with a lurch, fell into the ocean. Later, the bodies of Wilson and Antoine washed up on the rocks near Cohasset. They were buried in the same cemetery where many of the *Saint John* victims were laid to rest. At the funeral, keeper Bennett proudly noted that his crewmen had kept the Minot's Ledge light burning right up to the moment the tower fell into the sea.

The Minot's Ledge disaster was to claim another victim, this one in Washington DC, far from the storm-battered Massachusetts coast. Publicity generated by the collapse focused public attention on maritime safety and brought intense pressure on Congress to improve the nation's system of navigational lights. Little more than a month after the tower fell, Congress appointed a nine-member commission to investigate the status of America's navigational lights. The commission, led by Admiral William Shubrick, a highly respected naval officer, found the nation's lighthouse system in a shocking state of disarray. Crumbling towers leaned this way and that, keepers' dwellings were ramshackle and rotten, and light signals were weak if not altogether invisible. The commission concluded that, at best, American lighthouses and their beacons were vastly inferior to those in Great Britain and elsewhere in Europe. At worst, they were useless. Something had to be done.

Congress received the commission's report in October 1851 and took immediate action. Afterward known as the Lighthouse Board, the commission itself, with Shubrick at its head, was given authority over all American navigational aids and told to clean up the mess that Pleasonton had left behind. Pleasonton himself stepped away from a job he had often said he never wanted but to which he had clung for more than three decades.

Among the tasks confronting the new Lighthouse Board was construction of a replacement for the fallen Minot's Ledge tower. For obvious reasons, the board proceeded cautiously with the project, and construction did not begin until the late 1850s. The new tower was built with stone rather than iron, using a design similar to that of the Bell Rock and Eddystone lighthouses in Great Britain. Completed in 1860 at a cost of $330,000—

The military officers and engineers on the US Lighthouse Board placed great emphasis on orderliness and efficiency. Embracing the products of heavy industry, they used cast iron for construction of light towers such as the one that still marks Cape Neddick in Maine (opposite page upper). They also adopted rigid work rules for keepers—but these were not always followed. For instance, 1890s keeper William Brooks (opposite page lower) often earned pocket money by rowing tourists around the scenic cape in the station boat.

Bruce Roberts

Courtesy *Lighthouse Digest*

a fantastic sum at the time—it consisted of huge, interlocking granite blocks shaped in such a way as to grip one another when placed under pressure by storm-driven waves. In this case, at least, stone proved sturdier than iron; the tower has stood up to wind and the waves for more than 150 years. Its flashing beacon can still be seen. The characteristic one-four-three rhythm of the Minot's Ledge beacon has earned it the nickname the "i-love-you light."

The Victorian Era in America: 1852–1910

Admiral Shubrick's Lighthouse Board included some of America's foremost engineers and thinkers, among them Joseph Henry, a noted mathematician, physicist, and inventor and one of the founders of the Smithsonian Institution. Henry pressed Congress for money to fund optical research and to acquire large numbers of Fresnel lenses. This was done, and by the end of the 1850s, Fresnel lenses had been placed in nearly every American lighthouse.

Men like Henry were progressives who placed their faith in science and in the ability of human beings to control their environment. Deeply influenced by the Victorian movement in Britain, they took a highly organized approach to everything they did and believed in strict codes of dress and behavior. These attitudes soon found their way into what now came to be called the US Lighthouse Establishment.

The board mirrored the belief in strictness, organization, and scientific progress that characterized the second half of the nineteenth century in general. It divided the country into twelve lighthouse districts, placing each under the supervision of an inspector, usually a naval officer. Lighthouse keepers and crew were expected to wear uniforms and keep station property and equipment in spotless condition. Inspectors made unannounced visits to make sure everything was in peak condition, going over windowsills, storage cabinets, and even the floors of station residences with white-gloved hands, searching for traces of dust or grime. Keepers who failed to measure up to standards were summarily dismissed.

The board brought in US Army engineers to design and oversee construction of light towers and other facilities. Some, such as George Meade and Danville Leadbetter, were among the most talented and innovative builders of their era. Leadbetter designed and built a number of interesting towers along the Gulf Coast. The octagonal brick and concrete tower he erected at Sabine Pass, Louisiana, in 1852 had bizarre, finlike buttresses that spread the weight of the structure over the marshy ground alongside the Sabine River. Although abandoned more than a half century ago, the tower still stands in near perfect plumb. A Southerner, Leadbetter fought for the Confederacy during the Civil War and so was not allowed to return to US government service at war's end. He died in 1866 while designing lighthouses for Mexico.

Although the Minot's Ledge experiment with iron-skeleton construction had ended in disaster, Meade applied the concept successfully in the hurricane-prone Florida Keys. Meade built several tall skeleton towers in the Keys, anchoring them to reefs with screw piles. His Carysfort Reef (1852), Sand Key (1853), and Sombrero Key (1858) towers all remain in use after one and a half centuries of pounding by hurricanes. Meade is celebrated in history books for designing another

To establish permanent light stations in the open ocean, the Lighthouse Board turned to young military engineers such as Lieutenant George Meade, who as General Meade would later lead the Union Army at Gettysburg. Meade used screw piles and iron braces to erect skeleton towers atop wave-swept reefs. Several of Meade's reef lighthouses, such as the one on Florida's Sand Key (opposite page), have survived more than 160 years of pounding by hurricanes.
Bruce Roberts

Perhaps most impressive of the US Lighthouse Board's accomplishments was marking the nation's western seaboard where few, if any, lighthouses existed before 1852. Many of the western lights established by the board still shine, including the one on East Brother Island in San Francisco Bay. Built in 1874, this fully functioning lighthouse now charms B&B guests with its lovely Victorian architecture.
Bruce Roberts

hard-as-iron structure, the Union defensive alignment at the Battle of Gettysburg, where he was the Union commander. Robert E. Lee, who had also done work for the Lighthouse Board, was Meade's opponent at Gettysburg. When Lee unleashed his hurricane-like charge on the third day of the battle, Meade's carefully architected formations held fast and so, many believe, won the war for the North.

In the 1850s, the Lighthouse Board focused considerable attention on a long-neglected part of the country, the Far West. The board turned to a civilian engineer to jump-start an ambitious lighthouse construction effort, hiring Francis Gibbons to build eight towers on sites scattered along more than 1,000 miles of rugged coastline. Having brought a shipload of supplies from the East Coast to California by way of an arduous 12,000-mile voyage around the tip of South America, Gibbons built his first West Coast lighthouse on Alcatraz Island in San Francisco Bay. Completed in 1853 but not lit until the following year, Alcatraz Island Light featured a Cape Cod–style residence wrapped around a stout brick tower. Before long, similar structures stood on Point Loma near San Diego, Point Pinos near Monterey, and on Southeast Farallon Island, about 30 miles west of the Golden Gate Strait.

But the Gibbons project was about to strike a rock. While landing construction materials at Cape Disappointment in Washington, Gibbons's supply ship, the *Oriole,* foundered on the Columbia River bar, the very hazard the planned lighthouse was meant to mark. Gibbons never recovered financially from this mishap, but he did manage to gather more supplies and complete the remaining lighthouses covered by his government contract. All were eventually fitted with Fresnel lenses, and several remain in operation.

About two decades after Gibbons finished his work and returned east—more or less penniless—a crew of about a dozen workers took on the greatest challenge that ever confronted lighthouse builders in the American West. Tillamook Rock, a barren hunk of basalt rising like a fist from the Pacific about 20 miles south of the Columbia River's mouth, had threatened generations of mariners and taken the lives of more than a few. The huge waves that often swept the rock were so powerful that they sometimes tossed around loose boulders. Building a lighthouse in such a place had long seemed unthinkable, but in October 1879, a construction crew landed on the rock—with considerable difficulty—and started work. Living mostly in the open, and scurrying into crude shelters only when forced to by storms, the builders leveled a foundation with dynamite. Then, block by massive block, they erected a fortress of a lighthouse. The effort consumed fifteen months, more than $150,000, and at least one life, but mariners and maritime officials were convinced the result would be worth the effort.

Tragedy would prove them right when a Japanese freighter called the *Lupatia* struck Tillamook Rock and sank only a few days before its light signal was placed in service. No doubt, many other vessels would be spared the *Lupatia*'s fate by the station's warning beacon. The Tillamook Rock lighthouse served mariners for more than seventy-five years. Its beacon was deactivated in 1951, and the station eventually was abandoned. Today, the rock serves as a memorial and columbarium, where families deposit the ashes of deceased relatives.

As the US lighthouse system was extended to cover the rugged shores of Alaska, the beaches of Hawaii, and even the most remote offshore obstacles, lighthouse builders confronted many challenges such as the one at Tillamook Rock. The Lighthouse Board and its engineers met them all with characteristic Victorian confidence in solutions. A thing could always be done— one only needed to find the way. But with the approach of a new century came a new way of thinking. The twentieth century would bring with it electricity, cars, airplanes, and automation, along with a feeling that "solutions" had begun to overwhelm the world and even the engineers who had devised them.

Bruce Roberts

A CLOSER LOOK

Cape Hatteras's Lost Civil War Lens

During the spring of 1862, the Civil War threatened to turn the North Carolina coast into a wasteland. Hard-pressed by the Union with its vastly superior navy, Confederates on the Outer Banks dismantled the Fresnel lens at the Cape Hatteras lighthouse and carefully packed the pieces into forty-four pine boxes. The lens then took a strange trek inland by way of steamboat, special one-car train, and horse-drawn wagon. The journey ended—or so it seemed—more than 200 miles from the Atlantic in the small farming community of Townsville. There, the boxes were shoved into a warehouse to await better and safer times. But when the war finally ended some three years later, the boxes and the Henry-Lepaute crown glass lens they contained had vanished—or so legend would have it.

Thus began one of the great mysteries of American lighthouse history. For more than 130 years, the question of what happened to the original Cape Hatteras lens remained unanswered. Did the Confederates destroy it rather than have it fall into Union hands? Was it still hidden in a cave somewhere or buried beneath the waters of a mountain reservoir?

The mystery has now been solved, thanks to author and historical detective Kevin Duffus. After years of poring over old documents and Lighthouse Service records, Duffus has come up with the answer that eluded so many. He tells the complete story of the Cape Hatteras lens in his book, *The Lost Light: A Civil War History of Extinguished Southern Sentinels and Hidden Lighthouse Lenses* (Raleigh, NC: Looking Glass Productions). But here it is in brief.

The Civil War was still raging when the search for the Cape Hatteras lens began. Lacking an effective navy, the Confederacy extinguished the navigational lights along much of the southern coast. Whenever possible, the valuable lenses were removed and stored for safekeeping. Naturally, these efforts infuriated Union leaders who were trying to seal off southern ports with blockade fleets, and they were particularly angry about what they called the "theft" of the Cape Hatteras lens. In retaliation, Union forces drove the former Cape Hatteras keeper and his district superintendent into hiding. The picturesque waterfront town of Washington, North Carolina, which had once harbored the lens, was threatened with annihilation, and the steamboat that had transported it was eventually sunk. The lens became a pawn of war, a symbol both of Southern defiance and of Northern determination to preserve the Union.

As Confederate defenses crumbled during the closing months of the war, Union troops overran North Carolina, but they could not find

the Cape Hatteras lens. An enormous pile of lighthouse lenses and equipment was discovered in the state capitol building in Raleigh, but the Cape Hatteras lens was notably absent.

So what had become of it? Duffus's painstaking research uncovered the surprisingly simple answer to that question. In September 1865, about four months after the war ended, a Union patrol found the lens in its country hiding place. Without fanfare the lens was shipped across the Atlantic to Paris so that its manufacturers could make repairs. One year later, the lens was returned to the United States and stored at the Staten Island Lighthouse Depot in New York. When the modern Cape Hatteras lighthouse was completed in 1870, the station's original lens returned to its rightful place at the top of the tower. So ends the mystery. Where was the lens hiding all those years? In the Cape Hatteras tower right under the keeper's nose!

Likely as not, government bureaucrats thought there was nothing remarkable about the odyssey of the lens, and its story was buried in their files. In the 1920s a fire at the US Commerce Department in Washington destroyed many of the old Lighthouse Service records, further clouding the history of the lens. Meanwhile, the lens remained in use.

In 1936, the Lighthouse Service temporarily decommissioned the light. The lens was left unattended for several years, during which time it suffered greatly from vandalism. Many of the delicate glass prisms were chipped, broken, or taken away as souvenirs. Finally, in 1949, the National Park Service acquired the Cape Hatteras tower and removed the damaged lens. Today, the bronze framework and surviving prisms are on display at the Graveyard of the Atlantic Museum in Hatteras Village.

Era of the Civilian Lighthouse Service: 1910–1939

In 1886, the Lighthouse Board tried out an exciting new invention, placing an electric light in the torch of the recently completed Statue of Liberty. The board maintained the light as a New York City harbor beacon for more than fifteen years and by the turn of the twentieth century had begun the process of converting all its lighthouses to electric illumination. Having thus ushered in a new age of navigational technology, the Lighthouse Board had accomplished all it had set out to do when it was placed in charge of US maritime aids a half century earlier.

However, the world had become more complex since the 1850s, and so, too, had the US system of navigational aids. Under the Lighthouse Board, that system had grown to encompass more than 10,000 lighted aids, including considerably more than 1,000 lighthouses. Maintaining this enormous and far-flung system required a more centralized authority, and in 1910 Congress disbanded the Lighthouse Board and established the US Bureau of Lighthouses or, as it was more commonly known, the US Lighthouse Service.

Congress placed control of the new Lighthouse Service in the hands of a single individual, the Commissioner of Lighthouses.

To fill the new post, President William H. Taft named George R. Putnam, who had directed an extensive coastal survey in the Philippine Islands. Putnam must have liked the job—he served as commissioner for twenty-five years. During his quarter century at the helm of the Lighthouse Service, Putnam steered the agency on a steady course of growth and modernization, while never losing sight of the fact that its strength was in its workers. In his view, the heart of the Lighthouse Service lay in the ordinary people who kept the agency running and the lights burning. For Putnam, who often described the building and keeping of lighthouses as a "picturesque and humanitarian undertaking," the true lighthouse heroes were not scientists and engineers, but rather the lighthouse keepers and their families.

Putnam worked to improve the lot of keepers and other Lighthouse Service employees. He helped raise salaries, which had always been low compared with those of other federal workers; he

Built by immigrant laborers, the dramatic Split Rock Lighthouse (opposite page) near the far western end of Lake Superior was completed in 1910. That same year Congress placed responsibility for all US beacons in the hands of a civilian agency that would come to be called the United States Lighthouse Service.
Bruce Roberts

Bruce Roberts

coaxed a reluctant Congress to provide medical and retirement benefits; and he took measures to raise the morale of keepers and make them feel part of a vital and public-spirited endeavor.

Putnam resolved to keep personnel better informed of technological advances and of the activities of their compatriots throughout the service. In 1912 the agency mailed out the first issue of the *Lighthouse Service Bulletin*, a newsletter that appeared in the mail slots of keepers several times a year over the next quarter century. The *Bulletin* not only detailed important changes in equipment and procedures but also included letters and news items from service workers and their families. Readers learned of the heroic exploits of fellow keepers, the arrival of babies, and the passing of old friends.

The September 1926 issue ran an elegy for a dog named Sport who had "served" aboard the Great Lakes lighthouse tender *Hyacinth* for a dozen years. "Sport was just a dog," wrote the correspondent. "But he was always a good dog and a good shipmate . . . Sport came aboard this vessel back in 1914 when engineer Albert Collins pulled him out of the Milwaukee river during a thunderstorm . . . in a pitiful condition and practically skin and bones . . . In his prime there was no place on the ship he did not visit and nothing going on that he did not have a paw in. He swam and played baseball with the boys. No boat could go ashore without Sport, and on many occasions he carried a line to shore through the breakers when landing at some light station with

Ship Island Light
National Archives

our crew . . . Sport died of old age on July 19, 1926 . . . He was sewed in canvas and buried at sea . . . two miles off Ludington, Michigan . . . and thus ended Sport, the best dog I have ever known."

There was even poetry. For the benefit of *Bulletin* readers, keeper Frederick Morong Jr. lamented in verse the constant polishing required by his job in the following lines of verse: "Oh what is the bane of a lighthouse keeper's life, That causes him worry, struggle and strife, That makes him use cuss words and beat on his wife. It's Brasswork! The devil himself could never invent, A material causing more worldwide lament, And in Uncle Sam's service about ninety percent. Is Brasswork."

Over the years, many items of historic or technological importance appeared in the *Lighthouse Service Bulletin* and other publications and notices sent out to keepers. The Lighthouse Service and the profession of lighthouse keeping were changing rapidly during the first half of the twentieth century. For instance, in 1912 the Lighthouse Service launched an efficiency campaign allowing keepers who received high marks in their quarterly inspections to wear stars on their uniforms. By this time lighthouses were becoming popular destinations for outings. "Lighthouses and stations are of interest to the public," the Lighthouse Service instructed its keepers through the *Bulletin.* "Permission to visit them is often appreciated and is of educational value."

Technological innovations would continue. In 1915 the service announced the introduction of diaphone fog signals, a Canadian invention that produced a two-tone sound signal with compressed air. One year later, with the development of a device for automatically replacing burned-out electric lamps, the service took the first big step toward wholesale automation of lighthouses. Meanwhile, the importance of lighthouses to national security became more apparent. In August 1916 Congress approved a measure allowing for the mobilization of the Lighthouse Service during time of war. On

Named Commissioner of the US Bureau of Lighthouses upon its creation in 1910, George Putnam (above) assumed responsibility for a system of navigational aids that, in some respects, had changed little in over a century. Most beacons were powered by antiquated gas lamps, and living conditions, especially at isolated light stations such as the one on Mississippi's Ship Island (opposite page), remained quite rustic. Putnam electrified beacons, upgraded equipment, and improved conditions for keepers and their families.

Courtesy *Lighthouse Digest*

April 11, 1917, the United States entered World War I on the side of Britain and France, and almost immediately President Woodrow Wilson issued an executive order placing Lighthouse Service vessels and personnel under naval authority. Some Lighthouse Service personnel took an active role in the conflict. For instance, on August 6, 1918, a German submarine sank a lightship stationed at Diamond Shoals near Cape Hatteras, North Carolina. Having attempted to warn other vessels in the area, the crew abandoned ship and survived.

Once the war was over, the Lighthouse Service returned to civilian control and, despite ongoing budget constraints, modernization efforts resumed. The service reported that by the middle of 1919, telephones had been installed in 139 light stations, while dozens of lightships and tenders had received radio equipment. In 1920, the superintendent of the Fifth Lighthouse District made the first light station inspection by air. His hydroplane flight to the New River Inlet and Bogue Sound lighthouses in North Carolina took about two hours. Previously, those inspections would have taken at least four days.

Electrification of lighthouses proved to be the main driving force behind the move to automation. During the 1920s the service developed automatic timers to turn electric lamps on and off on a preset schedule. Efforts to automate lighthouse operation got a big boost in 1933, with the invention of a photoelectric control system that enabled some stations to operate without full-time keepers. A year later, the service introduced a remote-control system for operation of unmanned navigational aids by radio. In 1936 simplified timers were introduced, making it possible to automate even more lighthouses and fog-signal stations. All these changes were leading to a radical new approach to guiding mariners, one that would eventually make keepers all but unnecessary.

As with most lighthouses down through the centuries, the big white tower (opposite page) on Maine's Cape Elizabeth was paired with a residence. Throughout the Lighthouse Service era, typical light stations were not just navigational facilities but also homes where keepers or their spouses cooked in kitchens like the one above. This would change, however, as lights were automated and residences were boarded up. The pace of automation increased dramatically after the Coast Guard took charge of US maritime beacons in 1939.
Bruce Roberts

Cape Elizabeth
Bruce Roberts

The Keepers of the Lights

Little is known about the world's earliest lighthouse keepers. No doubt some of them were the family or friends of the mariners who relied on them for guidance. Perhaps they built fires on hillsides to call their loved ones home from the sea. During the Middle Ages, navigational lights often were kept by monks or nuns who regarded their efforts on behalf of mariners as "good works" likely to be rewarded by the Almighty.

While there always seems to have been sturdy men and women willing to faithfully tend navigational lights, the work was never high paying. George Worthylake, America's first full-time keeper, received only £50 per year and found he could not support his family on such a low income. During the nineteenth century, US keepers usually earned about $200 a year, but must have counted themselves lucky since their Canadian counterparts generally were paid less than half that of keepers on the other side of the border.

Despite the modest financial rewards, lighthouse keeping was always considered an honorable and even comfortable profession. After all, the job usually came with a house—almost by definition one with a spectacular ocean view. The work was steady and most certainly worthwhile.

As with some other professions, lighthouse keeping tended to run in the family. Once a man got a job as a keeper, he often held onto it for decades, and it was not uncommon for the same job to be passed on to his sons and even his grandsons. In Great Britain five generations of the Knott family kept one or another Trinity House light over an incredible unbroken stretch of 181 years. William Knott first tended the South Foreland Light in 1730; his great-great-grandson Henry Knott retired as keeper of the North Foreland Light in 1911. In the United States, War of 1812 hero John O'Neil and his descendants kept Maryland's Concord Point Light operating for nearly a century.

"We've all got the lighthouse fever in our blood," said Joseph Strout, keeper of the Portland Head Lighthouse from 1904 to 1922. Strout's father, Joshua, had been keeper of the same lighthouse from 1869 to 1904. Joseph Strout had grown up at the Portland Head light station and well understood that lighthouse keeping was a family affair. As a child he had pitched in along with the entire family to help with station chores. Even the Strout parrot Billy took part, announcing to one and all when thick weather set in: "It's foggy! It's foggy! Start the horn!"

Holidays and cherished rituals did not exempt keepers and their families from their duties, a fact that came home to the Strouts with a thump on December 24, 1888, just as they were settling down to enjoy their Christmas Eve dinner. The blizzard-bound three-masted sailing ship *Annie Maguire* crashed into the rocks, practically at the door of the keeper's residence. The Strouts hurried outside, where they managed to rescue everyone onboard the wrecked vessel.

It might be said that heroism was part of the keeper's job description. Even if they never participated in a daring rescue—and many did—keepers saved countless lives by faithfully tending their lights. Maritime history is filled with stories of keepers who stood by their posts through wartime assaults, crippling illnesses, mighty storms, or as was the case with original Minot's Ledge Lighthouse in 1850, even as the light tower itself was collapsing.

Some of the most heroic lighthouse keepers have been women. Perhaps the most famous American keeper of all time was Ida Lewis, who tended Rhode Island's Lime Rock Light and, over the years, pulled dozens of potential drowning victims from the waters off Newport. Port Pontchartrain keeper Margaret Norvell was said to have saved hundreds of lives in the storm-battered Louisiana lowlands.

Now that nearly all navigational beacons are automated, some might say the lighthouse keeper's profession is extinct, but not so. Even automated lights occasionally require attention, and someone must provide it. In the United States, members of US Coast Guard aids to navigation teams maintain the nation's maritime lights. Often called upon to repair or service lights on remote islands and narrow platforms that can only be reached by helicopter, these young Coast Guard servicemen display fortitude and dedication to duty at the very least equal to that of earlier keepers.

Additionally, the automation and deterioration of historic lighthouses over the last few decades have brought into being a whole new variety of keeper—the preservationist who works incessantly to save old light towers. Like the lighthouse keepers of old, their work is difficult but necessary, for they have taken upon themselves the task of keeping the lights burning for generations to come.

Known affectionately as "The First Lady of Light," Connie Small (right) receives support from a pair of US Coast Guard admirers at a dinner given in her honor during the 1990s. Connie and husband, Elson Small, served for decades at light stations along the rugged coast of Maine. Connie died in 2005 at the age of 103.

Courtesy *Lighthouse Digest*

The Coast Guard Era: 1939–Present

By 1939, 150 years after the first US Congress authorized its creation, the Lighthouse Service employed more than 5,300 workers, including 1,170 light keepers and assistants, 56 light attendants, and 1,995 officers or crew members on lightships and tenders. The service operated almost 30,000 navigational aids—fewer than 1,000 of them lighthouses—and 65 tenders.

At this point, the story of the Lighthouse Service came to an abrupt end. On July 1, 1939, President Franklin D. Roosevelt's Reorganization Plan No. 11 took effect. It provided that the Lighthouse Service and its functions be transferred to the US Coast Guard. President Roosevelt cited efficiency and economy as his rationale for dissolving the Bureau of Lighthouses and placing all maritime lights under the authority of the Coast Guard, but some historians recognize a broader strategic motive in the measure. With another war on the horizon, the president likely thought it prudent to place the nation's maritime lights in the hands of a military organization, just as President Wilson had done in 1917. Also, the reorganization allowed Roosevelt to increase the Coast Guard's budget without having to wring an extra appropriation out of a reluctant Congress.

Whatever the reason for its demise, there were many who lamented the passing of the Lighthouse Service. For most keepers and other

Among the last of America's old-time civilian keepers, William Demeritt stands with his family beside his lighthouse in Key West, Florida. Demeritt opposed dissolution of the Lighthouse Service and said so in an angry, face-to-face confrontation with President Franklin D. Roosevelt in 1939. Not surprisingly, the keeper lost the argument, and he retired soon after.

Courtesy Monroe County Public Library, Key West, Florida

agency workers, the service had been home. In fact, the shared sense of family within the service had been one of the key achievements of Commissioner Putnam, who retired from the service in 1935. The notion of working under military authority rankled more than a few.

Still, the change had been made, and the work of lighting the nation's coast had to continue. When the reorganization took effect, Putnam's successor, H. D. King, moved his office into Coast Guard headquarters in Washington and soon after retired. While some former Lighthouse Service employees resigned outright, most chose to stay, about half as civilians and half as newly enlisted members of the Coast Guard.

When members of the old Lighthouse Service retired or resigned and moved on to other jobs, their places were taken by young Coast Guard servicemen who had not necessarily signed up with lighthouse duty in mind. Even so, they took to the work with the same dedication as those who preceded them. Posted to cramped lightships or isolated light stations on barren rocks or desolate stretches of coast in Alaska, they demonstrated the characteristic willingness of lighthouse keepers in every era to put themselves in harm's way to safeguard the lives of others.

Nothing illustrates this so well as the fate of the five-man Coast Guard crew on duty at the Scotch Cap Light Station in the Aleutian Islands in the early morning hours of April 1, 1946. According to an adage popular among the peoples of the temblor-prone Pacific Rim, "Quakes shake, but tsunamis kill." Perhaps no force in nature is quite so powerful or so completely ruinous as a tsunami, the fast-moving tidal waves caused by undersea earthquakes. Literally a wall of water—sometimes more than 100 feet high—a tsunami can strike at near supersonic speed. Anything in its path for some distance inland will be smashed and then washed back into the sea, leaving little but scattered wreckage behind.

More than a few automated lighthouses have become popular tourist destinations. Visitors enjoy the view from the lofty gallery at Florida's St. Augustine Light.
Bruce Roberts

Bruce Roberts

1ST. REGT. N.Y. INDT.

Crown Point Lighthouse, Lake Champlain, N.Y.

Lake Champlain's grand Crown Point Lighthouse, depicted in the antique postcard (above), exists now only as a faded image on old photographs or in the memories of former keepers and their children. Far too many historic towers have vanished along with the invaluable maritime heritage they represent. Fortunately, the determination and hard work of preservationists are saving many others. Civil War buffs celebrate restoration of Georgia's Tybee Island Light (opposite page) and the important role the old tower played in the nation's history.

Courtesy *Lighthouse Digest*

There was never much at Scotch Cap in the first place, at least not structures that had been put there by humankind. Located beside the Bering Sea near the far outer edge of the Aleutian Islands on Unimak Island, Scotch Cap has been described as North America's last lonely outpost. The light station, established in 1903 to help mariners find a key channel linking the Gulf of Alaska with the Bering Sea, was so remote that it received mail and supplies only once or twice a year.

Keepers here needed a high tolerance for isolation and loneliness. Anyone not completely at home with themselves or with nature was unlikely to last long at Scotch Cap. According to Aleutian natives, who usually avoided the place, the island was haunted. They referred to Unimak as "the Roof of Hell," and Scotch Cap keepers likely had similar names for it themselves.

As a matter of policy, the Lighthouse Service and later the US Coast Guard limited Scotch Cap

Lighthouses in Miniature

During the last twenty years or so, lighthouse preservation has received a significant boost from an unexpected quarter—the collectibles market. Several companies now produce sculptures or models of lighthouses and sell them through catalogs, over the Internet, or in gift shops. The tremendous popularity of miniature lighthouses like those shown here has inevitably raised the level of interest in the full-size originals—and in efforts to save them from ruin.

Harbour Lights sculptures of South Africa's Cape Agulhas Lighthouse (above) and Germany's Bremerhaven tower (above left)

Harbour Lights sculpture of Canada's Cove Island Lighthouse (below)

Photos Courtesy Harbour Lights

assignments to only one year. This helped prevent some of the medical and psychological problems inherent in long stays at such an isolated place. In any case, most keepers did not object when reassigned to another duty station.

In 1946 the station's complement consisted of five young Coast Guard servicemen: Anthony Pettit, Leonard Pickering, Jack Colvin, Paul Ness, and Dewey Dykstra. Some were nearing the end of their scheduled tour on Unimak while others had just arrived. But as it turned out, none of the five would leave the island alive.

Anthony Pettit was the senior man at Scotch Cap, and he was known to take great pride in his work as a lighthouse keeper. Probably he was the one on duty during the important midnight-to-dawn shift on April 1, 1946, when an earthquake struck just after 1:30 a.m. It isn't known whether the station was damaged by the quake, but the real devastation was to come later, when a tsunami obliterated Scotch Cap. Experts have estimated that the wall of water may have been as high as a ten-story building and may have been moving at 500 miles per hour.

No doubt it was obvious to all five keepers that something terrible was about to happen. The sea bottom for some distance out from the station had been drained of water, and that could mean only one thing—that soon the water would come rushing back. Indeed, little more than half an hour after the station floors had stopped shaking, the water returned in the form of an enormous wave. Probably they never saw it at all, and even if they had seen it, they could not have escaped.

During the days and weeks after the disaster, rescue teams searched the beaches of Unimak Island as well as the former site of the Scotch Cap lighthouse. They found the bodies of two of the keepers and a bit of scattered debris but little else. Nothing at all remained of the former light station. Years later, a modest memorial for the victims was placed on the rocks where the lighthouse once stood. Today, the lost keepers are honored in a more active way by a US Coast Guard tender named the *Anthony Pettit,* which services buoys and light stations along the Alaskan coast.

Beacons in the New Millennium

While the heroism and dedication of lighthouse keepers has never been in question, their profession has dwindled—some would say it is all but extinct. This is true because the beacons they once tended so faithfully have changed dramatically and no longer require the full-time attention of keepers. All lighthouses in the United States and most others around the world are now automated.

In the United States the process of automating navigational beacons started in the early decades of the twentieth century, when a series of technological advances began to make it possible for navigational beacons to function reliably without much help from people. During and after World War II, the Coast Guard continued the development of new technologies and accelerated the pace of lighthouse automation. The lights of many old stone, brick, or wooden towers were extinguished and replaced by buoys or by automated beacons mounted on simple skeleton towers. In the 1960s the Coast Guard launched its Lighthouse Automation and Modernization Program (LAMP), which quickly reduced the number of manned light stations to fewer than sixty. By 1990 the number had dwindled down to one, and in 1999 Boston Harbor Light—America's oldest beacon—was finally automated.

While automation is cost-effective, it has taken a heavy toll on historic lighthouse properties in North America and throughout the world. Many old light towers have been demolished, and most of those that have survived show the scars of neglect. Without keepers to watch over them, their windows, walls, and delicate lenses have been

A Lifeline for Lighthouses

If lighthouses are no longer the cutting edge of navigational technology—and this is certainly the case—then why should we care what happens to them? Because the people who built them and kept their lights burning cared and because they form a link between caring people today and an unforgettable chapter in world history. Says *Lighthouse Digest* editor Timothy Harrison: "We must save lighthouses because they remind us of something we cannot afford to forget—our past." Time is running out on many of our nation's most historic lighthouses. When they're gone, it won't just be the structures themselves that we are losing; it'll also be their history and ours as well. With the passing of time, more of our lighthouse history is slipping away—lost forever. Future generations may never know the story of these structures and of the men and women who served at them. We may never fully understand the vital part they played in the saga of American, Canadian, and world maritime history.

Bruce Roberts

During the last few decades, as interest in lighthouses has grown, lighthouse preservation groups have sprung up all over the world. Most are small, dedicated to saving only one particular lighthouse, but a number of larger preservation organizations such as the US Lighthouse Society, the American Lighthouse Foundation, and the Great Lakes Lighthouse Keepers Association have also emerged.

In 2000 the US Congress passed the National Historic Lighthouse Preservation Act with the goal of giving away what remained of the Coast Guard's lighthouses nationwide to qualified nonprofits and other government agencies. Since then dozens if not hundreds of local and national organizations have taken advantage of the law to preserve still-standing lighthouses and celebrate their history.

damaged by the weather or vandalized. Some have deteriorated beyond repair.

Fortunately, even abandoned lighthouses are not completely friendless. In every country there are many people who honor the relics of past adventures and who count aged light towers among their nation's most important monuments. Dozens of national organizations and hundreds of local ones have been formed to help preserve old lighthouses and to make good use of them as bases for marine research or educational enrichment.

Some lighthouses have been converted into museums, hostelries, or bed-and-breakfast inns. Many others are cherished by local communities and businesses for the tourists they attract. In fact, lighthouses are enjoying a surge of popularity, and this is no accident. Unlike some public buildings—prisons, for instance—light towers have never suffered from an image problem. They have long been looked upon as romantic structures, representative of the very best instincts of humankind, and that is how they appear to us today.

Heceta Head Lighthouse. The bed-and-breakfast is on the far right.
Shutterstock.com

A LIGHTHOUSE
LEXICON

The following alphabetical listing of people, places, events, equipment, and specialized terminology is intended to bring lighthouses and their extraordinary story into clearer focus. Some of the characters and subjects you've already encountered in Part I are covered in greater detail in the lexicon, and it will introduce you to many others. We trust it will answer many if not most of your questions about navigational beacons and their history. Note that lighthouses in bold type are described in more detail in Part III of this book.

ACETYLENE LAMPS In 1892, while searching for an economical way to produce aluminum, Canadian inventor Thomas Willson stumbled across the electric arc process used to prepare acetylene. A highly flammable gas, acetylene could be stored under pressure in a tank, and when burned in a lamp, it yielded a pure white light and almost no smoke or soot. This made acetylene an ideal fuel for buoys and, occasionally, for the lamps in lighthouse lanterns.

Seeking a market for his new fuel, Willson himself designed and sold acetylene lamps and buoys, but he soon had competition from the American Gas Accumulator Company and similar firms. Before long, acetylene was being put to work in buoys and light stations along the coasts of nearly every maritime nation. In most cases the acetylene lamps could be left burning and required only occasional visits by tenders for refueling and maintenance. This made it much easier to maintain remote light stations where reliable electric power was unavailable. Acetylene technology also made it possible to automate certain coastal lights. Connecticut's **New London Harbor Light** was automated in this way in 1912.

Although acetylene had significant advantages over other fuels, it was costly, and because it was kept under pressure, there was always a danger of explosion. In 1913,

The sweeping seascape takes
in Ireland's Fastnet Lighthouse.
Copyright Jean Guichard

an acetylene buoy blew up on the US lighthouse tender *Hibiscus*. Fortunately, the vessel and most of its crew survived. In time, most national lighthouse services abandoned acetylene in favor of safer and less expensive energy sources, such as solar power. (See also Solar-Powered Optics.)

AEROMARINE BEACONS Developed for use at airports, aeromarine beacons began to replace the Fresnel lenses in some lighthouses after World War II. Relatively small, impervious to weather, and easy to maintain, they proved ideal for automated light stations. Aeromarine beacons are metal cylinders containing a lighting element with a lens at one end. Usually the cylinders are mounted in pairs, with the lenses facing in opposite directions. When the cylinders are rotated, the light appears to flash. Like the Fresnel lenses they replaced, aeromarine beacons are now considered out of date and in most cases have given way to Vega lights and other modern optics. **Cape Cod Light** (Truro, Massachusetts) employed rotating aeromarine beacons from about 1950 until 1998. (See also DCB Aerobeacons, Modern Optics, and Vega Lights.)

AIDS TO NAVIGATION TEAMS (ANTS) Coast Guard units assigned to operate and maintain lighthouses, channel lights, buoys, and other navigational markers are called Aids to Navigation Teams, or ANTs for short. In all, the Coast Guard has sixty-four ANTs to look after the approximately 400 lighthouses that now brighten the US

Cudillero Light crowns a cliff in Northern Spain.
Henry Gonzales

A trio of acetylene tanks (left) once fueled the light at Turn Point in Washington's San Juan Islands. The European-style aerobeacon (below) is in Hourtin, France.

Courtesy *Lighthouse Digest*

Egbert Koch

shoreline. Although all US navigational lights are now automated, they require periodic inspection and maintenance visits. Some visits to remote light stations still may take several days, if not weeks, giving team members a brief taste of the isolated lifestyles of old-time lighthouse keepers.

APOSTLE ISLANDS NATIONAL LAKESHORE

Every summer visitors flock to Wisconsin's Apostle Islands on the southern coast of Lake Superior to enjoy the natural beauty and vigorous outdoor activities they offer. However, the islands' biggest attractions may be their lighthouses. More than twenty islands and no fewer than six historic light stations are now part of the Apostle Islands National Lakeshore. Many visitors consider the area a veritable lighthouse museum.

Because the cluster of low, often fog-shrouded islands created a significant hazard to navigation, the US government began to mark them with lighthouses not long after the Soo Canal opened Lake Superior to shipping traffic from the other Great Lakes in the mid-1850s. In all, six light stations were established here, the first in 1857 (**Michigan Island Light**) near the eastern end of the chain. Other lighthouses were built on Raspberry Island (1863), Outer Island (1874), Sand Island (1881), Devils Island (1891), and Long Island (1895). Several of these lighthouses remain in operation, and most of the original structures still stand. Some are open to the public, and all can be seen and photographed from the water. With the help of volunteer actors, the National Park Service provides living history demonstrations at Raspberry Island Lighthouse.

A Lighthouse Lexicon   57

Maine's Saddleback Ledge (above) is occasionally visited by Coast Guard ANTs. Equally remote but far more inviting is the Sand Island Light (left) in the Apostles.
Bruce Roberts

ARGAND LAMPS In 1783, French inventor François-Pierre Ami Argand introduced a bright and relatively clean-burning lamp, which would see wide use in lighthouses around the world. The Argand lamp consisted of a fuel pan with a hollow, circular wick that allowed a free flow of oxygen to both sides. Argand lamps produced an intense flame, a very bright light, and hardly any smoke. European lighthouse services soon began to pair the Argand lamp with reflectors that further intensified the light. The most effective reflectors were parabolic or cone-shaped. Argand lamps eventually were replaced by a superior optical system relying on the advanced Fresnel prismatic lens.

ATTACHED DWELLINGS In some cases, the keeper's residence was attached to the tower. Often the residence was two stories tall and the tower rose from the front of the building or from one of its corners. Having the tower and residence attached

Courtesy Harbour Lights

This early tower at Marblehead (below) in Massachusetts likely employed an old-style Argand lamp and reflector. Established in 1818, Macquarie (left) is Australia's oldest light station.

Courtesy *Lighthouse Digest*

enabled the keeper to service the light regardless of weather conditions. Not surprisingly, attached residences were most common in northern climes, where a winter walk to a distant light tower might give the keeper a nasty case of frostbite. (See also Detached Dwellings and Keepers' Residences.)

AUSTRALIAN MARITIME SAFETY AUTH-ORITY Among the newest of the world's lighthouse administrative bodies, the Australian Maritime Safety Authority dates only to 1991, when it was created to coordinate all matters related to maritime navigation in Australia. The authority has a big job, since it must watch over nearly 24,000 miles of coastline and hundreds of major navigational aids. Australia has many historic light towers, with more than 120 built during the nineteenth century.

AUTOMATION With the introduction of electric power and reliable timers early in the twentieth century, it became possible to operate light stations without full-time keepers. By the 1930s, the US Lighthouse Service had begun to automate beacons and remove keepers from stations that were either extremely isolated or costly to maintain. Generally speaking, however, the service preferred to keep its personnel in place, and wholesale automation did not begin until responsibility for navigational lights was given to the US Coast Guard by presidential order in 1939.

Following World War II, remote-control systems, light-activated switches, and fog-sensing devices made automation an increasingly cost-

Many twentieth-century lighthouses, such as the Port Washington Breakwater tower (right) in Wisconsin, were designed with automation in mind. Bache's New Dungeness Light (below) is in Washington State.

effective and attractive option, and the efficiency-minded Coast Guard automated one light station after another. By 1970, only about sixty US lighthouses still had full-time keepers, and by 1990, all but one of those beacons had been automated. The first light station constructed in America, the **Boston Harbor Light**, was the last to give up its keeper.

An unfortunate if unintended consequence of automation was the rapid decline of lighthouse towers and dwellings. Usually, once the keepers were removed, little or no regular maintenance was done on light station buildings. Residences were particularly hard hit, and many deteriorated to the point of collapse. In recent years, lighthouse lovers and preservationists have stepped in to shore up walls, patch roofs, and, as funding permits, fully restore old lighthouses. The Coast Guard is now offering some light station residences and towers for sale or lease to well-intentioned individuals, groups, or local governments.

BACHE, HARTMAN A nineteenth-century US Army engineer, Hartman Bache designed the extraordinary screw-pile lighthouse at Brandywine Shoal in Delaware and also played a key role in lighting the American West Coast.

Screw-pile lighthouses were vulnerable to damage from river ice floes, especially in the Mid-Atlantic region. At the open-water Brandywine Shoal Light Station, Bache solved the ice problem by protecting the lighthouse with a forest of heavily braced iron legs. Usually, screw-pile towers rested on eight or ten legs, but the Brandywine Shoal tower had thirty. Completed in 1850, the Brandywine

60   The Lighthouse Encyclopedia

Hartman Bache's unusual design for the Brandywine Shoal Light (left) placed it atop a forest of piles.

National Archives

Keepers at Cape Henry in Virginia (below) could guide ships with three different type of beacon: light, sound, and radio transmissions.

National Archives

Shoal tower resisted the ice for more than sixty years. It was replaced by a caisson tower shortly before World War I.

In the mid-1850s Bache served as inspector of the Lighthouse Board's Twelfth District, which encompassed the entire West Coast. At the time the board selected Bache to head up its Western construction program about 1855, the West's only operating lighthouse was **Alcatraz Island Light** in San Francisco Bay. Within a few years Bache had at least fifteen additional light towers standing at strategic coastal locations from San Diego to Cape Flattery, at the entrance to the Strait of San Juan de Fuca in Washington. Bache insisted on the use of highly effective but expensive Fresnel lenses. Since the heavy and rather delicate lenses had to be imported from France, nearly half a world away, this delayed completion of several Western light stations.

Bache served as a Union topographical engineer during the Civil War and afterward returned to lighthouse-related duties in the East. He retired as a brigadier general in 1867.

BARBIER & FENESTRE See Fresnel Lens Manufacturers.

BEACONS Any light or radio signal intended to guide mariners or aviators can be referred to as a beacon. Often the word is used interchangeably with "light." Early beacons often were nothing more than a lantern hung from a pole, a candle kept burning in an upstairs window, or a fire built high

The National Historic Lighthouse Preservation Act

Does your group or agency want to acquire—and care for—a historic lighthouse? It's a big responsibility, but it may just be possible under the terms of the National Historic Lighthouse Preservation Act of 2000.

Passed by Congress and signed into law by President Bill Clinton, the Act provides an exciting mechanism for the protection and use of a vital resource—America's historic light stations. An amendment to the National Historic Preservation Act of 1966, the Act recognizes the cultural, recreational, and educational value of lighthouses as reminders of the nation's rich maritime heritage. It allows eligible federal or state agencies, local governments, and nonprofit groups to acquire ownership of historic lighthouses and lighthouse property at little or no cost. Transfer is contingent on compliance with certain conditions intended to ensure the lighthouses will be properly cared for and put to uses compatible with public interests. These conditions may include opening the lighthouse to the public at reasonable times.

The transfer process works as follows. The Coast Guard or other responsible federal agency identifies a surplus light station and reports it to the General Services Administration. Having provided advance notice and adequate time for prospective applicants to plan and organize preservation efforts, the GSA issues an official Notice of Availability. The National Park Service then provides applications to interested parties, reviews and evaluates them, and recommends approved applicants to the GSA. Once an applicant is selected, the property is transferred, but the new owners are required to meet stringent use and preservation standards. Several dozen historic lighthouses have been transferred in this way since the Act was passed in 2000.

on a hill overlooking the sea. Eighteenth-century light towers had very dim beacons produced by tallow candles or simple oil lamps, but over the years, lighthouse beacons grew increasingly sophisticated and effective. During the early nineteenth century, whale-oil lamps and silvered reflectors brightened their lights considerably. The invention of polished-glass prismatic lenses by Augustin Fresnel in the 1820s enabled lighthouse beacons to reach vessels at a distance of 20 miles or more. Radio beacons, introduced in 1921, extended the effective reach of a navigational station to several hundred miles. (See also Aeromarine Beacons, DCB Aerobeacons, Fixed Signals, Flashing Signals, Fog Signals, Fresnel Lenses, Modern Optics, Radio Beacons, Solar-Powered Optics, and Vega Lights.)

BIRDCAGE LANTERNS Early lanterns in the United States and elsewhere often had dozens if not hundreds of small panes of glass held in place by a thin metal frame. Consisting of numerous metal ribs extending from the gallery deck to the roof— usually a copper dome and ventilator—the frames gave these lanterns the appearance of a birdcage.

The small panes of glass in birdcage lanterns were difficult to keep clean and often of poor quality, limiting the brightness and effectiveness of the station's light signal. So, too, did the metal ribs, which blocked light and dimmed the beacon. Usually too small to accommodate Fresnel lenses, birdcage lanterns began to be phased out by the mid-nineteenth century and are now extremely rare. Birdcage lanterns remain in use at the Prudence Island Lighthouse in Portsmouth, Rhode Island, and Selkirk Lighthouse in Pulaski, New York, now a private aid to navigation. (See also Lanterns.)

US Coast Guard

Birdcage lanterns at Baileys Harbor in Wisconsin (below) and the long-vanished Cat Island Light (left) on the Gulf of Mexico.
Bruce Roberts

BOATS AND BOATHOUSES Not surprisingly, nearly all lighthouse keepers were familiar with the care and operation of small boats. Getting around in a harbor, on and off an open-water light station, or to and from a lighthouse tender required the deft use of small watercraft. Most early manned light stations had a boat, powered by oars or, on occasion, a modest sail. Later keepers or Coast Guard station crews had access to boats with outboard motors or small inboard engines.

Whenever possible, station boats were kept in a special storage building or boathouse. Usually, these were simple sheds with gabled roofs and iron or wooden rails to help with pulling the boat out of the water and into storage. Screw-pile, caisson, or other open-water stations suspended their boats from davits.

In times of emergency, keepers put their boats to good use. More than a few shipwrecked sailors owe their lives to the timely arrival of a keeper with his boat. During her decades of service at Rhode Island's **Lime Rock Lighthouse,** Ida Lewis was said to have saved more than a dozen persons by pulling them from the icy waters of Newport Harbor and into the station boat.

Ironically, the same boats that made it possible to save the lives of others sometimes became deathtraps for the keepers themselves. Of the keepers killed in the line of duty, and there have been quite a few, the majority lost their lives in boating accidents. George Worthylake, America's first lighthouse keeper, drowned in 1718 when his boat overturned while he was on his way from the mainland to Little Brewster Island, where he had tended the **Boston Harbor Light** for less than two years.

An early-twentieth-century light station boat and boat house (above) on White Island near Portsmouth, New Hampshire, and (right) at the Mamajuda Island Light on the Great Lakes. An iron-cylinder tower (opposite page) guards the Delaware Breakwater.

Courtesy *Lighthouse Digest*

BREAKWATER LIGHTS Harbors often are protected from high waves by a lengthy barrier of stone called a breakwater. Because they rise no more than a few feet above the surface, breakwaters are hard to see, especially at night, and may pose a threat to vessels entering or exiting the harbor. Breakwater beacons are meant to make mariners aware of this hazard so that they can safely navigate the harbor entrance. For obvious reasons, the light tower usually is placed near the end of the breakwater.

Engineers face unique challenges when building breakwater lighthouses. Since the foundations are nearly always unstable, these structures have to be relatively light but strong enough to stand up to high waves and wakes thrown up by passing ships. Since space atop the breakwater is limited, the keeper's residence usually is located on shore.

Over the years, many breakwater lighthouses have been demolished and replaced by pole lights or beacons mounted on steel towers. However, surviving breakwater lighthouses can be found at Rockland, Maine, in the Delaware Bay, and at several other locations along the US East Coast. The Great Lakes are especially rich in breakwater lights, with fine examples at Cleveland, Ohio, and Grand Haven, Michigan.

BRICK GIANTS The use of brick as a construction material dates from ancient times, but before the middle of the nineteenth century, very few brick buildings exceeded 100 feet in height. While many brick lighthouse towers had been built, particularly in the United States, they were seldom more than 80 or 90 feet tall. No doubt the builders, most of whom were not trained engineers, feared the extreme height would place too much stress on the walls.

Bruce Roberts

A hand-tinted postcard (above) features a century-old view of Maine's Portland Breakwater Light, a midget compared to the soaring, brick Shinnecock Bay tower (below) that once marked Long Island.

Courtesy Lighthouse Digest

Starting in the 1850s, the Lighthouse Board applied fresh engineering skill to the design and construction of light towers in the United States. In 1854 the 90-foot-tall **Cape Hatteras Light**, which had stood since 1803, was raised to a height of 150 feet. Some years later the original tower was torn down and replaced by a brick giant topping out at a breathtaking 193 feet.

Bricks were being stacked higher at other light stations as well, especially along the coasts of the southern United States, where there were few hills or cliffs to give light towers and their beacons a boost. Soaring brick lighthouses were built at Pensacola, Florida (a 160-foot tower completed in 1858), Fire Island, New York (a 180-foot tower completed in 1858), Bodie Island, North Carolina (a 163-foot tower completed in 1872), Ponce de Leon Inlet, Florida (a 168-foot tower completed in 1887), and ten other locations along the US Atlantic coast. These lighthouses were equipped with powerful Fresnel lenses to cast brighter light out to sea.

As testimony to the sturdiness of their construction, most of these tall brick lighthouses still stand, and their beacons continue to guide mariners. One that does not is the 170-foot tower of New York's Shinnecock Light. Completed in 1857, it was demolished in 1948 to make room for a parking lot.

BUG LIGHTS From a distance, lighthouses built on piles in open water look a bit like water bugs floating on the surface, hence the nickname "bug light." However, some old-time mariners claim the bug lights got their name because of the enormous numbers of insects attracted by their beacons.

Perhaps the best-known bug light of all time was Boston's Narrows lighthouse, built in 1856 and destroyed by fire in 1929. The fire started as keeper Tom Small was attempting to burn faded paint off the tower walls with a blowtorch. He set the tinder-dry structure ablaze and had no choice but to escape in the station boat and watch from a safe distance as his former home and workplace burned to the water line.

A very unusual bug light is located near the town of Greensport at the far eastern end of Long Island. Officially known as the Long Beach Bar Lighthouse, the two-story structure originally stood on spindly legs anchored to the bottom by screw piles. The original lighthouse burned down in 1963 but was rebuilt in the 1990s.

BULL'S-EYE LENSES Fresnel lenses often had two or more convex panels, or bull's-eyes, that concentrated light and caused the beacon to flash as the lens rotated. Clamshell or bivalve lenses, such as the one at Split Rock Light in Minnesota, have only two bull's-eyes. On the other hand, the big first-order Fresnel lens at the Point Reyes Light in California has twenty-four bull's-eyes. These radiate concentrated shafts of light that turn somewhat like the spokes of a wagon wheel as the lens is rotated. Although no longer used to guide

Depicted on this antique postcard (above), the Narrows "Bug" Light near Boston burned in 1929. A bulging bull's-eye (below) at the Cape May Light in New Jersey.
Courtesy *Lighthouse Digest*

mariners, the Point Reyes lens is sometimes lit up for demonstration purposes and the delight of tourists. (See also Clamshell [Bivalve] Lenses.)

BUREAU OF LIGHTHOUSES, US In 1910 Congress dissolved the Lighthouse Board (1852–1910) and established the US Bureau of Lighthouses, placing in its hands responsibility for construction, operation, and maintenance of all US navigational aids. The US Lighthouse Service was the operational arm of the bureau. George Putnam

Bruce Roberts

became the bureau's first commissioner and served in that capacity for twenty-four years.

At its height, shortly before World War I, the bureau maintained 1,462 lighthouses, 51 lightships, and more than 11,000 lesser maritime lights. Afterward, the size and complexity of the bureau and of the Lighthouse Service slowly declined. In 1939 the bureau's functions were taken over by the US Coast Guard. (See also Lighthouse Service, US and Putnam, George.)

BURGESS, ABBIE The story of young Abbie Burgess and her bravery in the face of a major winter storm has been told and retold. As a teenager, Abbie lived with her family at **Matinicus Rock Light,** located on a remote and mostly barren twenty-acre island more than 20 miles off the Maine coast. Abbie's father, Samuel Burgess, tended the lights in the station's twin granite towers.

During the second week of January 1856, keeper Burgess sailed off to the mainland to pick up supplies. While he was ashore, a major storm blew up out of the northeast, making it impossible for him to return. Several weeks passed before Burgess could safely make the crossing to Matinicus Rock. This left seventeen-year-old Abbie to keep the station's vital beacons in operation while caring for her invalid mother and two small sisters.

So ferocious was the storm that its waves washed completely over the rock and crashed into

Appropriately, a miniature light tower marks the grave of lighthouse heroine Abbie Burgess. Abbie's husband, Isaac Grant, lies nearby.

Courtesy *Lighthouse Digest*

The Whitehead Lighthouse was kept for nearly thirty years by Isaac and Abbie (Burgess) Grant. The Whitehead station is located on the central coast of Maine, only a few dozen miles from Matinicus Rock, site of Abbie's youthful exploits.

Courtesy *Lighthouse Digest*

the keeper's residence, forcing Abbie and her family to take refuge in the granite towers. Abbie later described the storm in a letter to a friend on the mainland:

"You have often expressed a desire to view . . . the ocean when it was angry. Had you been here on 19 January, I surmise you would have been satisfied. Father was away. Early in the day, as the tide rose, the sea made a complete breach over the rock, washing every movable thing away, and of the old dwelling not one stone was left upon another. . . . As the tide came, the sea rose higher and higher, till the only endurable places were the light towers. If they stood, we were saved; otherwise, our fate was only too certain. But for some reason, I know not why, I had no misgivings, and went about my work as usual. For four weeks . . . we were without assistance of any male member of our family. Though at times greatly exhausted with my labors, not once did the lights fail."

At one point during the storm, Abbie ran out to the chicken coop in an effort to save the family hens. "I ran out a few yards after the rollers had passed and the sea fell off a little, with the water knee deep, to the coop, and rescued all but one. It was the work of a moment, and I was back in the house with the door fastened, but I was none too quick, for at that instant my little sister, standing at the window, exclaimed, 'Oh, look! Look there! The worst sea is coming.' That wave . . . swept the rock."

"I cannot think you would enjoy remaining here any great length of time for the sea is never still and when agitated, its roar shuts out every sound, even drowning our voices."

A few years later, Abbie married a lighthouse keeper. She and her husband, Isaac Grant, spent nearly thirty years together at Whitehead Light, south of Rockland, Maine.

Secure on its stout caisson base, the Fourteen Foot Bank Lighthouse rises above the waters of Delaware Bay.

National Archives

CAISSON TOWERS Although inexpensive and in most ways practical, screw-pile lighthouses were fragile and prone to be swept away by storms and ice floes. For this reason engineers increasingly turned to caisson construction for offshore lighthouses. Essentially, a caisson is a hollow shell made of heavy, rolled-iron plates. Bolted together on land, the caisson was hauled to the construction site, sunk into the seabed up to a depth of about 30 feet, and then filled with sand, gravel, rock, or concrete. The caisson then provided a durable foundation for a lighthouse, usually of the iron-cylinder type. Because of their appearance, caisson lighthouses were sometimes called spark-plug or teakettle lights.

At many offshore lighthouse construction sites, the seabed required special preparation to clear obstructions and level the foundation. Pneumatic caissons developed in the mid-nineteenth century made it possible for crews to do this work below the surface in a more or less water-free environment. Open-ended caissons were lowered onto the seabed, and the water was pumped out to form a work chamber. Air was then pumped into the caisson continuously to maintain a high pressure level and keep water from seeping into the chamber. Workers entered the chamber through an air lock. Conditions inside the chamber were usually horrendous for workers, who had to contend with heat, humidity, and pressure as well as the back-breaking labor. Delaware's Fourteen Foot Bank Lighthouse was completed in 1887 using pneumatic caisson technology. The station remains operational.

As many as fifty caisson lighthouses were built in the United States, and a considerable number of these still stand. The Duxbury Lighthouse near Plymouth, Massachusetts, is said to be the oldest caisson tower in the United States. Other excellent examples are the Lubec Channel lighthouse in Maine (completed in 1890), the Orient Point lighthouse in New York (1899), and **Wolf Trap Light** in the Chesapeake Bay (1893). (See also Spark-Plug, Teakettle, or Coffeepot Lights.)

CAST-IRON TOWERS The introduction of cast iron as a building material in the 1840s was destined to revolutionize lighthouse construction. Stronger than stone and relatively light, cast iron made it possible to fabricate the parts of a tower in a far-off foundry and then ship them to the construction site for assembly. Cast iron was used for screw piles as well as for the legs, girders, and braces of skeleton structures, but it was most commonly used in the form of curved plating bolted together to form cylindrical towers.

A cylindrical structure assembled in 1844 on Long Island Head in Boston Harbor may have been the first all-cast-iron lighthouse. Eventually,

light towers of this type became a familiar sight on breakwaters, piers, and secured headlands. However, they were not considered sufficiently sound for more exposed locations. Occasionally, brick lighthouses were sheathed in cast-iron plates to protect the walls from weather damage.

CHANCE BROTHERS See Fresnel Lens Manufacturers.

CHARACTERISTIC The identifying feature of a lighthouse beacon is referred to as its characteristic. For instance, the light may be fixed and display a white, red, or green color. It may flash at regular intervals such as every six, ten, fifteen, or twenty seconds. It may display a single flash or series of quick flashes. Charts and published light lists help mariners identify the characteristic of a given light. Among the more famous lighthouse characteristics is that of the Minot's Ledge Light near Scituate, Massachusetts, which displays a single flash,

The cast-iron Nauset Beach tower (top) on Cape Cod was relocated with relative ease when threatened by erosion during the 1990s. The Bodie Island Light (above) shows off its flashing characteristic.

The shell-like shape of the Fresnel lens at Minnesota's Split Rock Light helps it funnel light into a single, powerful burst. Now a museum, the Split Rock station is no longer active, so this clamshell is lit only on ceremonial occasions.
Bruce Roberts

followed by four quick flashes, then three more. This one-four-three flashing sequence reminds some romantic observers of I-LOVE-YOU.

CLAMSHELL (BIVALVE) LENSES Most Fresnel lenses are round, but some have a slightly squeezed or flattened shape, somewhat like that of a clamshell. Known as clamshell or bivalve lenses, they nearly always feature a pair of bull's-eyes, or focal points, one on each side of the lens. The bull's-eyes enable the lens to display a pair of brilliant flashes with every complete rotation. Fine examples of the clamshell lens can be found at Split Rock Light in Minnesota and the Great Lakes Shipwreck Museum at Whitefish Point, Michigan. (See also Bull's-eye Lenses.)

CLOCKWORK MECHANISM Early rotating lighthouse lenses typically were driven by a set of gears, weights, and pulleys similar to those used in large clocks. Every few hours, the keeper had to rewind the machinery by pulling or cranking the weights to the top of the tower. Since the mechanism might need to be rewound at any time during the night, making regular sleep habits impossible, some keepers considered this an especially onerous chore. One of the early keepers at Minnesota's **Split Rock Light** is said to have slept on a pallet beneath the weight so that it would wake him when it reached the bottom and needed to be rewound.

COAST GUARD, CANADIAN Lighthouses in Canada are maintained and operated by the Canadian

Coast Guard, now part of the Department of Fisheries and Oceans. Canada's Coast Guard oversees approximately 260 major lighthouses and thousands of lesser navigational aids. Much like the US Coast Guard, the agency juggles an assortment of pressing duties and lacks the funds needed for extensive lighthouse preservation work. Also like the US Coast Guard, it relies on local governments and private groups to assist with restoration and maintenance of historic structures.

COAST GUARD, US Since 1939 lighthouses and other aids to navigation in the United States have been the responsibility of the US Coast Guard. As America's primary maritime agency, the Coast Guard plays a wide variety of roles, each of them vital to the security and well-being of the nation. In addition to the placement and maintenance of maritime aids, the Coast Guard also handles a vast array of assignments related to search and rescue, law

In addition to many other duties, the Canadian Coast Guard maintains active light stations like this one (above) on Prince Edward Island. To the south, the US Coast Guard likewise shoulders responsibility for lighthouses and other maritime aids. Two members of the US Cutter Service (below), as the Coast Guard was known before 1915, prepare to launch a small steamboat.

Courtesy *Lighthouse Digest*

With law enforcement and defense priorities draining its resources, the US Coast Guard can no longer spare personnel for the meticulous day-to-day maintenance lighthouses require (above). As a consequence, many historic light station properties are being turned over to parks, local governments, and preservationist groups.
Bruce Roberts

The cofferdam Detour Reef Lighthouse (above) on the Great Lakes nears completion in 1931.
National Archives

enforcement, environmental protection, preventive safety, and military preparedness. Each of these activities competes for a share of the Coast Guard budget and for the time of its personnel. Only about 20 percent of the agency's annual budget is devoted to maritime aids.

The Coast Guard is an amalgamation of five former federal agencies: the Revenue Cutter Service, the Lifesaving Service, the Steamboat Inspection Service, the Bureau of Navigation, and the Lighthouse Service. The Coast Guard was formed by an executive order from President Woodrow Wilson in 1915 when the Revenue Cutter Service and Lifesaving Service were brought together under its umbrella. Other agencies were

later added to the mix, the final one being the Lighthouse Service, which was absorbed by order of President Franklin Roosevelt shortly before World War II. Interestingly, the Coast Guard traces its history not to 1915 but rather to 1789, when the Lighthouse Service came into being.

For several decades the Coast Guard, like the old Lighthouse Service, operated under the auspices of the Treasury Department, but during World War I and World War II, it was placed under the authority of the Navy Department. In 1967 it became part of the Department of Transportation, which has been its home ever since.

The US Coast Guard is organized into nine districts, each with its own headquarters, commander, and geographic area of responsibility. Each Coast Guard district maintains Aids to Navigation Teams staffed by highly skilled technicians who look after navigational aids. Since all the nation's lighted maritime aids are now automated, team members need only visit them occasionally to make repairs and take care of routine maintenance. (See also Aids to Navigation Teams.)

COFFERDAM CONSTRUCTION When building lighthouses on very shallow sea or lake bottoms, construction crews sometimes employed the efficient and cost-effective cofferdam technique. Wooden walls were hammered together on shore and then hauled to the site, where they were used to build a box-shaped cofferdam. Once the walls were sealed, the water inside the cofferdam was pumped out, creating a relatively dry area where a sound foundation could be prepared. The cofferdam technique was used to build New York City's Robbins Reef lighthouse, completed in 1883, and Michigan's Detour Reef lighthouse, completed in 1931.

COLONIAL LIGHTHOUSES At least eleven major lighthouses were built during colonial times in what was to become the continental United States. Listed by year of construction, these were **Boston Harbor Light** (1716, Massachusetts); **Tybee Island Light** (1742, Georgia); Brant Point Light (1746, Massachusetts); Beavertail Light (1749, Rhode Island); New London Harbor Light (1760, Connecticut); **Sandy Hook Light** (1764, New Jersey); Cape Henlopen Light (1767, Delaware); Morris Island Light (1767, South Carolina); Plymouth Light (1769, Massachusetts); Portsmouth Harbor Light (1771, New Hampshire); and Cape Ann Light (1771, Massachusetts).

The history of the Tybee Island Light (above) can be traced back to the earliest days of colonial Georgia.

Bruce Roberts

A dozen fascinating Bruce Roberts lighthouse images appear on pages 72–73. They were taken at the following lighthouses (clockwise from the top of page 73): Cape Hatteras on the Outer Banks; Montauk Point on Long Island; Portland Head in Maine; Michigan City, Indiana; Cape Florida on Key Biscayne; Cove Point in Maryland; Tybee Island in Georgia; Frankfort, Michigan; Sand Key on the Florida Reef; Cape Neddick in Maine; and Grand Haven, Michigan.

Bruce Roberts

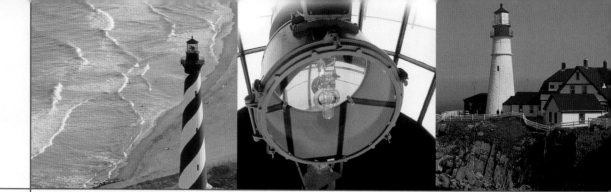

Seven Tips for Better Lighthouse Photos

One of the world's most celebrated and prolific photographers, Bruce Roberts has taken thousands of memorable lighthouse pictures, including many of the magnificent images in this book. His photographs capture not only the architectural outlines of a light tower and surrounding natural beauty but also the very essence of the place. Roberts offers the following tips to help you improve your technique and fill your photo album with pictures that will impress your family and friends.

1. The best times to photograph are dawn and dusk. The soft light just before sunrise and just after sunset usually makes better color pictures than the bright and harsh light of midday. In addition, the beacon from the lighthouse itself may be lit up and will add much to the quality of the picture. The low slant of the sunlight often illuminates vertical structures without fully lighting their surroundings. This will make the tower glow and stand out in your image.

2. Look at the lighthouse from as many angles as possible. Just because all the good photographs of a particular lighthouse have been taken from the same spot doesn't mean there isn't another excellent view. A telephoto lens may allow you to get back away from your subject and shoot from a number of vantage points that would be out of range for a normal or wide-angle lens. Keep trying and you may find a completely fresh and amazing point of view for your photograph.

3. Move to improve your line. When you change your position, everything in the picture also changes. Look carefully at all the objects in the frame—do they add or distract? Eliminate the distractions. By moving to the right or left, you can get telephone poles or other distractions out of the picture's frame.

4. Try different heights. You may also improve the picture by raising or lowering your point of view. We all tend to view things from 5 or 6 feet off the ground. The world changes when viewed from 1 inch off the ground or from an airplane looking down. Try getting close to the

surface of the water. To do this, you may want to shoot right from the water's edge or even take off your shoes and get in the water. (Even if the picture doesn't turn out as good as you hoped, everyone will be impressed by your dedication.) Shooting a lighthouse from the air is not always costly. A small plane like a Cessna 152 or 172 can be rented along with a pilot at many small airports for a rather modest hourly fee. You'll find that along the coast it's usually possible to fly low enough to get good pictures.

5. Add something else to the picture. Is there a boat that will pass by in the background? Or people coming or going? Or is there some interesting object that can be included in the foreground, such as a place sign or keeper's house? Some of the best lighthouse pictures tell something about the location or environment. For instance, a blanket of snow or even a few rain puddles can turn an ordinary picture into something extraordinary.

6. Look for special effects. Lighthouse keepers' dwellings nearly always had windows facing the tower so the occupants could easily check to see if the light was still burning. For photographers these windows offer another advantage: great reflections of the tower, flag poles, and other interesting objects. Move around until you see the reflection. If you see it, you should be able to photograph it. You also may find some fascinating reflections in ponds and puddles. If you can get inside the keeper's house, try using a window to frame your picture by shooting out through it.

7. Take your time, and use a tripod if possible. A tripod is a great asset. Not only does it let you shoot at slower shutter speeds into the darkening night, but it also gives you sharper pictures than the steadiest handheld camera. Particularly with telephoto lenses, camera movement is a major problem. A tripod also gives you time to see what you are really getting. Look at the edges in the viewfinder. Are you cutting off things at the right place? Check your composition. Do you really like it? Take your time. The longer you look, the more you see, and the better your pictures will be.

All photos by Bruce Roberts

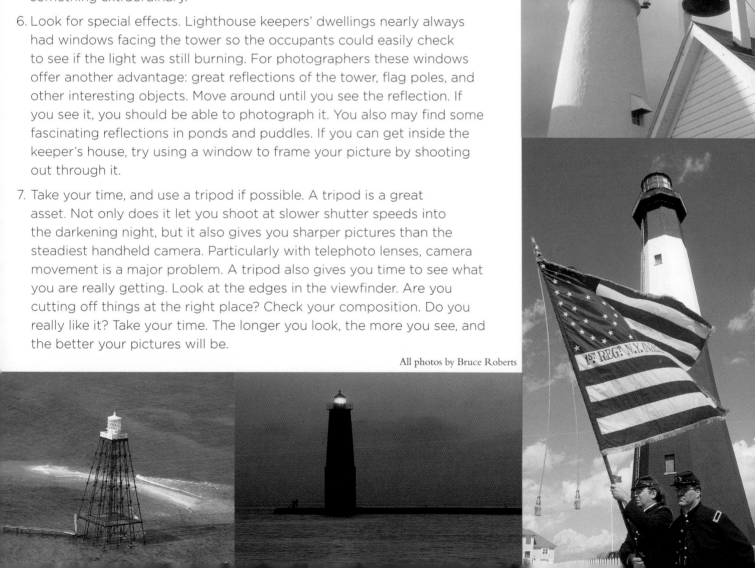

Its barrel-shaped tower built more than 800 years ago, Hook Head (above) is Ireland's oldest lighthouse. The York Spit Light (left), shown as it appeared in 1945, was one of many cottage-style light stations that once marked the Chesapeake Bay. Nearly all, including this one, have been removed.

Photos Courtesy *Lighthouse Digest*

Except for Cape Henlopen, all these light stations remain in operation, but only one, the Sandy Hook Lighthouse, retains its original tower. Mostly built of rough stone, America's eighteenth-century light towers lacked the durability of the brick and cast-iron lighthouses that were built later. The octagonal stone tower at Sandy Hook serves as a remarkable exception.

COLOSSUS OF RHODES Of the seven extraordinary structures described by the ancients as Wonders of the World, two were said to have been lighthouses. One of these was the Pharos tower at Alexandria, which guided mariners for at least 1,000 years. The other was the Colossus, an enormous bronze statue that once marked a key harbor on the Greek island of Rhodes in the Mediterranean. The statue was a likeness of the god Helios and stood at the harbor entrance. By some accounts the statue held a flame in its outstretched hand in a manner not unlike that of the modern Statue of Liberty. Said to have been toppled by an earthquake during the third century BC, the Colossus may or may not have actually served as a lighthouse, but it is interesting and instructive that the ancient writers thought so because it implies that navigational lights were already in use at that early date. (See also Pharos.)

COMMISSIONERS OF IRISH LIGHTHOUSES Responsible for all Irish aids to navigation, including those in Northern Ireland, are the Commissioners of Irish Lighthouses. Originally administered by the Dublin Port Authority, Ireland's light stations came under the authority of the commissioners in 1867. Currently, the commissioners oversee approximately eighty light stations. As is the case with lighthouses in England and Scotland, operating expenses are drawn from a general fund sustained by fees imposed on ships docking at ports throughout the British Isles.

COTTAGE-STYLE LIGHTHOUSES Consisting of a small, single-story wooden building with a light tower and lantern on the roof, cottage-style lighthouses were once quite common, especially in the bays and inlets of the American South. Combining the keeper's quarters, workrooms, and tower kept construction costs low and made these modest light stations relatively easy to maintain. Often octagonal or hexagonal in shape, the cottage-style lighthouses usually stood on piles in open water. Ultimately, cottage-style lighthouses proved vulnerable to storms, fire, ice, floods, and rot, and only a few remain, mostly in the Chesapeake Bay region.

CRIB FOUNDATIONS To provide an adequate if not rock-solid foundation for certain offshore light towers, builders assembled wooden cribs on land and then towed them to the construction site, where they were filled with broken stone. After settling securely on the bottom, the crib was capped with concrete and a tower erected on top of it. In ancient times the Romans used the hulk of an enormous Egyptian freighter as a makeshift crib for the light tower at Ostia.

Two thousand years later, American lighthouse builders made extensive use of cribs on the Great Lakes. The Spectacle Reef Lighthouse, built during the 1870s at the northwestern end of Lake Huron in Michigan, represents an impressive use of a crib foundation. Begun in 1870, the project cost the US government more than $400,000 and took 200 men more than four years to complete. The tower still stands, and its beacon, now solar-powered, continues to guide lake freighters safely past the reef.

DAYMARKS In addition to guiding mariners by night or in storms, light towers function as daymarks, landmarks that are visible from the sea during daylight hours. To serve as daymarks, light towers are brightly painted, often in distinctive colors or patterns. For this reason, deactivated light

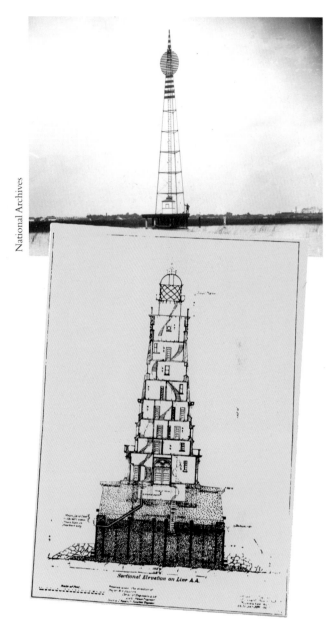

The architectural drawing (above) shows Michigan's White Shoal Lighthouse on its crib foundation. The distinctive tower (top) once served as a daymark for mariners approaching Green Bay, Wisconsin.
National Archives

towers are often left standing so that they can serve as daymarks. One such tower is New Point Comfort Light in Virginia. Although its light was snuffed out in the 1950s, the tower's stark white walls continue to help Chesapeake Bay pilots keep their vessels in safe waters. (See also Seamarks.)

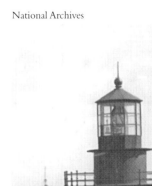

The hefty DCB aerobeacon (above) still serves Montauk Point in New York.

The largest and most active of the US Lighthouse Service supply depots was at Staten Island (above left). It had ample storage for oil, buoys, and equipment, wharves for tenders, and even its own lighthouse equipped with a powerful second-order Fresnel lens. Staten Island Depot workers (left) pause from their labors to pose in front of a warehouse doorway. On the right, the station dog and a local policeman squeeze into the picture.

DCB AEROBEACONS About 1950, the Carlisle and Finch Co. of Cincinnati, Ohio, introduced a new type of airport beacon known as the DCB series. A relatively simple device, it consists of one or more cast-aluminum drums 2 to 3 feet in diameter and housing a light source backed by a parabolic reflector. The drums emit a pencil beam of light, and they can be rotated so that, when seen from a distance, the light appears to flash. DCB aerobeacons are relatively easy to maintain because the housing is watertight and, therefore, weatherproof. This characteristic helped make DCB aerobeacons ideal not just for airfields but also for use in lighthouses. In the 1990s the US Coast Guard began to replace Fresnel lenses with DCB aerobeacons, especially at automated light stations.

Usually, DCB beacons are given a numerical designation indicating the number and size of the drums. For instance a DCB-24 has one 24-inch drum while a DCB-224 has two 24-inch drums. The larger model DCB-36 has a 36-inch drum.

Although once common, DCB aeromarine beacons are becoming increasingly rare. The US Coast Guard has replaced many of them with Vega lights and other self-contained, computer-controlled devices employing acrylic lenses. However, a few DCB aeromarine beacons remain in use in the Great Lakes and elsewhere. (See also Aeromarine Beacons, Modern Optics, and Vega Lights.)

DEPOTS The US Lighthouse Service maintained a number of depots, where supplies were stockpiled and equipment was readied for service or repaired. Often the depots encompassed extensive yards strewn with buoys, oil tanks, and construction materials. Usually, depots served as administrative centers and as home ports for the tenders that made regular visits to light stations scattered along the coasts. Key lighthouse depots were located in Baltimore, Detroit, San Francisco, and Ketchikan, Alaska, but the largest and most important was on New York's Staten Island. Once the headquarters for the entire Lighthouse Service, the Staten Island Depot is being restored and is now open to the public as the National Lighthouse Museum.

DETACHED DWELLINGS Lighthouse keepers rarely lived in the light tower itself, but rather in a separate dwelling. Sometimes the residence was attached to the tower or connected to it by a protected walkway, allowing the keeper easy access to the light even in foul weather. More often,

US Coast Guard

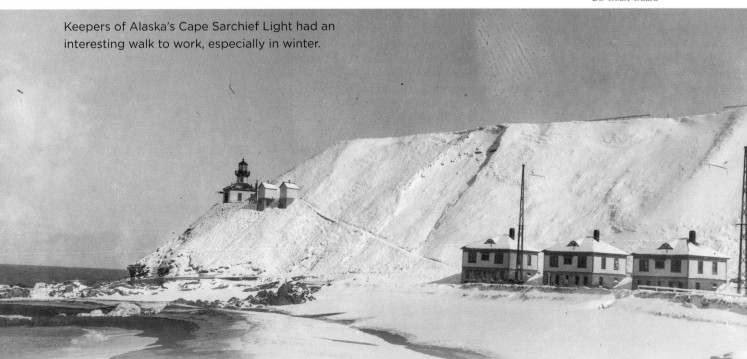

Keepers of Alaska's Cape Sarchief Light had an interesting walk to work, especially in winter.

Donohoo's Cove Point tower and adjacent bell house in Maryland.
Bruce Roberts

Canada's Point Abino Lighthouse, rising from its platform just above the winter ice of Lake Erie.
Bruce Roberts

however, the residence was detached and might be located a considerable distance from the tower. (See also Attached Dwellings and Keepers' Residences.)

DONOHOO, JOHN A very successful early-nineteenth-century government contractor, John Donohoo built several lighthouses on the Chesapeake Bay during the 1820s and 1830s. Donohoo's towers were solid structures of stone or brick, and a few, such as the one he built at Cove Point Light in Maryland (in 1828), still stand. During his tightfisted administration of the US lighthouse system, Stephen J. Pleasonton favored Donohoo largely because he was willing to work for little money. Donohoo received only $3,500 for

building Concord Point Light at Havre de Grace, Maryland, in 1827. Despite its bargain price, the Concord Point tower remains standing and still supports a navigational light.

DOUGLASS, NICHOLAS AND SIR JAMES Much like the celebrated Stevensons in Scotland, the Douglass family dominated the field of lighthouse engineering in England in the nineteenth century. Born in 1798, Nicholas Douglass did his first lighthouse construction work at an early age and became a Trinity House engineer. Among the lighthouses he designed was the Les Hanois Lighthouse in the Channel Islands. His son, Sir James Douglass, followed in Nicholas's footsteps as a lighthouse engineer, and in

1862 replaced the well-known and widely respected James Walker as engineer in chief of Trinity House. It was to Sir James Douglass that Trinity House turned when Eddystone Light had to be rebuilt in the 1880s. Constructed with dovetailed granite blocks, Douglass's Eddystone tower remains as solid today as when it was completed in 1883. Douglass also designed the remarkable light towers of Round Island, Longships, and Hartland Point on the southwest English coast. Sir James's brother, William Douglass, designed the Fastnet Lighthouse in Ireland.

ELEVATION In lighthouse parlance, elevation refers to the height of the signal emitted by the light tower. Fresnel lenses and most modern optical systems send out light signals in a narrow band known as the focal plane. Because the curvature of the Earth renders low-lying lights practically worthless for navigation, a coastal beacon must have an elevated focal plane. The height of the plane above the water's surface—usually from 40 to 200 feet—helps determine the range of the light. If their lights are bright enough, beacons shining from a height of 150 feet or more can be seen at distances exceeding 20 nautical miles.

In many cases, the light tower provides only a portion of the focal-plane elevation. The rest comes

A Canadian light tower at Battle Island (above) gets a substantial boost from high rocks on the shores of Lake Superior. An Eiffel Tower at sea, the Fowey Rocks Lighthouse (below) off Cape Florida has survived wind and waves since 1878.

The Ocracoke Island Light (above) on the North Carolina Outer Banks displays a fixed signal. Now lit mostly on ceremonial occasions, the Split Rock Light (below) has a focal plane of nearly 170 feet, but less than a third of that height is provided by the tower.

Photos by Bruce Roberts

from the site, which may be the top of a cliff, a hillside, or the top of a bluff. For instance, the tower of Oregon's cliffside **Heceta Head Light** is 56 feet tall, but its light has a focal plane of more than 200 feet.

Ironically, a beacon can be too high to be of practical use to mariners. Located on the summit of a lofty headland, the original 1856 Point Loma Light in San Diego signaled mariners from an elevation of 462 feet. This gave it an impressive range of 40 miles or more in fair weather. But the headland had a magnetlike attraction for low-lying clouds and fog, and its light was rarely seen by mariners. In 1891 the US Lighthouse Board ordered construction of a second Point Loma tower at a lower, more practical elevation. (See also Focal Plane.)

EXPOSED SCREW-PILE TOWERS The screw-pile construction techniques pioneered in England were widely used in shallow waters near the US mainland. Mid-nineteenth-century engineers such as I. W. P. Lewis and George Meade adapted those techniques for the harsh conditions along the wave-swept reefs of the Florida Keys.

Because mariners needed ample warning to help them avoid the deadly reefs, light towers here had to be tall and, therefore, quite heavy. To provide the necessary height while keeping weight to a minimum, Lewis designed an iron-skeleton tower for Carysfort Reef, south of Key Largo. Consisting of heavily braced iron legs, the 110-foot tower was anchored to the reef with screw piles. Broad iron plates at the upper end of the screw piles helped distribute the structure's weight. Brought in to oversee the construction of Carysfort Reef Light and other sites in the Keys, Meade successfully executed the Lewis design while making significant improvements.

Several exposed screw-pile lighthouses still guard the Florida Keys. In addition to the one at Carysfort Reef (completed in 1852), these include the Sand Key Light (1852), Sombrero Key Light (1857), Alligator Reef Light (1873), Fowey Rocks

Light (1878), and American Shoal Light (1880). (See also Screw-Pile Towers.)

FIXED SIGNALS A lighthouse beacon that shines constantly during its regular hours of operation is said to display a fixed signal. Most beacons flash or shine intermittently to help mariners distinguish them from nearby lights. Fixed signals are more often seen near the entrances of harbors or in relatively dark areas, where they are more easily spotted and identified. Owls Head Light near Rockland, Maine, displays a fixed signal, as does Dunkirk Light on Lake Ontario in New York.

FLASHING SIGNALS A lighthouse beacon that turns on and off or grows much brighter at regular intervals is called a flashing signal. Beacons with a flashing characteristic are readily distinguished from other nearby lights. Today the flashing characteristic of most maritime beacons is produced by a switch that turns the electric light on and off at the appropriate intervals. However, many early flashing beacons were generated by rotating Fresnel lenses. These funneled light into special panels, or bull's-eyes, that momentarily intensified the light and created the appearance of a flash. (See also Characteristic.)

FOCAL PLANE Most lenses and other devices used to generate navigational beacons bend light, funneling it into a narrow, concentrated band. The level or elevation of this band is known as the focal plane. To reach over the horizon to vessels at distances of more than a few miles, light signals must have a high focal plane. This, of course, is the main reason lights are placed in towers.

The focal plane of a beacon rarely is the same as the height of its tower. When lighthouses are built in open water, as in the Florida Keys, the focal plane is slightly lower than the height of the tower. For instance, the steel-skeleton Sombrero Key tower is 160 feet tall, while the focal plane of its light is 148 feet. On the other hand, when light towers are located on land, the elevation of the site gives the beacon a boost, sometimes of 100 feet or more. Minnesota's Split Rock Light tower is only 54 feet tall, but the elevation of its focal plane is nearly 170 feet because the tower sits on high ground. (See also Elevation.)

FOG SIGNALS When thick fog or heavy weather sets in, mariners may not be able to see or distinguish a light beacon shining from a tower. At such times a sound signal is used to warn vessels away from prominent headlands or navigational obstacles. A wide array of noise-making devices have been used as fog signals. Early keepers blew trumpets, fired off cannons, or rang heavy bells. A light station in Ludington, Michigan, once used the whistle of a parked locomotive to alert mariners. It is said that more than one vessel approaching the deadly rocks off Owls Head in Maine was saved by the incessant barking of the keeper's dog.

The world's earliest fog signals probably were used in Europe or the Middle East, where drums or bells likely helped mariners find safe harbor or warned them away from rocks. The first fog signal in America was a cannon placed at Boston Harbor Light in 1719.

While cannons could certainly be heard, it was not possible to load and fire them continuously over extended periods. Because fog could hang over a harbor for days at a time, a more practical signal was needed. First employed at Maine's West Quoddy Head Light about 1820, fog bells quickly became the sound signals of choice, and their use spread down the New England coast and along the Mid-Atlantic shore as far south as the Chesapeake Bay.

At first fog bells had to be struck by hand, but weary keepers soon found ways to make the task a little easier. Sometimes they attached a long cord to the clapper and ran it through an opening in the wall of the residence. That way, at least they could be comfortable while ringing the bell. One Maryland

A group of sound signal experts gather in 1929 at Michigan's Poe Reef Light, perhaps to discuss the rather chaotic state of foghorn technology at that time. Notice the hodgepodge of fog-signal devices behind them. US Coast Guard

keeper even trained the family dog to pull the cord. Within a few years, an array of weight-driven clockwork mechanisms and similar contraptions had been devised to handle the monotonous work of striking the fog bell. Some strikers could deliver as many as 10,000 blows, or up to four days' worth of ringing, on a single winding.

About the middle of the nineteenth century, fog bells began to be replaced by horns, trumpets, whistles, and sirens, most of them driven by steam. Among the earliest of these was an extraordinary device invented by C. L. Daboll during the 1850s. It directed compressed air or steam from a boiler over a reed, filling a large trumpet with sound. Some of Daboll's trumpets were enormous, measuring up to 17 feet in length and as much as 3 feet in width at the opening.

The Daboll trumpet was never widely used, but similar sound signals became common, and steam whistles or pump-driven horns could be heard along foggy coastlines everywhere. Some had a double-tone or diaphone signal, a system invented in Canada. The moaning of diaphone foghorns was once familiar to inhabitants of coastal communities everywhere. Many claimed to enjoy their calls—often deep-throated and sonorous—but others found them annoying. Some foghorn signals have been compared to the protests of a wounded moose or the complaints of a cow that needs milking.

The US Coast Guard has standardized the electrically powered, pump-driven horns it now uses to warn mariners. They come in three sizes, with audible ranges of 1 to 5 miles. These sound signals are turned on and off automatically by

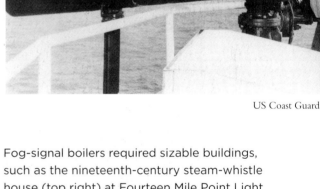

National Archives Photos

monitors that measure the level of moisture in the air with strobe lights and photoelectric sensors.

Usually, fog signals and the equipment required to produce them are housed in separate wooden, concrete, or cast-iron buildings. Early fog-signal buildings were square or pyramidal wooden bell towers, intended more to protect the bells than the keepers whose job it was to strike them. Often flimsily constructed, they were placed under considerable stress by the heavy bells, which could weigh a ton or more. Exposed to extreme levels of vibration and harsh weather conditions, the towers had to be replaced frequently and only a few survive, mostly in New England.

Offshore lighthouses often doubled as fog-signal buildings, an arrangement that could hardly have been comfortable for the keepers, especially those with sensitive ears. Caisson and screw-pile lighthouses sometimes had fog bells mounted on their outside walls. Either a member of the station crew or weight-driven striking machinery kept the

US Coast Guard

Fog-signal boilers required sizable buildings, such as the nineteenth-century steam-whistle house (top right) at Fourteen Mile Point Light in Michigan. Electric horns could be housed in smaller structures like the mid-twentieth-century foghorn shack (top left) on Alcatraz Island in San Francisco Bay.

A US Coast Guard keeper (above right) activates a powerful steam-driven foghorn. He wears protective headgear to guard against hearing loss. Throughout history most keepers had no such protection and simply tried to ignore the loud blasts of their horns, which often continued day and night through long stretches of fog.

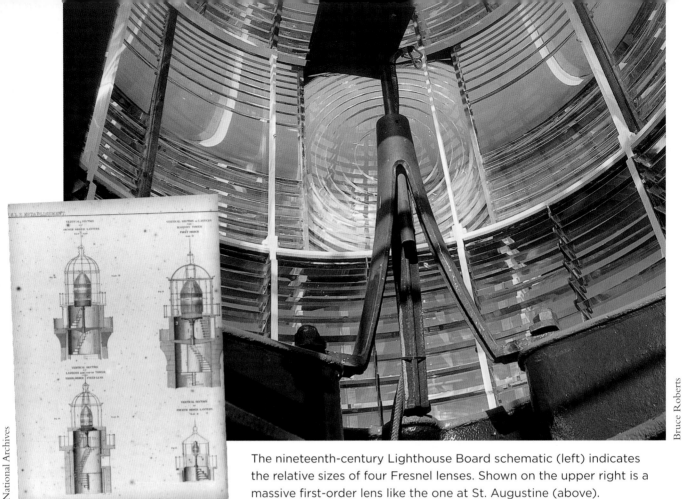

National Archives

Bruce Roberts

The nineteenth-century Lighthouse Board schematic (left) indicates the relative sizes of four Fresnel lenses. Shown on the upper right is a massive first-order lens like the one at St. Augustine (above).

bells ringing through stretches of foggy weather, which might last for days.

When steam-powered horns were introduced in the latter half of the nineteenth century, fog-signal buildings became far more substantial structures. Sometimes nearly as large as the station residence, they housed an impressive array of boilers, wheels, pulleys, horns, and whistles, all of which made them look like small factories. A large supply of coal had to be kept on hand either in the fog-signal building itself or in a nearby storage structure to heat the steam-generating boilers.

Electric foghorns replaced steam-driven devices in the early twentieth century, and sizable buildings no longer were needed to house the fog-signal equipment. Even so, many fog-signal buildings were left standing for use as workrooms, storehouses, or garages. With the growth in popularity of light

stations as tourist attractions, a few old fog-signal buildings have been pressed into service as museum display spaces or even gift shops.

FRESNEL, AUGUSTIN JEAN French physicist Augustin Fresnel invented the light-gathering prismatic lens that was the lighthouse optic of choice for more than a century. Born the son of architect Jacques Fresnel in 1788, Fresnel was fascinated by light and studied the way it was bent or refracted as it moved though solid materials, such as glass. In 1819, Fresnel's discoveries won him the grand prize awarded each year by the French Academy of Science.

Fresnel applied his mathematical skills and formulas to the challenge of improving lighthouse beacons, and, by the end of 1822, he had created the first of his beehive-shaped lenses.

An open flame loses nearly all of its brightness over even relatively short distances. Fresnel discovered that by gathering and concentrating the light with prisms, he could conserve more than 80 percent of its brightness. Soon French companies were manufacturing Fresnel lenses and selling them to governments all over the world. Unfortunately, Fresnel did not live long enough to savor the fame and wealth his invention had earned him. Having struggled against ill health all his life, he died of tuberculosis in 1827 at the age of thirty-nine.

FRESNEL LENSES Devised in 1822 by Augustin Fresnel, the Fresnel lens concentrates light into a powerful beam that can be seen over great distances. Usually Fresnel lenses consist of individual hand-polished glass prisms arrayed in a bronze frame. The lenses were complex and expensive to make, but demand for them was great in the nineteenth century, and they were manufactured by a number of French or British companies. Fresnel lenses were classified by their different sizes, or orders. A first-order Fresnel lens is the largest; it may be more than 6 feet in diameter and 12 feet tall. A sixth-order lens is only about 1 foot wide and not much larger than an ordinary gallon jug.

Although now thought old-fashioned, Fresnel lenses represented the finest available lighthouse technology of their day. Remarkably, they still work as well as or better than most of the modern optics that in many cases have replaced them.

Increasingly, lighthouses are being acquired by nonprofit groups or government agencies and opened to the public as historic attractions. As part of this process the new owners often replace modern optics with antique Fresnel lenses to add to the historic allure of the old towers. Sometimes the lens is the original one that served the lighthouse from the time of its construction in the nineteenth or early twentieth centuries. Other such lenses are acquired from private owners, museums, or Coast Guard storage facilities. These historic lenses don't

A handsome brass plate beneath the huge first-order lens at Point Reyes, California, identifies the manufacturer as Barbier & Fenestre of Paris. The same company made many other Fresnel lenses used in the United States and throughout the world.
Bruce Roberts

come cheap. Even when the lens is donated, the cost of repairing it and establishing it in a light tower can be very high indeed and run to $100,000 or more.

FRESNEL LENS MANUFACTURERS During the nineteenth century, Fresnel lenses were rightly considered a first-rate, high-technology product, and as such they commanded extremely high prices—up to the equivalent of $1 million in today's money. Although the technical problems involved in manufacturing these complex devices were daunting, there was plenty of money to be made on them.

Looking just a bit like a multilayered wedding cake, the Rawley Point tower (right) in Wisconsin features not one but three separate galleries. The cast-iron railing of the lower gallery is beautifully detailed. Francis Gibbons's Point Loma Lighthouse (above) is near San Diego. Its tower rises through the roof of a modest Cape Cod-style dwelling.

Over the years, a number of companies managed to turn handsome profits casting, polishing, and selling the delicate glass prisms that made them work.

Not surprisingly, most Fresnel lens manufacturers were French. Makers such as François Soleil Jr., Letourneau & Co., Henri LaPaute Co., and Barbier & Fenestre produced lenses at facilities in and around Paris. It is said that some of these companies paid children and destitute street people a penny or so per day to polish the glass prisms. The names of these manufacturers can be found on brass plates attached to the frames of Fresnel lenses throughout the world.

Eventually, manufacturers in other countries began to make prismatic lighthouse lenses, with or without patents from the French. They included, among others, the Chance Brothers Co. in England, the Wilhelm Weuke Co. in Germany, and the Macbeth-Evans Co. of the United States. By far the most prolific and successful of the non-French

Fresnel lens makers was Chance Brothers. Founded in 1824 by James Timmius Chance as a manufacturer of glass products, Chance Brothers turned out its first lighthouse lenses at its Birmingham factory in 1851. Before long, Chance Brothers was outselling its French competition and became the world's leading producer of lighthouse optics. Chance Brothers also produced helical lighthouse lanterns and clockwork drives to rotate the heavy lenses. The company remained in business for more than 150 years, finally closing its doors in 1977. Interestingly enough, some of the Chance Company's lenses have lasted even longer than the company that made them. Several Chance Brothers lenses remain in use in the United States, one of them at Point Cabrillo Light in northern California.

GALLERY Many light towers have a circular walkway with a metal railing around the lantern. Known as a gallery, this walkway gives keepers

Bruce Roberts

convenient access to the outside of the lantern for painting, repair work, and cleaning the windows of the lantern room, a vital task since even a thin film of grime on the glass can sharply reduce the effectiveness of the beacon. The railing, usually of cast iron, provides an opportunity for playful decorative touches, as at Cape Neddick Light in Maine, where miniatures of light towers are perched on the railing's balusters.

GIBBONS, FRANCIS As an engineer and government contractor, Francis Gibbons built a dozen or more lighthouses, many of them on the US Pacific coast. In the early 1850s, the newly created Lighthouse Board launched a major construction effort in the West. The board hired Gibbons, who had built lighthouses on North Carolina's Outer Banks and elsewhere, to build up to a dozen light towers. The board hoped to save money by working

The harbor light at Grand Marais (above) competes with a Minnesota sunset, while an 1874 maritime notice (below) bears the name of Lighthouse Board Chairman Joseph Henry.

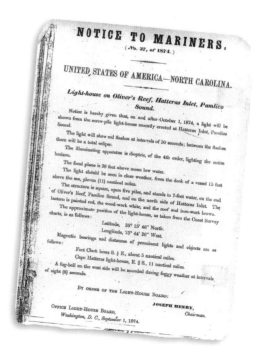

Courtesy Lighthouse Digest

US Coast Guard

More than twice as tall as a man, the massive hyper-radial Fresnel at Makapuu Point (above) on Oahu is the largest lens ever used in a US lighthouse. In contrast, the Thunder Bay Light in Canada (top) has an optic not much bigger than a rain barrel.

with a single contractor, but a corrupt scheme left Gibbons with a tight budget and little margin for error in order to make a profit.

Gibbons set up shop in California and began operations late in 1852. Gibbons organized the project with machine-like efficiency, and by August 1854 he had built Alcatraz Island Light in San Francisco Bay, Point Loma Light near San Diego, and six other towers. Unfortunately, any hope Gibbons had of profiting from the venture sank along with his supply ship *Oriole,* lost on Washington's Columbia River bar in 1853.

Most of Gibbons's lighthouses were Cape Cod–style structures of brick or stone with an integral central tower. His Alcatraz lighthouse was destroyed in the 1906 San Francisco earthquake, but several others still stand, including the Old Point Loma Lighthouse (now a national monument exhibit) and the Point Pinos Light in Pacific Grove, California, which is still in use.

HARBOR LIGHTS Not intended to serve as major coastal markers, early harbor lights often consisted of little more than a lantern hung from a pole. However, many were official light stations with a tower and residence for the keeper. Many of these relatively modest beacons, such as Derby Wharf Light in Salem, Massachusetts, and Grand Marais Light in Minnesota, remain in operation. (See also Lever Lights and Range Lights.)

HENRI LAPAUTE CO. See Fresnel Lens Manufacturers.

HENRY, JOSEPH Among those appointed to the new Lighthouse Board in 1852 by President Millard Fillmore was Joseph Henry, one of America's foremost scientists and thinkers. Henry served as the first official secretary of the Smithsonian Institution, and he helped found modern meteorology. A noted mathematician and physicist, he is credited with dozens of inventions, including the electromagnet and electric motor. He made key contributions to the development of the telegraph and telephone and even found time to help Congress find better ways to heat and light the deliberative chambers of the US Senate and House of Representatives.

As a member of the Lighthouse Board, Henry used his considerable political influence to coax appropriations out of Congress to purchase expensive Fresnel lenses and fund optical research. Henry's interest in the board's activities was, thus, not limited to improving navigational lights and increasing safety. The board's annual budget exceeded $500,000, approximately sixteen times that of the Smithsonian, and Henry was able to ensure that some of the money was spent on research. Even so, he refused to accept a salary for his work on the Lighthouse Board, which consumed as much as two months of his time each year. Henry replaced Rear Admiral William B. Shubrick as chairman of the Lighthouse Board in 1872 and served in that capacity until his death in 1878.

HYPER-RADIAL LENSES Some specially designed lighthouse lenses are even larger and more powerful than the massive first-order Fresnel lenses. One such hyper-radial lens is located at Makapuu Point Light at the eastern end of the Hawaiian island of Oahu. More than 12 feet high and 9 feet in diameter, this amazing Fresnel lens is the largest lighthouse optic in the United States. Put in place when the lighthouse was built in 1909, it continues to serve mariners.

INTERNATIONAL ASSOCIATION OF LIGHT-HOUSE AUTHORITIES (IALA) Established in 1957, the IALA is a nonprofit international technical association with members from approximately eighty nations. The association's goal is to "harmonize aids to navigation worldwide and to ensure that the movements of vessels are safe, expeditious, and cost-effective." The IALA works through a number of standing committees that study and disseminate information on lights, buoys, radio navigation services, and maritime traffic management. It also has become increasingly involved in efforts to preserve historic lighthouses.

INVESTIGATION OF 1851 A rash of shipwrecks along the US coast during the late 1840s focused public attention on the generally poor quality of American lighthouses. After the recently constructed Minot's Ledge Lighthouse collapsed in March 1851, killing two assistant keepers, Congress was under intense pressure from maritime interests to take action. On May 21, 1851, Congress appointed a committee headed by Rear Admiral William B. Shubrick to investigate the nation's aids to navigation. Within months, the Shubrick committee had compiled and submitted a 750-page report confirming what many in Congress already believed—that the US lighthouse system was at best shoddy and at worst a tragedy. The following year, Congress made a radical change in the way US aids to navigation were administered, placing responsibility for coastal beacons, buoys, and other navigational aids in the hands of a nine-member Lighthouse Board, which Shubrick headed.

The IALA advises governments concerning operation of an extraordinarily varied worldwide lighthouse system. Examples of its diversity: Aruba's California Light in the West Indies (above left); India's Alleppey Light (above center); the diminutive Laag Light in Belgium (above right); and the La Entallada Light (below) in the Canary Islands

IRON-PILE TOWERS Like wood-pile and screw-pile lighthouses, straight iron-pile towers were built on sites unsuitable for conventional masonry buildings. In this case, cast-iron or wrought-iron piles (see illustration, p. 89) were driven deep into surface or subsurface mud, sand, or stone and then used to anchor a tower—usually an iron-skeleton structure. American Shoal Light off Florida's Sugarloaf Key is a tower of this type. It was erected in 1880 and remains in operation.

KEEPERS The person responsible for operating a navigational beacon and maintaining the buildings, property, and equipment at a light station is known as the keeper. Early keepers often received their appointments in return for exemplary military service or as a political favor. Even so, the work was hard and the pay—often little more than ten dollars a month—hardly enticing. Still, keepers had a regular income, a place for themselves and their families to live, and no rent to pay.

Until 1939 US lighthouse keepers were civilian employees of the Lighthouse Service, Treasury Department, or some other government agency. After 1939, most lighthouses were staffed by US Coast Guard crews. Since most lighthouses around the world have been automated, the lighthouse keeper's profession has all but disappeared. In the United States there are no more full-time resident keepers—at least none employed as such by the government. (See also Burgess, Abbie; Knott Family; Lewis, Ida; Moore, Catherine; Norvell, Margaret; and Worthylake, George.)

KEEPERS' RESIDENCES The presence of a keeper's residence is what turned a light station into a lighthouse. In many cases, light stations were placed on islands or other remote places that could not easily be reached from a town or even a small village. Because of the nature of their work, keepers needed to be available all night and, in foggy weather, during daylight hours as well. In the days

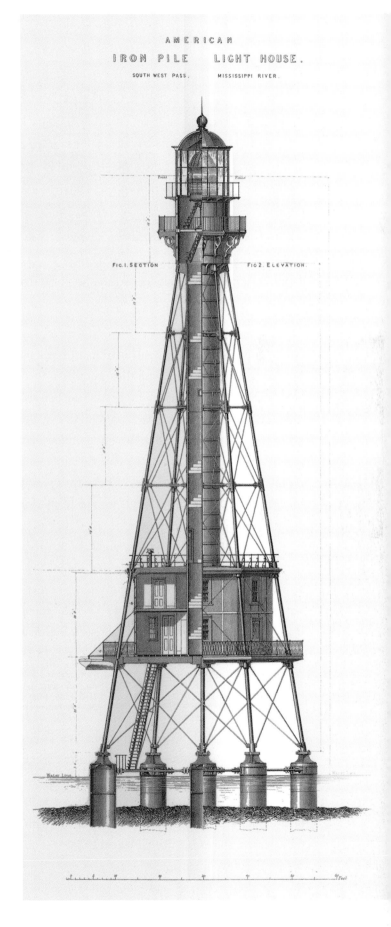

AMERICAN
IRON PILE LIGHT HOUSE.
SOUTH WEST PASS. MISSISSIPPI RIVER.

FIG.1. SECTION   FIG.2. ELEVATION.

Keepers (left to right) Charles Henry, Bishop & Clerks Light in Massachusetts; Ted Pederson, St. Elias Light in Alaska; and Douglas Larrabe, Isle of Shoals Light in New Hampshire

before automation, this meant there had to be on-site residences for keepers and their families.

Keepers were never paid very well, but in most cases, their homes were provided rent-free. Most keepers' dwellings were modest but comfortable, and of course, they nearly always had a great view. A typical dwelling was a one-and-a-half-story wood or stone structure built in a style similar to that of other modest homes in the area.

As light stations grew larger and more complex with the addition of Fresnel lenses, fog-signal machinery, and other equipment, keepers were given one or more assistants to help them handle their growing list of chores. Additional living quarters were provided to house the extra crew. Some keepers' residences built during the late nineteenth or early twentieth centuries were duplexes or even triplexes.

As the great wave of automation swept over the world's lighthouses in the mid-twentieth century, keepers were removed from one lighthouse after another. In most cases the dwellings were boarded up, and since there was little use for them, they became the most vulnerable part of the station. While the towers remained in use and were kept in reasonably good repair, the unneeded dwellings

were allowed to deteriorate. More than a few burned down, rotted away, or were demolished. Some were sold to private owners and removed from public lands.

Ironically, when lighthouses are restored for use as museums or historical attractions, the dwellings become extremely useful for the offices and display spaces they provide. In a few instances, preservation organizations have rebuilt razed lighthouse dwellings so that they can be used as gift shops or small museums. Some of the larger dwellings have been converted for use as hostelries, inns, or bed-and-breakfasts. (See also Attached Dwellings, Detached Dwellings, Privies, and Storehouses.)

KIMBALL, SUMNER See Lifesaving Service, US.

KNOTT FAMILY Few families have devoted themselves to a single profession—other than farming—for longer than the Knotts, who tended one or another of Britain's coastal lights for nearly two centuries. In 1730 William Knott agreed to tend the South Foreland light, near the entrance to the Thames River. Four generations of his descendants also served as keepers of British lighthouses. In all, the Knott family's continuous line of lighthouse service

Typical light station residences were well furnished though not always as warmly as the living room above, with its Edison phonograph, organ, and ornate stove. Keepers at the Grand Traverse Lighthouse in Michigan must have enjoyed many afternoons in these pleasant surroundings.

lasted 181 years, longer than some of Britain's royal dynasties. The last of the line was William Knott's great-great-grandson, Henry Knott, who retired from his post as keeper of North Foreland Light in 1911. Perhaps the family's best-known member was George Knott, a third-generation keeper who tended the lights at Eddystone, Bull Point, North Foreland, and elsewhere. A constant tinkerer and artist, George Knott made meticulously detailed models of the lighthouses in which he served.

LAMP-AND-REFLECTOR SYSTEMS For several decades prior to the introduction of the Fresnel lens, lighthouse beacons were intensified by means of lamp-and-reflector systems. These combined a

Life at remote light stations could be quite lonely, but to this keeper, his young wife, and their friendly mutt, Washington's isolated Cape Flattery Light station may have seemed a paradise.

A Lighthouse Lexicon   97

REVOLVING
APPARATUS
ON THE
CATOPTRIC
PRINCIPLE.

A diagram of a catoptric or reflecting optic (above) hints at the size and complexity of some such mechanisms. Oil hungry, inefficient, and hard to maintain, most lamp-and-reflector systems were replaced by dioptric or refracting optics like the one at Split Rock (right). The big clamshell lens is the most prominent feature of the glowing Split Rock lantern.

bright-burning lamp, such as the one invented by François-Pierre Argand in 1783, and a polished mirror shaped to concentrate the light. In 1810 American Winslow Lewis introduced such a system, incorporating a parabolic mirror of his own design. Lewis managed to sell US maritime officials on the merits of his system, and although Lewis's design quickly became outdated and inefficient, it remained in wide use until the 1850s. (See also Argand Lamps.)

LANTERNS The glass-enclosed space at the top of a light tower is known as the lantern. The lantern houses the lens or optic and protects it from the weather. Often the lantern is topped by a cone-shaped metal roof and encircled by a narrow walkway called the gallery. Many lanterns are of cast-iron construction and have a number of separate window panels.

The birdcage lantern, a style dating to the early 1800s, consisted of a large number of metal ribs running from the roof down to the gallery. Eventually, lighthouse designers abandoned the birdcage style because it tended to block light and reduce the effectiveness of the beacon. Usually too small to accommodate Fresnel lenses, most birdcage lanterns were replaced by the mid-nineteenth century.

The lanterns that replaced them were usually made of cast iron. Hexagonal, octagonal, or even ten-sided, they held large panes of glass that could be easily cleaned or replaced. Often, one or more panels were hinged to allow better ventilation and to serve as a door opening onto the gallery. (See also Birdcage Lanterns.)

Bruce Roberts

Lighthouse engineer Danville Leadbetter (right). The contraption (above) is a swape, or lever, for hoisting a basket of blazing coal. European harbormasters once used these simple devices to signal ships.

Egbert Koch

LEADBETTER, DANVILLE As a US Army engineer, Danville Leadbetter designed and built a number of lighthouses along the coast of the Gulf of Mexico. Several of his towers featured interesting structural innovations. With its stabilizing finlike buttresses, his Sabine Pass Light tower in Louisiana is considered a masterpiece of lighthouse design. Leadbetter served rather unsuccessfully as a general in the Confederate Army during the Civil War and died a broken man in 1866.

LEVER LIGHTS European port cities often used lever lights, or swapes, to guide vessels moving into and out of their bustling harbors. These rather simple navigational markers consisted of iron baskets attached to long poles or levers. At night, the harbormaster built a bright coal fire in the basket and used the lever to raise it high enough to be seen from the decks of approaching vessels. When the fire began to burn low, the basket was lowered and its fuel replenished. About 1625 Danish inventor Pedersen Grove devised an effective lever light system called a *vippefyr*. It made use of a very long pole attached to a stout wooden frame. The English employed many such lever lights, which they referred to as swapes. (See also Harbor Lights.)

Harper's Weekly told America and the world about Ida Lewis's heroic rescues. As a result the shy New England keeper received bags full of mail and as many as a dozen marriage proposals—none of which she accepted. Eventually, Lewis married a local fisherman, but their union was not a happy one. After a few weeks of Ida's company at the Lime Rock Lighthouse, her husband put to sea and never returned. The emergency equipment stored in the structure at the bottom of the next page was once maintained by the US Lifesaving Service.

LEWIS, IDA Likely the most famous lighthouse keeper of all time, Ida Lewis earned international acclaim not for her more than fifty years of faithful service at Rhode Island's Lime Rock Lighthouse but for rescuing people from the chilly waters of Newport Harbor. She made her first daring rescue at the age of sixteen in 1858, when she looked out the window of the keeper's house and saw four young men flailing in the waves beside their overturned sailboat. Moments later, Ida was pulling hard on the oars of the station boat. Having reached the scene of the accident, she managed to get all four men safely ashore. Ida would save many more lives before her career as a lighthouse keeper and heroine was over.

Idawalley Zorada Lewis was born in 1842 and was still a young girl when hard times overtook her family. Ill health forced her father, Captain Hosea Lewis, to give up his career as the pilot of a revenue cutter and take a less strenuous and far less lucrative position as keeper of a harbor light. Captain Lewis's health continued to deteriorate, and he had to rely on his daughter to help him manage his chores at Lime Rock. Ida tended the light, kept up with her schoolwork, looked after her younger siblings and mother—also weakened by illness—and, on occasion, saved lives.

Ida had already made several dramatic rescues when she attracted national attention in 1869 by racing to the aid of a pair of drunken soldiers whose boat had capsized well offshore. Newspapers around the country picked up the story, and soon engraved pictures of Ida and the Lime Rock lighthouse had appeared in *Leslie's* magazine and on the cover of *Harper's Weekly.*

Three years after this incident, Captain Lewis died and Ida was named official keeper of Lime Rock Light. Although she had become a national celebrity, she rarely left the light station, and she remained on duty until she died in 1911. It is said that on the day of her death, the bells of vessels in Newport Harbor tolled far into the evening.

LEWIS, ISAIAH (I. W. P.) Civil engineer Isaiah Lewis served as a lighthouse inspector in the mid-nineteenth century. A nephew of lighthouse contractor Winslow Lewis, the younger Lewis wrote an official report that was highly critical of his uncle's work. Isaiah Lewis advocated construction of iron-skeleton light towers, especially in areas where storms and high winds were a threat. His design for Carysfort Reef Light in the Florida Keys called for a lofty, 110-foot skeleton tower anchored by screw piles. George Meade executed the Lewis design, adding a few innovations of his own.

LEWIS, WINSLOW A former New England sea captain, Winslow Lewis built dozens of US lighthouses during the first half of the nineteenth century. Lewis's bids for these projects often were quite low, and as a consequence, his lighthouses were built on unrealistically tight budgets. Many of these structures were of poor quality, but a few of them still stand. A brick-and-mortar tower built by Lewis in 1820 on Georgia's Little Cumberland Island was later moved to Amelia Island in Florida, where its beacon continues to guide mariners.

Lewis maintained a long-term and mostly favorable association with Stephen J. Pleasonton, a Treasury Department auditor who was responsible for the nation's lighthouses from 1820 to 1852. Pleasonton consistently awarded construction projects to Lewis in large part because of Lewis's low bids. Lewis's nephew, I. W. P. Lewis, also a lighthouse contractor, accused his uncle of collusion with Pleasonton, but no firm evidence was ever put forward to prove the existence of a corrupt relationship.

Lewis was best known for the lamp-and-reflector system he introduced in 1810. A modified version of a French-designed optic at that time widely used in Europe, the Lewis system was adopted for use in most if not all US lighthouses. Like many of the towers he built, Lewis's optics often proved inadequate. The Lewis lamp was not nearly as bright as its French counterpart, designed by François-Pierre Ami Argand, and his parabolic reflectors tended to warp when exposed to heat, ending up almost spherical. (See also Lamp-and-Reflector Systems.)

Engineer I. W. P. Lewis designed the spider-legged but sturdy Carysfort Reef Light (above) off the Florida Keys. Lewis was highly critical of his uncle Winslow's lighthouse work, and the two men were not on friendly terms.

FOR EMERGENCY USE (

Lifesaving stations like this one (above) served as the base of operations for many daring rescues. For many years the St. Croix Lighthouse (below) near Calais, Maine, stood at the top of the official Coast Guard Light List. The wood-frame building burned to the ground in 1976.

LIFESAVING SERVICE, US The crews of ships that run aground on sandbars, reefs, and beaches often need help to safely reach shore. For centuries this assistance, if it arrived at all, came in the form of impromptu rescue efforts thrown together by untrained locals. Around 1850 the US government began to place lifesaving stations along dangerous stretches of coast, especially in the Northeast. Although well stocked with surfboats, ropes, rockets, and other equipment, these stations had no full-time staff and were run much like volunteer fire departments.

After a deadly storm in 1870 left East Coast beaches littered with broken ships and bodies, Congress finally responded to calls for a more comprehensive and professional approach to maritime lifesaving. Funds were appropriated to employ six-man crews at existing stations and to establish many new ones. In 1878 all these stations were gathered under the wing of a new federal entity, the US Lifesaving Service, an agency of the Treasury Department. Sumner Kimball headed the agency during its entire thirty-seven-year history. Kimball retired when the service was absorbed by the US Coast Guard in 1915.

Although it existed for less than four decades, the Lifesaving Service made its mark on maritime history. Many sailors owed their lives to the quick work of service lifesavers. Usually, when a vessel wrecked near shore, lifesaving teams rushed to the rescue of passengers and crew in their nearly unsinkable surfboats. In some cases lifesavers used a gun or carronade to fire a line across the deck of the stranded ship. Once the line was secured, it could be used to ferry people ashore.

LIGHT LISTS As part of its effort to upgrade the performance of US navigation aids and to increase their usefulness to mariners, the Lighthouse Board issued an annual publication known as the *Light Lists*. It contained the precise location and characteristic of each official government light. A ship's captain in possession of an up-to-date *Light*

Like the shell of a chambered nautilus, a staircase winds upward through the 210-foot La Coubre light tower in France.

Lists could navigate the nation's coastal waters with relative confidence. Special bulletins were issued when new lights were commissioned, old ones were deactivated, or characteristics were changed. The US Coast Guard still publishes the *Light Lists* following much the same system as the one adopted by the Lighthouse Board.

LIGHT STATIONS, ADAPTIVE USES The roles played by navigational lights in general and lighthouses in particular have changed dramatically. Over the last century, the introduction of electric power and automated switching and monitoring devices made it possible to remove the full-time keepers from nearly every lighthouse in the world. Often, once the last keepers moved away to take up other assignments, their former residences were boarded up and more or less abandoned. This inevitably led to their decline and, in too many cases, their destruction.

Fortunately, many adaptive uses have been found for old keepers' residences, towers, oil houses, and fog-signal buildings. Since they are by nature historic, these structures make fine locations for museum displays, especially those with maritime themes. Some of the world's finest maritime museums can be found at automated but still-operating light stations, such as Michigan's Whitefish Point Lighthouse, where the Great Lakes Shipwreck Museum draws large crowds every summer. Universities and other educational institutions are also making good use of former

As the pictures on this and the opposite page illustrate, every light tower is different. Each is built to fill a particular need and meet the demands placed on it by a unique set of conditions.

lighthouses, especially those located offshore or in environmentally sensitive areas. For instance, the University of Florida maintains a research station at Cedar Key Lighthouse in the Gulf of Mexico. Other such facilities can be found at light stations in Alaska, Europe, and Australia. The keepers' residences of more than a few lighthouses have been converted for use as hostelries or bed-and-breakfast inns. Still others have been purchased for use as private homes.

While many productive uses have been found for old lighthouses, some preservationists believe they serve best as reminders of the world's rich maritime heritage. Since national government agencies often lack the time or resources to maintain historic buildings such as lighthouses, local governments, preservation organizations, and private individuals are stepping in to do the job.

LIGHT SOURCES See Acetylene Lamps; Fresnel Lenses; Lamp-and-Reflector Systems; Modern Optics; and Vega Lights.

LIGHT STATIONS See Lighthouse.

Above left: a block tower on a block dwelling at Avery Rock in Maine. The octagonal brick Montauk Point tower (left) in New York. On page 101: light towers don't get much simpler than the poll-hoisted box lantern (opposite left) that once guided mariners past Turn Point in Washington's San Juan Islands. Representing wholly different worlds and eras are Canada's Michipicoten Island tower (opposite upper) on Lake Superior and the seventeenth-century stone Flamborough tower (opposite lower) in England.

Courtesy *Lighthouse Digest*

Courtesy *Lighthouse Digest*

LIGHT TOWERS Because of the curvature of the Earth, objects or lights at or near sea level cannot be seen from more than a few miles away. Ancient people built signal fires on hills to make them visible over greater distances. A light tower is, in essence, an artificial hill, designed to raise the height of the beacon.

People have been building light towers for more than 2,000 years. The first known to history was the Pharos, a giant, 450-foot stone structure near the entrance of the harbor at Alexandria, Egypt. It is said vessels were guided to the city by a fire blazing on the Pharos roof.

Light towers of the modern era are used to support a lantern, which houses a lamp, electric beacon, or some other lighting device. The height of the tower may be as little as 20 or as much as 200 feet, and this in part determines the range of the beacon. Typically, light towers are cylindrical, square, or octagonal and constructed of stone, brick, cast iron, or steel. A stairway of wood or iron—lighthouses rarely feature elevators—provides access to the lantern room. Tower interiors can be quite dark, but many have a few windows to provide a little daylight for the stairs. Near the top of the tower is the watch room, where keepers once did much of their work. From the watch room, keepers reached the lantern room and optic by way of a ladder or narrow iron staircase.

Some light towers are an integral part of the station residence. Keepers at lighthouses of this type were able to do their work without braving the elements, an attractive feature at light stations in harsh climates. Other towers are stand-alone structures, usually located a short distance from the keeper's residence and other station buildings. Today, in the era of automation, more than a few keepers' residences have fallen into ruin, and in

Lighthouses may take almost any shape or form and do not always include an actual residence. It's hard to say what the Toledo Harbor Light (below) suggests—perhaps a Russian Orthodox church but probably not a house. Nonetheless, keepers lived and worked here for many years. Established in 1904 to assist commercial shipping in western Lake Erie, the station was automated in 1966 and its keepers were removed.
US Coast Guard

some cases the tower may be all that remains of the old light station. (See also Breakwater Lights, Colonial Lighthouses, and Keepers' Residences.)

LIGHTHOUSE The term lighthouse has been applied to a wide variety of buildings constructed for the purpose of guiding ships. Often it is used interchangeably with similar or derivative terms, such as light tower, light station, or simply light. The traditional concept of a lighthouse is that of a residence with a light tower either attached or located a short distance away, but many so-called lighthouses never really fit this description. Historians often describe the Pharos tower built in Alexandria during the third century BC as the world's first true lighthouse, but no evidence exists that keepers ever used any part of this colossal stone building as a residence. The Statue of Liberty's torch once helped guide New York City harbor traffic, but is the big bronze lady really

a lighthouse? Some would say so. Others maintain that a real lighthouse must, naturally enough, have a residence associated with it.

In 1915 the US Bureau of Lighthouses saw the need to carefully define some of the terms commonly used in its published manuals and regulations. The bureau defined lighthouse as a "light station where a resident keeper(s) is employed." Bureau lighthouses usually included one or more residences, a light tower (either attached to or separate from the keeper's dwelling), a storage facility for oil and other supplies, and sometimes a separate building to house fog-signal equipment. To help the keepers feed themselves and their families, the property often had a garden patch, chicken coop, and even a barn for cows.

Today, the US Coast Guard refers to all major beacons simply as lights, and many of these are a far cry from what once might have been described as

TWIN LIGHTS
CHATHAM MASS

A CLOSER LOOK

Just Memories

Lighthouses speak to the romantic side of human nature, and their scenic attributes have long been recognized by travelers. That is why light towers have been and remain to this day a favorite subject for postcards. These three delightful antique cards show lighthouses not so much as they actually looked at the time but as tourists would have liked their friends to imagine they appeared. Each is depicted in dreamy pastels, as if it were being remembered rather than seen.

Unfortunately, memories are all that remain of the lighthouses shown here. Mississippi's Ship Island Light (above) burned to the ground in 1972. Built in 1906, Wisconsin's Racine Reef Light (below right) was demolished in 1961. The Egg Rock Light just outside Lynn, Massachusetts, came to an especially ignominious end. After decades of service, its beacon was discontinued and the building sold to private owners who hoped to move it to the mainland. As the structure was being lowered onto a barge, it broke away and fell into the sea.

EGG ROCK, LYNN, MASS.

2189 Racine Reef Lighthouse, Three Miles from Shore

Racine, Wisconsin

The Diamond Shoals Light (above), about 12 miles from Cape Hatteras, looked more like an oil platform than a lighthouse. More traditional is the Chatham Lighthouse on Cape Cod. Once a twin-towered station, it now features a solo light (left).

a lighthouse. For instance, the Lehua Rock Light, located on a remote part of Hawaii, consists of little more than the metal casing of an automated optical device known as a Vega light. Perched hundreds of feet above the Pacific on the knife-edged rim of an ancient volcano, the Lehua Rock Light occupies a space far too small for even a modest building. No keeper has ever made a home in this precarious place, and fortunately, no one needs to live here. The light's operations are monitored by remote control from a far-off Coast Guard base. When something goes wrong, members of a specially trained Aids to Navigation Team head to Lehua via helicopter and make repairs.

LIGHTHOUSE BOARD In 1851 a 750-page report on the condition of America's maritime beacons proved so critical of Treasury Department Fifth

Auditor Stephen J. Pleasonton and his management of the US lighthouse system that Congress soon took responsibility for the nation's navigation aids away from him. In October 1852 authority over what came to be known as the Lighthouse Establishment passed to a nine-member Lighthouse Board composed of civilian and military officials. Headed by Rear Admiral William B. Shubrick, a widely respected naval officer, the semiautonomous board exercised complete authority over the US lighthouse system and nearly all matters relating to it. The board reported to the Secretary of the Treasury, who served as its ex-officio president but in reality had little influence on its activities.

Creation of the Lighthouse Board brought a fresh professional spirit and penchant for innovation to the administration of US aids to navigation. Shubrick and his board launched a wide-ranging

Photos by Bruce Roberts

The seal (right) at Montauk Lighthouse in New York lists the members of the US Lighthouse Board in 1860. It includes the names of noted military men, engineers, and scientists such as Joseph Henry, who promoted the use of advanced Fresnel optics like the big first-order lens (above) at the Seguin Island Lighthouse in Maine.

LIGHT HOUSE BOARD
1860
HON. HOWELL COBB.
COMMODORE W. B. SHUBRICK, U.S.N.
BRIG. GEN! J. G. TOTTEN, U.S.A.
CAP! A. A. HUMPHREYS, U.S.A.
PROFESSOR A. D. BACHE.
PROFESSOR J. HENRY.
COMMANDER E. G. TILTON, U.S.N.
COMMANDER R. SEMMES, U.S.N.⎫ Sec!
CAP! W. F. SMITH, U.S.A.⎭
COMMANDER A. M. PENNOCK, U.S.N.
INSPECTOR 3ᴿᴰ DISTRICT.
CAP! W. F. SMITH, U.S.A.
ENGINEER 3ᴿᴰ DISTRICT

modernization program that would, in time, make US lighthouses among the best in the world. Substandard towers were repaired or rebuilt, while many new light stations were established to fill in troubling dark stretches along America's coasts. The organization of the lighthouse system was changed as well. To oversee the maintenance and operation of navigational lights and buoys, the board created twelve districts, placing an experienced military officer—usually an engineer—at the head of each.

Perhaps the board's most telling change was adoption of the Fresnel lens as the standard US lighthouse optic. Far superior to the outdated—but much cheaper—lamp-and-reflector optics that Pleasonton had favored, the French-made prismatic lenses were imported in large numbers and eventually fitted into the lantern rooms of nearly every lighthouse in the country.

The Lighthouse Board remained the governing authority for US light stations for more than a half century. In 1910 the board was dissolved and replaced with the purely civilian Bureau of Lighthouses.

LIGHTHOUSE DIGEST A highly informative periodical devoted entirely to lighthouses and

Bruce Roberts

National Park Service

lighthouse preservation, this magazine has been published regularly since 1992 by Foghorn Publishing. Founding editor Tim Harrison fills its pages with articles highlighting historic lighthouses, lightships, lighthouse keepers, and general maritime history. The magazine also keeps readers up to date on current lighthouse-related events and maintains a "Doomsday List" of endangered light towers and keepers dwellings.

LIGHTHOUSE SERVICE, US While many writers and historians refer to the American lighthouse system prior to 1939 as the Lighthouse Service, that name never had official status. However, during the era of the US Bureau of Lighthouses—1910 to 1939—its operational arm was widely known as the Lighthouse Service. An employee newsletter called the *Lighthouse Service Bulletin*, first published in 1912, firmly established the term, which eventually found its way into common usage and even onto coffee mugs and dinner plates. The Lighthouse Service vanished

These ten gentlemen (above left) all worked as keepers or assistants at Lighthouse Service facilities on Wisconsin's Apostle Islands. When stricken by the sniffles or other more serious health problems, keepers relied on US Lighthouse Service medicine chests like the one (above right) at the Ponce de Leon Inlet Lighthouse Museum in Florida.

along with the Bureau of Lighthouses in 1939, when President Franklin D. Roosevelt reassigned responsibility for construction, maintenance, and operation of lighthouses to the US Coast Guard. Today, lighthouse lovers and preservationists tend to look back on the era of the civilian Lighthouse Service as a "golden age" when America's lighthouses flourished in the care of faithful keepers. (See also Bureau of Lighthouses, US.)

LIGHTHOUSE SERVICE BULLETIN Beginning in 1912, the US Bureau of Lighthouses published a

Courtesy *Lighthouse Digest*

This open-water tower (above) took the place of the Frying Pan Lightship near the mouth of North Carolina's Cape Fear River in 1966. The Lightship Overfalls (below) heads for its station in the Delaware Bay. Crewmen assigned to the Lightship Portsmouth slept in bunks (opposite page) when not guiding mariners into the Chesapeake Bay.

US Coast Guard

substantial newsletter known as the *Lighthouse Service Bulletin*. It contained letters from keepers, tidbits about the comings and goings of service personnel, and newsworthy items about the construction and, occasionally, destruction of lighthouses. The *Bulletin* succeeded in building esprit de corps while promoting professionalism among keepers and other bureau employees. When keepers were involved in rescues or heroically stood by their lights through hurricanes, their exploits invariably turned up in the newsletter. The *Bulletin* went out of existence along with the bureau in 1939.

LIGHTSHIPS Lightships were essentially floating lighthouses equipped with their own beacons that usually were displayed from a tall central mast. They marked shoals or key navigational turning points where construction of a permanent light tower was either impossible or prohibitively expensive.

The world's first lightships are thought to have been ancient Roman galleys with elevated baskets in which fires were kept burning. The first lightship of the modern era was the *Nore,* outfitted by British merchant Robert Hamblin in 1731 to mark the entrance to the Thames. The *Nore* carried two elevated oil lamps spaced about 12 feet apart. Similar vessels were soon afloat off the coasts of nearly every maritime nation.

In the early 1820s as many as five small lightships were placed on station in or near the Chesapeake Bay, and by 1823, another was operating off Sandy Hook to help mark the approaches to New York Harbor. At one time or another over the next 150 years, the US government placed lightships on duty at more than 100 locations along the US coasts. The size of the US lightship fleet peaked in 1910, when the Bureau of Lighthouses listed fifty-six such vessels. Afterward, the usefulness of lightships declined, and over the years, the US fleet dwindled. The *Nantucket Shoals,* the last active US lightship, was taken out of service in 1983.

Although large enough to hold foghorn equipment and support one or two light masts, often topped with a revolving optic, most lightships were quite small, usually only a few dozen tons in displacement. This meant that quarters for the crew were cramped and uncomfortable. Crewmen might serve onboard for months at a time with practically no contact with land and little to eat but salt beef and potatoes.

Lightship crewmen often faced grave danger, especially when raging storms blew in and tossed their little vessels around like corks. In 1913 *Buffalo Lightship Number 82* foundered in a mighty November gale that had swept across Lake Erie. Before his ship went down, dragging everyone on board to the bottom, the captain had just enough time to scratch a desperate message on a board. It read "Goodbye, Nellie, ship is breaking up fast—Williams."

Most likely ice crushed the hull of *Cross Rip Lightship Number 6,* which vanished with all hands off Martha's Vineyard during the winter of 1918. A hurricane can be blamed for the destruction of *Vineyard Sound Lightship Number 73,* lost with her entire crew in 1944. Many other lightships have been lost or damaged by wind, weather, and ice, but nature was not the only danger they faced.

Outweighed by hundreds to one, the *Nantucket Lightship Number 117* got by far the worst end of a collision with the 47,000-ton British passenger liner *Olympic* in 1934. A sister ship to the more famous *Titanic,* the giant liner emerged from a dense fog to slice right through the hull of the hapless *Nantucket,* which plunged to the bottom like a stone, carrying seven of her eleven crew members with her.

The loss of the *Diamond Shoals Lightship Number 71* in 1918 off Cape Hatteras, North Carolina, was no accident. Having spotted a marauding German submarine, the vessel's radioman sent out an urgent warning to all nearby freighters. Unfortunately for the lightship, the submarine received the transmission, surfaced, and blasted the vessel with a deck gun. The

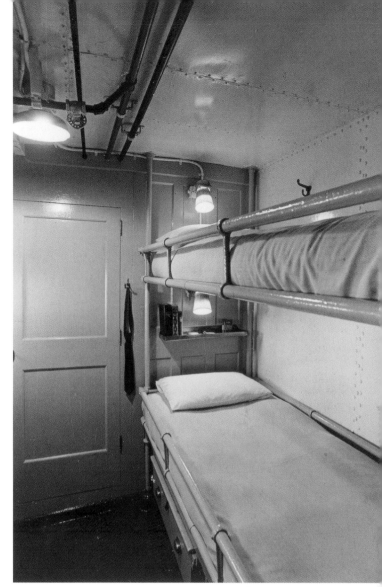

Photos by Bruce Roberts

LIGHTSHIP PORTSMOUTH

George Meade
Courtesy Library of Congress

submarine commander allowed the crew to abandon ship before he opened fire.

MEADE, GEORGE He is remembered today as the Union general who led the Union army to victory over Robert E. Lee's Confederates at Gettysburg, but even before the Civil War, George Meade had earned himself an honorable mention in history books as a builder of lighthouses. In the 1850s, Meade won the respect of fellow engineers and the gratitude of the fledgling US Lighthouse Board by erecting sturdy light towers on several very unpromising sites, mostly in the hurricane-prone Florida Keys.

Meade's first project in the Keys was at Carysfort Reef Light near Key Largo, where he supervised construction of the soaring iron-skeleton tower designed by I. W. P. Lewis. Meade not only executed Lewis's design but also added a number of personal innovations, including an enlarged foot plate that prevented the tower's screw piles from sinking under the structure's enormous weight. Completed in 1852, the 100-foot Carysfort Reef tower still stands and remains in use. So do Sand Key Light near Key West, Absecon Light in Atlantic City, New Jersey, and the Jupiter Inlet lighthouse on the Florida mainland, all built by Meade.

MERCURY BATHS To minimize friction, rotating lenses can be floated in a tub filled with mercury. It is a hazardous arrangement, and more than a few keepers were poisoned by the mercury vapors. While the technique is effective for protecting lenses, concerns for the safety of keepers led to the replacement by rotation devices with rollers or linked metal wheels known as chariots. A few mercury lighthouse optics remain in use, mostly in Europe.

MODERN OPTICS Most navigational beacons are now produced by so-called modern optics. The term refers to a broad array of lightweight, mostly weatherproof devices, such as the Vega light. Most

Catherine Moore's Black Rock Harbor Light in Connecticut
Courtesy *Lighthouse Digest*

Bruce Roberts

The golden glow of the East Brother Light (above) in San Francisco Bay adds warmth to a California sunrise. Interestingly, this so-called modern optic makes use of nineteenth-century Fresnel technology to concentrate light. Unlike old-fashioned Fresnel lenses, however, it is relatively inexpensive, compact, fully automated, weatherproof, and easy to maintain.

modern optics employ refraction to concentrate their beacons but rely on acrylic rather than glass lenses. Although rarely more effective than the Fresnel lenses they have replaced, modern optics are relatively low in cost and easy to maintain.

MOORE, CATHERINE For more than fifty years, Catherine Moore tended the Black Rock Harbor beacon near Bridgeport, Connecticut. For much of that time, she assisted her father, Stephen Moore, who was the keeper of record from 1817 until 1871. When her father fell ill during the later years of his life, Catherine handled all the work of maintaining the lighthouse. She was named the official keeper

in 1871 and served until 1878. Catherine Moore has been credited with rescuing twenty-one shipwrecked mariners.

NORTHERN LIGHTHOUSE BOARD The agency that administers aids to navigation in Scotland is known as the Northern Lighthouse Board. Its history can be traced to the 1780s, when a series of destructive storms left the shores of Scotland littered with wrecked ships and the bodies of drowned sailors. Alarmed by the magnitude of these disasters, in 1786 Great Britain's Parliament created the Northern Lighthouse Board and empowered it to establish navigational lights and

A Lighthouse Lexicon 115

Cloch Point Lighthouse (above) on the River Clyde, one of nearly 200 important light stations maintained by Scotland's Northern Lighthouse Board. Margaret Norvell served at a number of Louisiana light stations much like, though not including, the Bayou Bonfouca Lighthouse (below).

collect fees from the vessels that relied on them. Parliament provided no funding, so the board had to borrow money to build its first four lighthouses—at Eilean Glas, Kinnaird Head, Mull of Kintyre, and North Ronaldsay. These light stations and many others built afterward soon paid for themselves. Today the Northern Lighthouse Board oversees the maintenance and operation of about 200 lighthouses. The Northern Lighthouse Board was the stronghold of the Stevenson family, famous for its lighthouse builders and engineers. (See also Stevenson Family.)

NORVELL, MARGARET For more than forty years, Margaret Norvell kept the lights burning at various navigational stations in the southern United States. She began her Lighthouse Service career in 1891 at the critical Head of Passes lighthouse in Louisiana's lower Mississippi River delta and ended it in 1932, when she retired from her post as head keeper at the West End lighthouse in the Louisiana bayous. Norvell spent much of her career at Port Pontchartrain Light near New Orleans, where she served as keeper from 1896 to 1924.

Norvell earned praise for her daring rescues of shipwrecked mariners on Lake Pontchartrain.

She also was known for assisting the homeless whenever hurricanes drove floodwaters into low-lying residential areas near the lake. During an especially destructive 1903 storm, she cared for more than 200 people who sought refuge at Port Pontchartrain Light.

OCCULTING LIGHTS There are several ways to produce a beacon that appears to flash. One is to occult, or block, the light at regular intervals with an opaque panel. Usually the panel rotates around the outside of the lens. Fenwick Island Light in Delaware displays an occulting light (also known as an eclipsing light), as does Bass Harbor Head Light in Maine.

OIL HOUSES Before the coming of electricity, whale oil, coal oil, kerosene, and other flammables were used to power lamps at light stations. These fuels posed a severe fire hazard, especially when stored inside the residence or tower, and more than a few lighthouses burned to the ground when their fuel supplies were accidentally ignited. The obvious solution for this problem was to store the fuel in a separate building.

In the late nineteenth century the Lighthouse Board began to add oil houses to light stations. This process became more urgent as relatively inexpensive but highly volatile kerosene became the lighthouse lamp fuel of choice. In 1902 the US Board of Lighthouses informed all its keepers that all mineral oil belonging to the Lighthouse Service be kept in an oil house or a room by itself. The oil house was to be visited daily by the keeper to detect loss by leakage, and keepers were required to take every precaution for the safekeeping of the oil.

Most oil houses were small, fireproof structures made of brick, concrete, or cast iron. Although they were highly functional in design, some received architectural detailing similar to that of the station dwelling or tower. After electricity replaced kerosene in lighthouse lantern rooms,

At night or in inclement weather, Delaware's Fenwick Island tower (above) displays its occulting light. This brick oil house (below) allowed keepers at the Marblehead Light in Massachusetts to store flammable fuels well away from the tower, residence, and other important structures that might be damaged by fire.

Photos by Bruce Roberts

Courtesy *Lighthouse Digest*

Modern lighthouses like the Faro Pedaso (above) inherited the task once handled by Ostia and other ancient beacons—they guide mariners along the rugged and often dangerous coast of Italy. The Servizio dei Fari, or Italian Lighthouse Service, maintains fifty-seven lighthouses and a variety of other navigational aids.

oil houses typically were used for odds-and-ends storage. Since they were solidly built, many old oil houses survive to this day.

OSTIA Like Alexandria and several other ancient cities, Rome had its own great light tower. It marked the harbor of Ostia, the primary port of the imperial capital. Although neither as tall nor as massive as Alexandria's Pharos, the Ostia tower was nonetheless impressive, with a height estimated at 100 feet or more.

According to ancient sources, the emperor Claudius had the tower built about AD 50 atop the sunken hull of a giant Egyptian freighter that had been used by his predecessor, Caligula, to haul an enormous obelisk from Egypt. While this may seem unlikely, it has been verified in part by modern archaeological excavations that found pieces of a huge ship at the former site of the Ostia Lighthouse. Apparently the Romans filled the hull with concrete and stone, creating an early version of a crib foundation.

Ancient architects often designed tall stone structures with tiers to ensure stability; the Ostia tower had four such stepped levels. The three lower levels were square, while the upper one was cylindrical. Signal fires were lit atop the upper level each evening until the lighthouse was destroyed, likely during the sixth century. The Ostia tower is known today largely from 2,000-year-old coins, mosaics, reliefs, and graffiti.

PATENTS British monarchs sold patents to groups or individuals, granting them the right to build and maintain lighthouses and then collect fees from ships docking at nearby ports. These arrangements could be quite lucrative for both the crown and the investors who established the lights.

In some cases the expectation of profit prodded remarkable innovations. About 1775 a Liverpool dockmaster named John Phillips obtained a patent to build a lighthouse on the Smalls, a wave-swept scrap of rock several miles offshore. To build the lighthouse, Phillips hired Henry Whiteside, who had previously earned his living by making fine musical instruments. Despite his lack of construction experience, Whitehead designed and built a light tower such as the world had not seen before. It stood on wooden piles well above the tides and ultimately proved strong enough to last for eighty-five years. Initially, however, the project was not a successful investment. Its considerable costs emptied the pockets of Phillips, who turned to Trinity House, Britain's de facto lighthouse authority, to bail him out financially. Meanwhile

Whitehead became marooned at the station when a storm carried away his boat, and the unfortunate man had to throw a note into the sea in a bottle to attract attention to his plight.

Both men eventually were rescued—Whitehead literally and Phillips financially. In time the Smalls lighthouse became such a moneymaker that Trinity House was willing to pay more than £170,000 for the patent rights to it. (See also Trinity House.)

PHAROS Historians generally agree that the world's first true light tower was the Pharos, an enormous stone tower located on an island near the harbor entrance of Alexandria, Egypt. Built about 280 BC during the reign of Ptolemy, founder of Egypt's Macedonian dynasty, the Pharos tower was considered one of the Seven Wonders of the World. The tower had a base some 360 feet wide, and its lower walls were perhaps 100 feet wide. The two upper levels were smaller but still quite substantial.

Believed to have been as much as 450 feet tall, the Pharos, no doubt, was intended to impress, but it had a practical purpose as well. Alexandria was the busiest port in the world at the time the tower was built, and approaching merchant ships had difficulty navigating along the shores of the flat Nile delta. The lofty Pharos gave mariners an obvious seamark that could be seen for miles. At night, fires lit on the tower's upper level produced a beacon with a range of up to 30 miles.

Although not always used as a lighthouse, the great tower survived more than 1,500 years. It finally succumbed to an earthquake during the fourteenth century. Recent underwater archaeological expeditions have located Pharos tower blocks in the harbor of modern Alexandria.

PLEASONTON, STEPHEN J. A remarkable though little-known figure in American history, Stephen J. Pleasonton maintained a firm—some would say choking—grip on the US lighthouse

Many British lighthouses like the one at Southstack (above) were established by investors who obtained royal patents allowing them to collect fees from passing ships. The fee collected by operators of the ancient Pharos Lighthouse, depicted (below) as a Harbour Lights sculpture, was two books for the famed Alexandria Library.
Photos Courtesy Harbour Lights

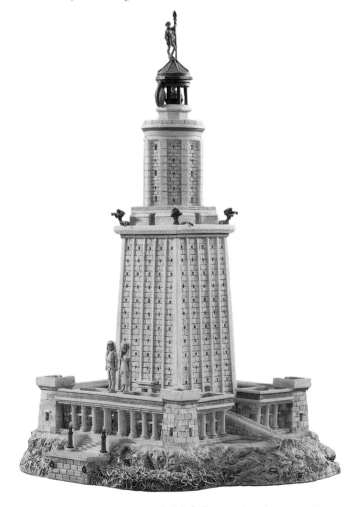

Some historians say Stephen Pleasonton made US coasts unnecessarily dangerous by resisting new technologies that would have improved the national lighthouse system but greatly increased its cost. Pleasonton might have replied that he did the best he could with the resources at hand. He welcomed experimentation when it served the purpose of efficiency as in 1844 at Long Island Head (above), where builders used cast iron to erect the nation's first all-metal light tower.

US Coast Guard

system for thirty years. A consummate bureaucrat who was destined to hold the position of Fifth Auditor of the Treasury through a half dozen presidential administrations, Pleasonton was handed responsibility for the nation's lighthouses in 1820. He did not relinquish his authority over the system and its purse strings until Congress created the Lighthouse Board in 1852, effectively forcing Pleasonton from his post.

Most historians agree that Pleasonton's tightfistedness led to low construction standards and delayed US adoption of the advanced optical technology for many years. Pleasonton hired cut-rate contractors even when their previous work had been shown to be of poor quality. He equipped light stations with Winslow Lewis's outdated but relatively low-cost lamp-and-reflector system long after the far superior but more costly prismatic Fresnel lenses became available.

Some have suggested that a corrupt relationship existed between Pleasonton and Lewis, but no such malfeasance has ever been proven. In fact, a more benign interpretation can be put on Pleasonton's parsimonious behavior. It is important to remember that, during the Pleasonton era, America was largely agricultural and by no means a rich nation. It may be that the Fifth Auditor was merely doing the best he could with the resources he had at hand. Still, it cannot be denied that numerous ships and lives were lost due to the inadequacies of US coastal beacons prior to 1852.

A fascinating footnote to the Pleasonton story was his role in saving a number of his nation's most cherished historic treasures. Pleasonton was a young government clerk working in Washington DC, when the British burned the capital during the War of 1812. While others panicked, Pleasonton loaded up a wagon with important documents, hitched it to a team of horses, and drove it to safety in the Virginia countryside. Among the papers Pleasonton managed to save were the original copies of the Declaration of Independence and US Constitution.

POLE LIGHTS Probably the simplest form of lighted aid to navigation, a pole light consists of a long iron or wooden pole with a small, self-contained beacon at the top. Pole lights frequently are used in shallow water as channel markers. Occasionally, they are used to replace a retired lighthouse beacon. (See also Harbor Lights.)

PRIVATE AIDS TO NAVIGATION This term refers to privately owned and maintained navigational lights. It is often used to describe formerly deactivated beacons that have been reestablished for historic or aesthetic purposes. These reactivated lights are considered part of the navigational aid system, but they receive no government funding or maintenance. Selkirk Light on Lake Ontario in Pulaski, New York, now functions as a private aid to navigation.

PRIVIES When nineteenth- and early-twentieth-century lighthouse keepers heeded nature's call, they took care of necessities in the same manner as other rural people the world over—in an outdoor privy. For the most part, these were rudimentary, wood-frame structures, but some were made of brick or even of iron. Currituck Beach Light on North Carolina's Outer Banks had a rather fancy privy built in a Queen Anne style that matched the architecture of the keeper's residence.

Keepers of offshore lighthouses had fewer options when it came to such matters. The privy holes of screw-pile lighthouses often dropped directly into the water. Given modern sensibilities and environmental laws, such an arrangement would be unthinkable today. The privies of caisson-style lighthouses were much like those on ships and no more friendly to the local water quality than those at screw-pile stations. Because they were made of metal, the privies of caisson lighthouses were used as electrical grounds and hooked directly to the station lightning rods. Needless to say, keepers avoided the places during thunderstorms. (See also Keepers' Residences.)

PUTNAM, GEORGE A mapmaker, surveyor, and engineer, George Putnam worked on US government projects in various parts of the world. In the Philippine Islands he directed a highly successful coast survey, which attracted the attention of his superiors in Washington. In 1910, President William H. Taft chose Putnam to administer the newly created Bureau of Lighthouses. Putnam served as the agency's commissioner for twenty-five years, finally retiring in 1935.

An able administrator, Putnam increased the efficiency of Lighthouse Service operations while

Bruce Roberts

New York's historic Selkirk Light (above) is now a private aid to navigation. Another structure (below) once served New England keepers as a private aid of a different sort.

Courtesy *Lighthouse Digest*

Among the improvements championed by George Putnam was the introduction at many light stations of radio beacons. These gave mariners an efficient way to pinpoint their locations but, like other new technologies, sometimes caused confusion. In 1923 crossed radio signals led to one of the worst peacetime naval disasters in US history when several destroyers slammed into the rocks near the Point Arguello Lighthouse and sank with a loss of nearly two dozen lives.
National Archives

raising standards for employee safety, working conditions, benefits, and pay. He also championed new technologies that led to the automation of many light stations.

RADIO BEACONS Radio beacons are directional signals broadcast by radio transmitters from navigational stations, enabling mariners to plot their course accurately even when they are too far away to see a light or hear a foghorn. First used in 1921, radio beacons greatly enhanced the operative range of the light stations that used them. Consisting of an identification signal sent in Morse code, radio beacons could reach vessels at distances of up to several hundred miles. Shipboard navigators equipped with radio direction finders could use the signals to determine their position.

Bureau of Lighthouses Commissioner George Putnam was a champion of radio beacons, and at his urging as many as 200 transmitters were placed at light stations on US coasts and lakeshores. But radio beacons were not a fail-safe technology. One or more fixes on a radio beacon was required to accurately plot a position, and it was possible to mistake one signal for another. On at least one occasion, confusion over the source of a radio beacon led to a maritime disaster. In 1923 a flotilla of fourteen US destroyers headed south along the California coast misread a radio beacon and turned directly into the fog-shrouded rocks off Point Arguello. In all, seven of the destroyers were lost along with twenty-three sailors. Ironically, the wrecks took place only about a mile from the Point Arguello lighthouse.

Made obsolete by radar and global positioning systems, all US radio beacons have been taken out of service by the US Coast Guard. (See also Beacons.)

RANGE LIGHTS Displayed in pairs, range lights help mariners keep their vessels safely within the narrow navigable channels that crisscross estuaries or lead in and out of harbors. The rear range light is higher and farther from the water than its partner, the front range light, which is often located at water's edge. When viewed from mid-channel, the lights appear in perfect vertical alignment. If the rear light appears to be either to the right or the left of the front light, the pilot must steer in the opposite direction to correct course.

The idea for range lights is credited to Dewitt Brawn, the son of a lighthouse keeper in Saginaw, Michigan. As a teenager, Brawn spent a lot of time on the water, and he noticed how the perspective of two objects changed as he floated past them. Brawn's insight was given a practical application with construction of the Saginaw River Range Lights in 1876. Its rear range tower stood 61 feet high and a considerable distance from a modest front range tower down on the riverbank. Functioning in tandem, the two beacons helped pilots steer a straight course through the river's channel.

Liston Rear Range Light in Delaware Bay is a steel skeleton some 120 feet tall with a focal plane more than 170 feet in elevation. The Liston Front Range tower, on the other hand, is a simple metal structure located in front of the old keeper's residence and rises only 45 feet above the water.

Dewitt's range light system continues to be used throughout the world whenever pinpoint navigation is essential. Range lights are common in the Great Lakes where towers are often arrayed in pairs on breakwaters or piers and used to guide vessels into harbor.

REINFORCED CONCRETE TOWERS When concrete is reinforced with iron bars or mesh, it becomes very strong, especially in relation to its weight and cost. Early in the twentieth century,

Like the US Navy destroyers lost nearby during the 1920s, California's Point Arguello Lighthouse (above) no longer exists. Delivering its message in the form of light, not radio waves, the Grand Haven Pier Lights (below) signal ships in the midst of a Lake Michigan thunderstorm. By lining up both lights, mariners can be sure they are in a safe channel.

Bruce Roberts

Looking a bit like an oversize oil drum, the Munising Rear Range tower (top) stands on a Michigan hillside ablaze with fall color. At night its light pairs with a second beacon located down closer to the harbor. Built with reinforced concrete after a 1906 earthquake destroyed an earlier tower, California's Point Arena Lighthouse (bottom) remains sound to this day.

Photos by Bruce Roberts

budget-minded maritime officials seized on reinforced concrete as a construction material for lighthouses. When the light station at Point Arena, California, was flattened by an earthquake in 1906, the replacement tower was built with reinforced concrete. Later, this very adaptable material was widely used in Alaska, where a number of extraordinary Art Deco–style towers were built in the 1920s and 1930s.

Lighthouse builders were still using reinforced concrete as recently as 1958, when Oak Island Light in North Carolina was completed. The tower's 169-foot height offers proof of the material's enormous strength.

RELOCATION Despite constant exposure to harsh coastal environments, lighthouses are surprisingly durable structures. Built with massive blocks of stone, iron, and other tough materials, many lighthouses have withstood batterings from coastal storms for centuries and can be counted among the oldest and most historic edifices on many lists of national landmarks. However, in part because of their longevity, light towers are quite vulnerable to another force of nature—erosion. Shorelines inevitably change, beaches erode, cliffs crumble, and sandy bluffs blow away with the wind, and when the ground beneath then fails, lighthouses are in jeopardy.

Usually, when lighthouses are threatened by erosion, the only solution for preservation is relocation, the physical moving of the structure to safer ground. Only a few decades ago, people would have scoffed at the notion of relocating a brick or stone structure, possibly 150 to 200 feet tall and weighing 3,000 tons or more. During the 1990s, however, several such moves were successfully completed. The most famous of these lighthouse rescues was that of the erosion-threatened Cape Hatteras Light in North Carolina. Completed in the summer of 1999, this $12 million project involved the relocation of the tallest brick light tower in the United States.

In 1996 $1.5 million in government and private funding made it possible to save the 140-year-old Cape Cod Light from falling over the edge of a rapidly weathering bluff. Using what has been called a "combination commonsense and high-tech approach," the movers shoved the old tower backward over rails, much as they would later do at Cape Hatteras. In 1993 Block Island Southeast Light was saved in a very similar manner.

SCREW-PILE TOWERS Piles driven straight into sand, mud, or soft clay often failed to provide a sufficiently stable foundation for lighthouses. In the 1830s British engineer Alexander Mitchell proposed a solution to this problem. Instead of driving piles, he attached a propeller-like blade to one end and then twisted it into place as if it were a giant screw. In 1841 Mitchell used this technique to build a lighthouse near the entrance to the harbor at Lancashire, England.

The technique soon made its way to the United States. In 1850 a screw-pile lighthouse was built at Delaware's Brandywine Shoal, where an attempt to install a straight-pile lighthouse had failed some decades earlier. The screw-pile structure proved much sturdier than its predecessor and stood until 1914, when it was replaced by a caisson tower.

US lighthouse builders used cast-iron screw piles fitted with spiral flanges that made it easy to screw the piles into the soft sedimentary material underlying shallow water construction sites such as those on the Chesapeake Bay. Usually, light wooden buildings were placed on top of the piles. Because they were relatively inexpensive and could be placed in open water directly over a shoal, lighthouses of this type proved quite popular with both mariners and the government agencies that paid for them. In the second half of the nineteenth century, as many as 100 screw-pile lighthouses were built in bays and inlets throughout the American South.

Because of their vulnerability to ice damage, screw-pile towers were far less common in northern

One of many cottage-style, screw-pile light towers that once marked inland waterways along the US East Coast, the Hooper Strait Lighthouse is shown at its station in the Chesapeake Bay. In 1967 the building was moved ashore and restored for use as a museum display.

areas. Only one screw-pile tower was erected in the Great Lakes, and it was crushed by ice during its first winter. Even in the relatively warm Chesapeake, fast-moving ice floes proved a serious problem, and eventually, the screw-pile design was abandoned in favor of far more durable caisson towers. Today only one screw-pile lighthouse remains on regular duty in the Chesapeake, the Thomas Point Shoal Light near Annapolis, Maryland. Other fine examples can be found on display in Maryland at the Baltimore Inner Harbor (Seven Foot Knoll), the Chesapeake Bay Maritime Museum (Hooper Strait Light), and Calvert Maritime Museum (Drum Point Light), all in Maryland, and in Alabama (Mobile Bay Light). (See also Exposed Screw-Pile Towers.)

Saving Cape Hatteras Light

No event in recent memory has attracted so much attention to the lighthouse preservation movement as the relocation of the Cape Hatteras tower in 1999. The thought of moving Cape Hatteras Light even a few feet—let alone more than a half mile—is a daunting one, even now, more than a decade after it was accomplished. Standing 198 feet tall and weighing in at about 4,800 tons, Cape Hatteras is one big lighthouse, and yet, it was pushed and shoved some 2,900 feet to the southwest with barely the loss of a single brick, a feat that earned a place in *Guinness World Records.* More importantly, however, it was etched in the memories of everyone who witnessed it—and thanks to extensive television coverage, many did.

The move was made necessary by erosion, often the worst enemy of lighthouses and other historic structures along the coast. Cape Hatteras Light, a venerable signpost of North Carolina's Outer Banks, stood for many years on the brink of disaster. The barrier islands that make up the Outer Banks are slowly and continually shifting westward. When the lighthouse was completed in 1870, it stood about 1,600 feet from the shore, but by 1987, the distance had been cut to only 120 feet. Despite $17 million spent to control the erosion that threatened to undercut the old tower, it seemed certain the Atlantic would soon claim its victim.

Many thought the only practical way to save this national treasure was to move it. Eventually, the government approved a relocation plan along with an $11.8 million appropriation to pay for it.

The relocation process got under way in the spring of 1999. First, workers prepared the lengthy corridor over which the lighthouse and two keepers' houses would travel.

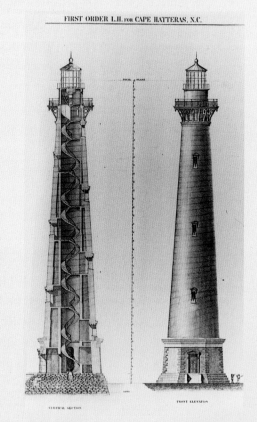

Outer Banks History Center

Next came the difficult task of removing the tower from its old foundation. A wire saw with a diamond cutting cable separated the tower from its underpinnings. Then, over a span of several weeks, workers carefully removed the granite foundation one 2-foot section at a time. As space opened up, steel beams were inserted and welded together to evenly spread the enormous weight. Super-powerful hydraulic jacks were used to lift the tower and its platform of steel beams onto a set of rails.

Not long afterward the long-armed jacks began to push the tower an inch or two at a time along the rails, which, interestingly enough, were lubricated with ordinary Ivory soap.

Beginning on June 17, 1999, the tower's epic journey took twenty-two days. Reporters and photographers from all over the world came to Cape Hatteras to witness this painstakingly slow but nonetheless dramatic process. Thousands of spectators were on hand to watch as the tower finally reached its destination during the second week of July and was lifted onto its new, rock-solid foundation some 1,600 feet from the Atlantic. Structural engineers predict that the new setting, a safe distance from the ocean's ravenous waves, will ensure the survival of Cape Hatteras Light for the next 100 years.

Outer Banks History Center

Photos by Bruce Roberts

This 1902 photograph of Maryland's Love Point Lighthouse (above) illustrates the vulnerability of screw-pile structures to ice. Interestingly, the besieged building survived that year's brutal winter and many others only to be demolished by the Coast Guard in 1964. The rather bizarre, privately constructed tower (opposite page) at Playa Del Carmen in Mexico is sufficiently distinct to make it an excellent seamark.

SEAMARKS Seamarks are easily recognizable objects that help mariners get their bearings. A seamark can be either a natural object, such as a distinctive rock formation, or a man-made one, such as a church steeple.

In the early days of seafaring, mariners relied heavily on seamarks because there were very few coastal lights to guide them. Mariners with well-marked charts or an intimate knowledge of local waters could make their way safely along the coast by steering from one seamark to the next. In some cases they might line up a pair of seamarks one behind the other and use them much as range lights are used today.

Even today seamarks remain an important, even if old-fashioned, tool for navigators. To make them easier to use as seamarks, some light towers are painted with stripes, spirals, or other special markings. (See also Daymarks.)

SHUBRICK, WILLIAM B. In 1851 Rear Admiral William B. Shubrick headed a committee appointed by Congress to appraise the condition of US aids to navigation. Shubrick's committee found the nation's coastal beacons to be outdated and poorly administered, and its 750-page report to Congress led to a complete overhaul of the US lighthouse system. To make improvements and govern a rejuvenated system, Congress created the nine-member Lighthouse Board and appointed Shubrick as its chairman.

A distinguished naval officer, Shubrick brought military-like efficiency to what he called the Lighthouse Establishment. Crumbling lighthouses, some of them built during the colonial era, were repaired or rebuilt, and many new towers were erected. Keepers and other lighthouse personnel were expected to wear uniforms and adhere to rigid standards for cleanliness and behavior. Keepers who failed to follow regulations laid down by Shubrick and his board were dismissed.

During his nineteen-year tenure as chairman of the Lighthouse Board, Shubrick presided over what could be called an American lighthouse revolution. By importing large numbers of Fresnel lenses, Shubrick's board vastly improved the range

Admiral William B. Shubrick (above) became chairman of the US Lighthouse Board upon its creation in 1852 and served in that capacity for nearly twenty years. Under his leadership, the board launched many innovative projects such as construction of skeleton light towers. Completed in 1852 and still in service today, the Carysfort Reef Lighthouse (below left) has proven all but impervious to hurricane-driven winds and waves. England's Maplin Sand Lighthouse (below right) was among the first skeleton towers ever built.

and overall quality of US beacons. Shubrick is also credited, in part, for encouraging engineering innovations such as the use of cast-iron screw piles and the construction of skeleton towers.

SKELETON TOWERS Skeleton light towers are so named because of their design. They consist of four or more heavily braced metal legs (either iron or steel) topped by workrooms and/or a lantern. Relatively durable and inexpensive, they were built in considerable numbers in the second half of the nineteenth century. Because their open walls offer little resistance to wind and water, skeleton towers proved ideal for offshore navigational stations, such as those in the stormy Florida Keys.

Skeleton towers often were fabricated in a foundry and then shipped to the site in pieces for assembly. Should the tower need to be heightened at some later date, additional sections could be added to the bottom. The light weight of skeleton towers made it possible for them to soar skyward, and many are quite tall. At 191 feet, Virginia's Cape Charles Light is the tallest skeleton light tower in the United States. The tower, built in the 1890s, remains in use, as do many other skeleton towers.

Plate V

Marblehead Light in Massachusetts and Sand Key Light near Key West, Florida, are fine examples of skeleton towers.

SMITH, THOMAS The owner of a successful whaling operation and a manufacturer of whale-oil lamps, Thomas Smith adapted the Argand lamp for use in lighthouses. This brought him to the attention of Scotland's Northern Lighthouse Board, which hired him to build and provide optics for several light stations in Scotland. The board eventually appointed Smith as its official engineer.

Having recently married into the Stevenson family, Smith took his young stepson, Robert Stevenson, with him when he started work on Kinnaird Head Light. This experience laid the foundation for Stevenson's long career as a lighthouse engineer. It also helped launch the Stevenson family's engineering dynasty, which was to include several generations of renowned lighthouse builders. (See also Stevenson Family.)

SOLAR-POWERED OPTICS Many remote lighthouse beacons are now powered by batteries recharged during the day by solar panels. Surprisingly, this technique is used even in Alaska, where skies often are cloudy and days are short in winter. The Art Deco–style Sentinel Island Light on Frederick Sound near Juneau has a large array of solar panels on its roof, as does Cape Hinchinbrook Light near the entrance to Prince William Sound. Even some lighthouses in less remote locations make use of solar panels, including Race Point Light near Provincetown, Massachusetts, and East Pierhead Light in Cleveland, Ohio.

SPARK-PLUG, TEAKETTLE, OR COFFEEPOT LIGHTS Many open-water lighthouses in northern climates are built on round, concrete-filled caissons, which protect them from fast-flowing water and ice floes. Usually, the wide caissons are black, while the narrower cylindrical iron towers on top of them

Courtesy Lighthouse Digest

Solar panels (above) at Race Point in Massachusetts. Look closely at the photograph below and you'll see that the teakettle-style Goose Rocks Lighthouse near Maine's Vinalhaven Island is also equipped with solar panels.

Courtesy Lighthouse Digest

The Rockland Lake coffeepot tower (above) in New York looked as if it had sprung a leak. Essentially, it had, and in 1923, Lighthouse Service crews gave up trying to straighten the leaning tower and demolished it. Alan Stevenson (below right) was the noted lighthouse designer and promoter of refracting technology for maritime optics.

are painted white for visibility. Their distinct shape and two-tone paint job give these structures an odd appearance, somewhat like that of an automobile sparkplug. As a result, lighthouses of this type are widely referred to as spark-plug lights.

Most spark-plug lights are located in relatively shallow water near the shore. Many were too small to provide living quarters, so their keepers often commuted to work by boat from a separate residence on land. This was the case at the sparkplug–style Lubec Channel Light in Maine, which still is in use but is now completely automated.

Sometimes open-water, cast-iron towers are referred to as coffeepot or teakettle lights. Orient Point Light off the northeastern end of Long Island has been nicknamed "The Old Coffee Pot" by locals. (See also Caisson Towers.)

STEVENSON FAMILY The Stevensons figured prominently in Scotland's maritime history.

The family's involvement in lighthouse design and construction actually began with Thomas Smith, the stepfather of Robert Stevenson and an engineer with Scotland's Northern Lighthouse Board. Robert Stevenson oversaw the building of almost twenty lighthouses in Scotland, including Bell Rock Light, completed in 1811. His sons Alan, Thomas, and David (father of writer Robert Louis Stevenson) followed in their father's line of work.

Alan Stevenson was fascinated by the prismatic lenses designed by Augustin Fresnel. The famous French physicist had died by the time Stevenson traveled to France in the early 1830s to study the lenses. Stevenson returned from his visit deeply impressed by the Fresnel optical technology and later persuaded the Northern Lighthouse Board to install a Fresnel lens in the important Skerryvore Lighthouse in the Inner Hebrides. This ensured the widespread use of Fresnel-type lenses throughout Great Britain and its colonies.

Alan Stevenson designed the Skerryvore tower, completed in 1844, and many other noted British lighthouses, including those at Little Ross (1843), Covesea Skerries (1846), Chanonry Point

Courtesy Northern Lighthouse Board

(1846), Cromarty (1846), Cairn Point (1847), Noss Head (1849), Sanda (1850), Heston Island (1850), Hoy (1851), and Amish Point (1853).

Although he preferred literature to engineering, Robert Louis Stevenson shared the family affinity for lighthouses, and it is said the area around Scotland's Fidra Lighthouse inspired his classic novel *Treasure Island*. Stevenson not only wrote fiction but also travelogues, and lighthouses turned up frequently in his writings. While visiting California in 1879, he spent considerable time at Point Pinos Light in Monterey. (See also Smith, Thomas.)

STOREHOUSES Just as many homeowners do today, lighthouse keepers needed lots of extra storage, and some stations had a separate building designated for this purpose. These utilitarian frame or masonry storehouses might be filled with paint, building materials, spare parts, fuel, or provisions stockpiled just in case the tender missed its next delivery. It is hard to say just what might have been found in a light station storehouse. No doubt the keepers and their families sometimes used the space as if it were an attic, shoving into it old clothes and other discards they could not bring themselves to throw away. However, they could not afford to be untidy even in the station storehouse or the lighthouse inspector was sure to upbraid them at his next visit.

Storage posed a chronic problem at offshore lighthouses, where space came at a premium. Caisson lighthouses had large cellars where fuel and provisions could be stored, but cramped screw-pile lighthouses had even less space than the ships they served, so everything had to be kept ship-shape. Still, screw-pile keepers found ways to store extra items and materials outside their elevated cottages. Often this was done on a separate platform slung below the station.

Where light station storehouses have survived, they continue to be used in much the way they always

have—for storage. Historical societies, preservation organizations, and educational institutions that now maintain many lighthouses have found their station storehouses to be treasure troves of artifacts such as old magazines and newspapers and even US Bureau of Lighthouses buttons and caps.

SWAPES See Lever Lights.

The smaller structures shown in this picture of Cape Neddick Lighthouse in Maine were likely used for storage.
US Coast Guard

TENDERS Throughout its history, the US Lighthouse Service maintained a fleet of small, specially outfitted tenders used to deliver construction materials and supplies to light stations. Throughout much of the nineteenth century, of course, these vessels were sailing ships. Later, steam- and diesel-powered ships were used as tenders.

When the US Coast Guard took charge of the nation's aids to navigation in 1939, the Lighthouse Service handed over its fleet of sixty-four tenders. A Coast Guard engineering digest published at the time described these vessels as follows: "Lighthouse Tenders are used for general duty, which consists mainly of servicing navigational aids and supplying necessities to lighthouses and lightships. In order to perform these duties, the vessel must be able to

Its deck loaded with enormous buoys, the lighthouse tender *Tulip* approaches a dock in Philadelphia during the 1920s.

National Archives

carry personnel, cargo, fuel, and water. In addition to the above, the vessel must have adequate deck space for working, storing, and servicing buoys. . . . The vessels are of medium speed, in general rather shoal draft, and are usually twin screw due to the draft limitation. The initial stability is of necessity quite high, due to the requirement of handling heavy weights over the side, coupled with a low freeboard requirement. The larger tenders are designed for open sea work, a smaller type being used for bays and sounds, and a still smaller type for protected waters. Vessels are powered with steam, diesel, and diesel-electric drives."

Many Lighthouse Service tenders were named after flowers, fruits, or trees. For instance, the *Marigold, Amaranth, Orchid, Azalea,* and *Spruce* serviced light stations in the eastern United States and on the Great Lakes. The Coast Guard later continued this tradition, launching tenders such as the *Mistletoe, Sweetgum, Sweetbrier, Red Birch,* and *Papaw.*

TOLLS Most nations operate their lighthouses with money provided by the government, but this has never been the case in Great Britain, where navigational aids are paid for by fees imposed on shipping. Originally, these fees amounted to a few pennies per ton on ships arriving at British ports. An early Trinity House fee schedule levied tolls of six pence for two-masted ships, four pence for one-masted vessels, and two pence for all others. Today the fees are calculated according to a complex formula based on the size of the vessel and the type of cargo it carries. (See also Patents.)

TRAMWAYS Light stations often received foodstuffs and supplies from lighthouse tenders that steamed into sight only once every few months. Since deliveries were infrequent, large amounts of oil, coal, food, and other necessaries had to be delivered at each visit. Sailors either brought the goods ashore in small boats or, when the tender could move in close, offloaded them directly onto the station dock. This left the keeper and others at the station with the task of lugging heavy boxes and barrels to storage areas. More often than not light stations were located a considerable distance above the water, making the job even more strenuous.

Some stations were equipped with tramways to ease the burden. A light rail line linking the dock with the station made it possible to load supplies onto small wheeled carts and move them to storage areas with relative ease. In many cases the tramway was built before the lighthouse itself. This simplified the process of bringing in construction materials and equipment. Lighthouses equipped with tramways include Point Reyes Light in California, Sentinel Island Light in Alaska, and Split Rock Light in Minnesota.

TRINITY HOUSE In Great Britain, responsibility for managing navigational aids belongs to Trinity House. A corporation that functions much like a government agency, Trinity House began as a medieval mariners' guild concerned primarily with the welfare of old seamen and of widows and orphans of sailors lost at sea. Most English ports had guilds of this type, but the one on the Thames in London—originally known as The Brethren of Trinity House of Deptford Strond—became increasingly influential, especially in matters of navigational policy. Reorganized during the sixteenth century under a royal charter from King Henry VIII, Trinity House eventually was placed in charge of lighthouses, buoys, and the enforcement of shipping regulations in and around the United Kingdom. Trinity House built its first lighthouse at Lowestoft in 1609, and over the years, many more would follow. Nowadays, Trinity House maintains approximately seventy lighthouses.

The corporation received no government funding, but it was allowed to defray its costs by collecting tolls from ships. During its early years Trinity House came into conflict with the crown over the monarchs' practice of selling royal patents to private individuals for the operation of lighthouses and the collection of associated duties. British monarchs regarded these sales as a welcome source of income, but by making it difficult to enforce uniform standards, they had the effect of diminishing the overall quality of British lights. During the 1800s, the sale of private lighthouse patents was discontinued, and Trinity House was given the right to buy out and operate all privately owned beacons.

Today Trinity House serves a number of important functions. In addition to its lighthouse duties, the organization oversees the placement and maintenance of foghorns, buoys, and other fixed or floating seamarks throughout Britain. It helps train seamen and harbor pilots, and, much as it did 500 years ago, it also serves as a charitable organization

The Hook Head Lighthouse in Ireland and all other major light stations throughout the British Isles are funded by tolls imposed on shipping.

A tramway leads from the water to an elevated engine house at the Eldred Rock Lighthouse in Alaska. The tramway is long gone as are the station's keepers who were removed when the light was automated in 1973.

US Coast Guard

An antique postcard view of the twin lights at Chatham, Massachusetts (above), now a single tower station

Courtesy *Lighthouse Digest*

concerned with the welfare of needy mariners and their families. (See also Patents.)

TWIN LIGHTS A few lighthouses, such as Cape Elizabeth Light in Maine, Cape Ann Light in Massachusetts, and Highlands Light in New Jersey, were equipped with two separate lights to help mariners distinguish them from other prominent nearby lights. Usually tended by the same keeper, these twin lights were displayed from separate towers spaced several hundred feet apart.

The first twin beacon in the United States was Gurnet Light, established in 1769 in Plymouth, Massachusetts. Unlike later twin lights, the Gurnet beacons were displayed from the roof of the same wooden structure, an arrangement that may

have contributed to the destruction of this early American lighthouse. In 1801, the oil supply caught fire and burned the building to the ground. Soon afterward, it was replaced with two separate towers spaced about 30 feet apart.

In 1924 the US Bureau of Lighthouses decided to convert all US multiple lights to single lights. This policy was enforced even at Plymouth, where one of the historic Gurnet towers was torn down. The other tower remains in use to this day.

UNDERWATER FOUNDATIONS When fast currents made more conventional construction methods impossible, lighthouse builders sometimes attempted to create man-made foundations by dumping enormous quantities of rock on underwater ledges. Usually, hundreds of shiploads and thousands of tons of stone were required to build up these artificial islands, a process that could take several years. The cost of this technique was often so prohibitive that it was not even considered. Even when it was attempted, the effort was not always successful. Often the currents washed away or scattered the stone almost as soon as it was dumped.

At Race Rock near the northeastern end of Long Island Sound, it took five years to create a 10,000-ton foundation. Three more years were needed to build the lighthouse itself, which was completed in 1879 at a then-exorbitant cost of $278,716. Roughly 90 percent of this amount, $250,000, was spent on the foundation alone.

VEGA LIGHTS Among the many modern optics now used to guide mariners and mark navigational obstacles is a self-contained rotating beacon commonly known as a Vega light. Manufactured by Vega Industries of Porirua, New Zealand, these completely automated lights combine powerful halogen lamps with old-fashioned Fresnel prismatic technology to produce intense beacons visible over distances of 15 to 22 nautical miles.

The optical equipment is housed in a waterproof cylinder that can be placed in a conventional light tower or on an open platform exposed to the weather. The cylinder is rotated by a low-speed, direct-drive motor. Both the lamps and the rotation drive can be operated and monitored by radio signal from a remote location. Sometimes Vega lights are installed in pairs so that if one fails, the other can take over until repairs can be made.

As long as it has a source of electric power, a Vega light can operate on its own for months, if not

Courtesy Harbour Lights

Established in 1724, Les Casquets Lighthouse (above) in the Channel Islands is one of more than seventy key light stations funded and maintained by England's Trinity House. The mostly underwater foundation (below) is all that remains of this Great Lakes lighthouse.

Courtesy *Lighthouse Digest*

years at a time. Its low maintenance requirements have made the Vega light a favorite of lighthouse services and coast guards around the world. The US Coast Guard has made extensive use of these beacons, particularly in remote locations where regular maintenance is all but impossible. (See also Beacons and Modern Optics.)

A Lighthouse Lexicon   137

Monument to a Mad Emperor

To commemorate a bizarre, imaginary battle in which he pitted his legions against the sea god Neptune, the mad Roman emperor Caligula ordered construction of a tower on a cliff in northwestern Gaul (now France) overlooking the Straits of Dover. Built in twelve slightly tiered stages of red brick and stone, it was an octagonal building about 125 feet tall. Known as the Tour d'Ordre, it was used as a lighthouse on and off for nearly 1,600 years. About AD 800 Charlemagne is said to have ordered repairs on the structure. Nothing remains of the tower today; the cliff beneath it gave way and collapsed into the sea in 1644.

Rising from bare rock off the coast of Brittany (below right), this French beacon looks out over the British Channel as did the long vanished Tour d'Ordre tower built by the demented Roman Emperor Caligula.
Photos Courtesy Harbour Lights

WAESCHE, RUSSELL RANDOLPH Born in Maryland in 1886, Russell Waesche entered the US Revenue Cutter Service School in 1904 and graduated two years later as an ensign. He became a member of the US Coast Guard when it absorbed the Revenue Cutter Service in 1915. Having attained the rank of rear admiral, Waesche was appointed Commandant of the Coast Guard in 1936. Admiral Waesche became the nation's head lighthouse keeper when President Franklin D. Roosevelt dissolved the Lighthouse Service in 1939 and handed responsibility for US maritime lights and other aids to navigation to the Coast Guard.

Integrating the operations of a purely civilian agency with those of a military organization was by nature a ticklish process, but Waesche made sure the transition was a smooth one. Even more impressive was Waesche's efficient administration of the Coast Guard during World War II, when the fleet he commanded grew from a few hundred to several thousand ships. Waesche retired in 1946 and died a few months later.

WALKER, JAMES Born in 1781 in Falkirk, Scotland, James Walker served for many years as Engineer in Chief for Trinity House. Walker designed a number of impressive British light towers, including Bishop Rock Light and Beachy Head Light. He also designed and built the Westminster Bridge in London, the Victoria Bridge in Glasgow, and many other noted structures in England and Scotland. He was elected President of the Institution of Civil Engineers in 1834.

Bishop Rock Light is probably the most widely celebrated of the towers designed and built by Walker. Exposed to high winds and constant pounding by waves, this exposed open-water ledge presented Walker with what was almost certainly his greatest challenge. Having made an unsuccessful attempt to erect a screw-pile tower on the rock in 1849–50, Walker turned to the more familiar technique of building with interlocking granite blocks. The latter approach proved highly successful, and although the tower took seven years to build, it was able to withstand even the most ferocious gales. Completed in 1858, Walker's Bishop Rock tower—renovated by Sir James Douglass during the 1880s—still serves mariners.

WATER COLLECTION AND SUPPLY

Among the many challenges that confronted lighthouse keepers and their families, none was more

A Vega light atop a volcanic island in Hawaii.
Courtesy John Grant

ironic than the scarcity of fresh water. Although constantly washed by ocean waves and threatened by floodtides during storms, most lighthouses existed in what could reasonably be described as virtual deserts. Keepers had the same problem as the unfortunate narrator in Samuel Coleridge's *The Rime of the Ancient Mariner,* who said, "Water, water, everywhere, Nor any drop to drink." There was plenty of water around all right—far more than enough, in fact—but it was not fit for consumption.

Whenever possible, light stations made use of spring water or wells. Some piped in water from lakes or springs located at a higher elevation. All too often, however, keepers had to rely on rainwater collection systems to provide water for drinking, cooking, and washing. Sometimes keepers also used rainwater to charge the boilers of steam-powered fog signals.

Stations built on barren islands or rocky points were often entirely dependent on rainwater. In such cases, the roof of the keeper's dwelling and perhaps other buildings as well were used as water collectors. The gutters and downspouts channeled rainwater into a large cistern. Stations in areas where rain was spotty or infrequent, such as the coast of southern California, often had extensive catchments and enormous cisterns. The Point Loma Light cistern held up to 10,000 gallons. The cistern at California's Anacapa Island Light could store up to 130,000

Coast Guard Commandant Russell Waesche
Courtesy *Lighthouse Digest*

gallons, but the island's sparse rainfall could never fill the station's huge redwood tanks and cistern. Instead they were filled with water pumped into them during occasional visits by tenders.

WAVE-SWEPT TOWERS Some offshore lighthouses were built on rocks either completely submerged or swept by waves at high tide. Perhaps the most famous light tower of this type is Eddystone Light, a few miles off the coast of Plymouth, England. Although four earlier towers marked the rock—the first during the late seventeenth century—the existing lighthouse today dates to 1882. Its massive, interlocking masonry blocks have enabled it to withstand the giant waves thrown at it by more than a century of gales blasting through the English Channel.

Perhaps the best-known wave-swept lighthouse in US waters is Minot's Ledge Light, southwest of Boston. An earlier attempt to mark the ledge with a skeleton tower failed when the structure collapsed in a storm, carrying two assistant keepers to their deaths. Completed in 1860, the existing lighthouse is a solid-walled cylinder somewhat similar to the Eddystone tower. Its interlocking granite blocks grip one another when placed under pressure by waves.

The notable engineering feat of building the Minot's Ledge tower was more than matched

The wave-swept lighthouses of England, France, the United States, and other nations surely rank among the most dramatic structures ever built. California's St. George Reef Lighthouse is shown here under construction during the early 1890s. An Atlantic wave crashes into the French Kéréon Lighthouse (opposite page).

National Archives

at construction sites off the US West Coast. One of these, St. George Reef Light near Crescent City, California, was built in the early 1890s at a then record cost of $704,633.

WICKS AND WICKIES Before electric power made lighthouse work much cleaner and simpler, nearly all navigational beacons were produced by oil or kerosene lamps. Most of these lamps had wicks that required constant care and trimming. Consequently, lighthouse keepers often referred to themselves somewhat humorously as "wickies." When speaking of a friend or associate who worked for the US Bureau of Lighthouses or kept lights for the US Coast Guard, a former keeper may describe him as an "old wickie."

WILLSON, THOMAS See Acetylene Lamps.

Lighthouse wicks and mantles

Bruce Roberts

WOOD-PILE TOWERS The best way to mark shoals, reefs, and other open-water obstructions is to place a light directly over them. To build such light stations offshore, however, a way had to be found to protect the structure along with its occupants and equipment from water and storm damage. One way to do this was to place the living quarters, workrooms, and lantern on an elevated platform beyond the reach of tides and waves. Often this was accomplished by building on stiltlike wood piles driven securely into the subsurface rocks or sediment.

An early use of this technique came in the mid-1770s at Smalls Rock, a threatening obstacle in the St. George's Channel off the west coast of Wales. When local merchants decided to mark the rock with a lighthouse, they put the project in the hands of Henry Whiteside, who was a maker of musical instruments rather than an engineer. Instead of a conventional masonry tower, likely to fall apart and collapse after only a few years, Whiteside concocted a revolutionary design. His lighthouse was built atop a small forest of oak posts, each of them 2 feet thick and 40 feet long. Completed in 1775, Whiteside's lighthouse stood for more than eighty years.

A number of wood-pile lighthouses were built in the United States. One of these, completed in 1828 at Brandywine Shoal in Delaware Bay, was destroyed by ice after only a few months of service. A wood-pile lighthouse built at Lambert Point in Virginia stood for twenty years before it began to sink into the mud at the bottom of the Elizabeth River and was abandoned.

Most nineteenth-century lighthouse engineers found iron a much more reliable material for piles. By the middle of the twentieth century, the last US wood-pile towers had been dismantled. (See also Exposed Screw-Pile Towers, Iron-Pile Towers, and Screw-Pile Towers.)

WORTHYLAKE, GEORGE Generally recognized as America's first lighthouse keeper, George

An example of a wood-pile lighthouse is at Carquinez Strait in California. Having served mariners for many years, the building was eventually lifted from its forest of wooden supports and moved to land for use as headquarters of a private marina.
National Archives

During the early 1700s when George Worthylake tended this light station at the entrance to Boston Harbor, the place was even more rustic than it appears in this early photograph. Worthylake held the job for only a year before drowning in a boating mishap. There have been more than sixty other keepers since.

Worthylake accepted a job tending Boston Harbor Light on Little Brewster Island in 1716. Assuming that he could supplement his income by raising sheep and serving as a harbor pilot, colonial officials agreed to pay Worthylake only fifty British pounds a year for the task of keeping the station's tallow candles lit. Unfortunately, the keeper found his duties much more arduous than expected, and he had little time left over for piloting. To make matters worse, the luckless keeper lost a herd of sheep in a winter storm and was soon penniless.

Worthylake pleaded for a salary increase, and early in 1718 his employers finally relented, granting him an extra twenty pounds a years. The keeper and his family then happily went ashore to collect his pay. On their way back to Little Brewster Island, their boat overturned, and the entire Worthylake family drowned. A thirteen-year-old Benjamin Franklin wrote a poem about the incident called "Lighthouse Tragedy" and earned pocket money by hawking it on the street.

Part
III

LIGHTHOUSES
AROUND THE WORLD

Lighthouses are found on the coasts of every seafaring nation, and it can be said that they make the world a safer and friendlier place. Part III of this book offers a tour of key light stations from Cape Hatteras in North Carolina to Cape Agulhas in South Africa, from Peggy's Cove in Nova Scotia to Dondra Head in Sri Lanka, from La Laterna on the blue Mediterranean to Split Rock at the far end of Lake Superior. While you'll find more than 180 US, Canadian, and international lighthouses described and photographed here, this listing is selective rather than comprehensive. The lighthouses included were chosen because of their extraordinary beauty, historical significance, or maritime importance. For each lighthouse described here, key facts, such as the height of the tower and the date the light station was established, are provided. Enjoy your tour.

South Carolina's Morris Island Lighthouse.

istockphoto.com

The Michigan City Lighthouse at sunset. Some might count this Great Lake range light among the most evocative and beautiful structures in the world.
Bruce Roberts

Absecon Light

Location: Atlantic City, New Jersey

Established: 1857

Tower height: 189 feet

Elevation of focal plane: 167 feet

Optic: Fresnel lens (first-order)

Status: Reactivated in 1997

Handsomely restored and returned to service in 1997, Absecon Light now displays the brightest light in Atlantic City—a first-order navigational beacon. Named for a local Indian tribe, the station was established in 1857 and served until 1933, when its light was decommissioned. The US Coast Guard planned to demolish the tower but relented in the face of public protests. Although the tower occasionally received a coat of paint, little other maintenance was done for many years, and in time, it took on a scarred and dilapidated look. In the 1990s a local preservation group attracted public and private funding for a full-scale restoration effort. Today the tower is back to the ship-shape condition of its glory years, complete with a historically correct replica of the station's dismantled keeper's residence, which now serves as a museum and visitor center. ::

Alcatraz Island Light

Location: San Francisco, California

Established: 1853

Tower height: 84 feet

Elevation of focal plane: 214 feet

Optic: Modern

Status: Active (automated in 1963)

Seabirds often flock to Alcatraz Island in the evening. That's how the island got its name, which is derived from *alcatraces,* the Spanish word for pelican. However, the island is most widely known for birds of a very different feather—jailbirds like Al Capone, who served time at the island's maximum-security federal penitentiary.

Bruce Roberts

Absecon Light

Because of its notorious prison, the island has a dark reputation, but mariners see the place in a more positive light. For more than 160 years, vessels have followed the Alcatraz Island beacon through the Golden Gate Straits and into San Francisco Bay. The federal government established the West's first official light station on Alcatraz Island in 1853. Built by contractor Francis Gibbons, it consisted of a Cape Cod–style masonry residence with a tower rising through the center of its roof. Equipped with a third-order Fresnel lens, the Gibbons structure served until 1906, when an earthquake ravaged it along with much of San Francisco.

An 84-foot reinforced concrete tower took the place of the shattered original in 1909. It still stands and remains in operation, but nearly everything else on the island has changed. Closed during the 1960s, the island's empty prison now attracts a steady stream of tourists who cross over from San Francisco's Fisherman's Wharf via ferry. Most want to see the historic lighthouse as well as the penitentiary, although little remains of it but

Once a federal prison and now a destination for curious tourists, Alcatraz Island served as a military base (above) during the Civil War.
Bruce Roberts

Courtesy *Lighthouse Digest*

the 1909 tower and lens. The two-story keeper's residence burned during occupation of the island by Native American activists in 1970. ::

Alfanzina Light

Location: Carvoeiro, Portugal
Established: 1920
Tower height: 52 feet
Elevation of focal plane: 206 feet
Optic: Fresnel lens (third-order)
Status: Active (automated in 1984)

Standing high atop the Algarve cliffs of Portugal's southern coast, the square, stone Alfanzina Light guides vessels to the port of Carvoeiro. The station is maintained by the Portuguese Lighthouse Service (Navy Department) and displays two white flashes every eleven seconds. Its light signal can be seen from nearly 30 miles at sea. ::

Alfanzina Light
Courtesy *Lighthouse Digest*

Au Sable Point Light

Location: Grand Marais, Michigan

Established: 1874

Tower height: 86 feet

Elevation of focal plane: 107 feet

Optic: Modern (solar powered)

Status: Active (automated in 1958)

Mariners still dread the miles of dark, rock-strewn shoreline stretching westward from Whitefish Point along Michigan's Upper Peninsula. For many years, there was no light to guide vessels along these treacherous shores, but in 1874 the Lighthouse Board moved to fill this dangerous void. The conical brick tower and two-story brick keeper's residence built on remote Au Sable Point at that time still stand. Although no longer focused by the station's original third-order Fresnel lens, Au Sable Point Light continues to warn ships to keep well away from shore. The station is located in Pictured Rocks National Lakeshore and has been carefully restored by the National Park Service. The lighthouse now looks much as it did when its light first shined in 1874. ::

Barnegat Light

Bruce Roberts

Barnegat Light

Location: Long Beach Island, New Jersey

Established: 1835

Tower height: 172 feet

Elevation of focal plane: 165 feet

Optic: Modern

Status: Reactivated in 2009

Designed and built in 1857 by US Army engineer George Meade, later a key Civil War general, the 172-foot tower replaced an earlier lighthouse that had marked Long Beach Island since 1835. (The original structure, which Meade assessed as being "built of inferior materials," was so deteriorated that its lens fell into the sea the year before it was rebuilt.) A first-order Fresnel lens focused the Barnegat beacon until 1944 when the station was discontinued. A $666,000 restoration in 1991 returned the tower to like-new condition, and "Old Barney" began a new career as a tourist attraction on the New Jersey shore. As an added attraction to visitors and lighthouse lovers alike, the old lighthouse has been reactivated and it once more serves as an official aid to navigation. The station's original Fresnel lens is on display at a nearby museum. ::

Au Sable Point Light

Bruce Roberts

Bass Harbor Head Light

Location: Near Bass Harbor, Maine

Established: 1858

Tower height: 32 feet

Elevation of focal plane: 56 feet

Optic: Fresnel lens (fourth-order)

Status: Active (automated in 1974)

Clinging to the edge of a red-granite cliff with its back to a forest of blue-green firs, Bass Harbor Head Light surely ranks among the most picturesque lighthouses in America. The white brick cylindrical tower and attached residence have stood since 1858. The station's light still guides fishermen home from the open and often turbulent waters of Blue Hill Bay.

Although the light has been automated since 1974, the station's original fourth-order Fresnel lens remains in place. Instead of flashing, its light is occulted briefly every few seconds. Tinted panels placed outside the lens create the light's red color.

Known for its fleet of brightly painted lobster boats, Bass Harbor bustles with tourists as well as fishermen. During the summer, Acadia National Park visitors flock here to sample the fresh, flavorful

Bass Harbor Head Light
Bruce Roberts

local catch, and often stop at the lighthouse where they are allowed to walk the station grounds but not enter the light tower. The main building still serves as a residence for Coast Guard personnel. ::

Beachy Head Light

Location: Near Eastbourne, England

Established: 1902

Tower height: 142 feet

Elevation of focal plane: 103 feet

Optic: Modern

Status: Active (automated in 1983)

England's Beachy Head Light tower stands, appropriately enough, on the beach. It was built in 1902 to replace the older Belle Tout Lighthouse,

The cliffs above the Beachy Head Lighthouse continue to crumble.
Courtesy *Lighthouse Digest*

located on the lofty but erosion-prone cliffs overhead. The chalky cliffs dwarf the tower, which is itself unusually tall and contains 3,660 tons of Cornish granite. Converted to solar power in 2000, the station guides mariners with a flashing beacon visible for 8 nautical miles. ::

Beavertail Light

Location: Jamestown, Rhode Island

Established: 1749

Tower height: 45 feet

Elevation of focal plane: 68 feet

Optic: Aeromarine beacon

Status: Active (automated in 1972)

During the 1600s the infamous pirate Captain William Kidd used Beavertail Point as a hideout. In 1749 this site achieved a claim to fame of a different sort when it became home to America's third fully functional lighthouse (after Boston Harbor Light and Brant Point on Nantucket), installed to mark the southern end of Conanicut Island and the entrance to Narragansett Bay. British troops burned the lighthouse during the Revolutionary War, and it was not repaired and put back into operation until 1790.

The Narragansett is prone to fog, so early Beavertail keepers warned mariners with blasts from a small cannon—perhaps America's earliest fog signal. During the mid-1800s, keepers employed a horse-power foghorn. When fog set in, a horse walking on a treadmill drove the pump for the horn.

In 1856 the station's square, granite tower was fitted with a third-order Fresnel lens that was used until a modern plastic optic was installed in 1991. Flashing white every six seconds, the beacon continues to warn mariners. ::

Big Sable Point Light

Location: Ludington, Michigan

Established: 1867

Tower height: 112 feet

Elevation of focal plane: 106 feet

Optic: Modern

Status: Active (automated in 1968)

Big Sable Point Light
Bruce Roberts

Beavertail Light

The severe weather of the Great Lakes region causes brick structures to crumble, particularly brick light towers such as the one at Big Sable Point on Lake Michigan. Three decades of exposure to storms blowing across the lake from the west nearly ruined the tower. But in 1900 the structure was encased in a shell of iron plates to protect it from further deterioration, a measure that proved highly effective in saving not only Big Sable Point Light but several other lake towers as well.

During the nineteenth century the Big Sable Point station made use of a highly unusual fog signal. When fog or heavy weather set in, helpful Ludington residents fired up the boiler of an old steam engine and blew its whistle to warn mariners. ::

Biloxi Light

Biloxi Light

Location: Biloxi, Mississippi

Established: 1848

Tower height: 61 feet

Elevation of focal plane: 48 feet

Optic: Fresnel lens (fifth-order)

Status: Decommissioned in 1968

A suit of cast-iron armor has protected the Biloxi Lighthouse from weather and war for more than 160 years. Thought to be the American South's oldest cast-iron light tower, it survived the Civil War as well as Katrina, the monster hurricane that blasted the Gulf Coast in 2005.

Several of the keepers at this Gulf Coast station were women. Maria Younghans took over as keeper following the Civil War and tended the beacon for more than fifty years. Her daughter Miranda Younghans served as keeper from 1918 until 1929. Biloxi Light was decommissioned by the Coast Guard in 1968, and the station is now owned and operated by the city of Biloxi. Located in the median of US 90, the stark white tower is a familiar sight to coastal motorists. ::

Bishop Rock Light

Location: Near St. Agnes, England

Established: 1858

Tower height: 161 feet

Elevation of focal plane: 144 feet

Optic: Fresnel lens

Status: Active (automated in 1991)

The dangers posed by Bishop Rock and other hazards near the Isles of Scilly are legendary. An entire squadron of British warships and more than 2,000 sailors were lost here during a single storm in 1703, and there have been many other maritime calamities in these waters. However, building a lighthouse on this narrow, open-ocean ledge was long believed impossible.

Bruce Roberts

Bishop Rock Light
Courtesy Library of Congress

a new lighthouse around the old one. Completed in 1887, the Douglass tower has remained solid ever since. Full-time keepers served at this isolated station until 1992. ::

Block Island Southeast Light

Location: Block Island, Rhode Island
Established: 1875
Tower height: 52 feet
Elevation of focal plane: 261 feet
Optic: Fresnel lens (first-order)
Status: Active (automated in 1994)

Rising prominently from the often turbulent waters east of Long Island Sound, Block Island marks the site of a seventeenth-century Indian massacre. A raiding party of Mohegan warriors

In the late 1840s Trinity House resolved to mark the rock with a first-rate light station. Unpredictable weather combined with the difficulties involved in delivering materials and maintaining a construction crew at the site would make this one of the most challenging projects ever undertaken by British lighthouse builders. On the advice of engineer James Walker, Trinity House opted for a screw-pile structure, and after two years of hard work and an expenditure of £12,000, the tower was almost ready to receive its lens. Then, early in 1850, a titanic gale descended on the isles and swept away the entire station.

Trinity House decided to try again. Abandoning the idea of a screw-pile tower, Walker drew up plans for a masonry structure instead. Since the base of the tower would be underwater, workers had to build a cofferdam to keep the rock face dry. Storms repeatedly pummeled the site, slowing progress to a crawl. In all, it took seven years, 2,500 tons of dressed stone, and £34,500 to complete the 110-foot tower, but by 1858, it was ready for duty.

Despite its considerable bulk, the tower suffered from constant pounding by the sea, and during the 1880s it had to be substantially renovated. The restoration plan prepared by Sir James Douglass strengthened the tower by encasing it in 3,200 additional tons of stone. Essentially, Douglass built

During the 1990s the aged, redbrick Block Island Southeast residence and tower became the focus of a monumental preservation effort.
Bruce Roberts

were overwhelmed by local tribesmen and driven over the towering cliffs on the southeast side of the island. In the late twentieth century, a similar fate almost befell the historic lighthouse built atop the Mohegan Bluff in 1875.

Lighthouse preservationists count Block Island Southeast Light as one of their success stories. Originally, the Victorian-style brick structure stood more than 200 feet from the precipice, but by the 1990s erosion had brought the building to the edge of destruction. To keep the old lighthouse from falling into the sea, preservationists raised more than $2 million to have the 2,000-ton structure moved back several hundred feet from the rapidly eroding cliff. Conducted by the International Chimney Corporation—the same firm that later moved the Cape Hatteras Lighthouse—the relocation proved successful, and the station is now once again in service.

The original optic was a first-order Fresnel lens lit by a whale-oil lamp with four circular wicks. Barrels of oil were stored at the base of the tower, and the lamp burned up to 900 gallons of this expensive fuel each year. Later the station's lamps were converted to burn kerosene, which was far less expensive than whale oil. Today, electric bulbs provide the light focused by the powerful lens.

When the lighthouse was moved in 1990, its 134-year-old lens was retired and replaced by a more serviceable first-order Fresnel lens once used at Cape Lookout Light in North Carolina. The station displays a flashing green light with a range of approximately 20 miles.

Several miles to the north of Block Island Southeast Light sits its sister light, an even older structure located in a sandy game preserve. Built in 1867, Block Island North Light served for more than a century before being taken out of service in 1970. In 1998 a $400,000 federal grant enabled Shoreham Township to restore the granite structure and relight its beacon. ::

Bodie Island Light

Location: Bodie Island, North Carolina
Established: 1848
Tower height: 163 feet
Elevation of focal plane: 156 feet
Optic: Fresnel lens (first-order)
Status: Active (automated in 1939)

So many ships were destroyed by the shoals and shallows off the North Carolina Outer Banks that the area earned the nickname "Graveyard of the Atlantic." As many as 3,000 large vessels have been lost on or near these barrier islands. Understandably, marking these deadly shores with adequate navigational lights has been a major concern for the US maritime authorities, but early efforts to do so often proved less than satisfactory.

Bodie Island Light
Bruce Roberts

In 1848 the government paid contractors $11,000 to erect a lighthouse at the south end of Bodie Island, which sits at about the midpoint of the Outer Banks chain. The result was an unsightly pile of bricks stacked atop a foundation so unstable that the structure was demolished and replaced after only a few years of service. The second Bodie Island tower had its career dramatically shortened by the Civil War. Less than two years after it was completed in 1859, it was blown up by Confederate forces to keep it out of Union hands.

The war was still a painfully recent memory when the current Bodie Island Light was built in 1872. Painted with bold black and white bands, the 163-foot brick tower has served at least a half dozen generations of seamen. With a granite foundation set atop iron pilings, the building has weathered numerous sea storms and hurricanes. The station's first-order Fresnel lens focuses a flashing white beacon with a range of up to 18 nautical miles.

Located only a short distance from the popular coastal resort town of Nags Head, the lighthouse attracts its share of tourists. The National Park Service maintains station structures as part of the Cape Hatteras National Seashore. The two-story, wooden keeper's residence houses a museum and gift shop. ::

Boston Harbor Light

Location: Boston, Massachusetts
Established: 1716
Tower height: 89 feet
Elevation of focal plane: 102 feet
Optic: Fresnel lens (second-order)
Status: Active (automated in 1999)

By far the oldest light station in the United States is the one on Little Brewster Island near the entrance to Boston Harbor. The light station here was established in 1716 to attract commerce and improve maritime safety and was maintained by

The existing Boston Harbor tower (above) has served since 1783 when it replaced an earlier structure built in 1716. In contrast the light towers on Nantucket's Brant Point (opposite) were not known for durability. As many as ten separate towers have stood here since the station was established in 1746.

Bruce Roberts

means of a penny-per-ton tax on vessels delivering goods to Boston wharves.

The Boston Harbor Lighthouse became one of the early victims of the Revolutionary War. The British initially used the tower to guide their warships, but they blew it up before retreating from Boston early in the war, and the lighthouse was not rebuilt until the war ended in 1783. The new stone tower, built with £1,450 supplied by the Massachusetts Legislature, was given walls 75 feet high and more than 7 feet thick at the base. During the nineteenth century the tower was raised to its current height of 89 feet.

Although Boston Harbor Light is now automated, it still has a full-time crew of resident Coast Guard keepers. They are kept on duty at Little Brewster Island, in part as a historical gesture.

The station also retains its second-order Fresnel lens, which focuses a 1.8 million-candlepower light that is visible for 16 miles. ::

Brant Point Light

Location: Nantucket Island, Massachusetts
Established: 1746
Tower height: 26 feet
Elevation of focal plane: 26 feet
Optic: Modern
Status: Active (automated in 1965)

Brant Point Light is the nation's second-oldest light station. However, the modest wooden tower that marks the Nantucket Harbor entrance today dates only to 1901. In fact, as many as ten different towers or beacons have guided whaling ships and other vessels into Nantucket's harbor.

Several early towers either burned down or were bowled over by storms. In 1774, a Boston newspaper included this report: "We hear from Nantucket that on Wednesday the 9th of March Instant at about eight o'clock in the Morning, they had a most violent Gust of Wind that perhaps was ever known there, but it lasted only about a Minute. It seemed to come in a narrow Vein, and in its progress blew down and totally destroyed the Light-House on that Island, besides several Shops, Barns, etc."

Early towers on Brant Point signaled mariners with candles or lamp-and-reflector systems like the one introduced by Winslow Lewis, but the 47-foot brick tower built in 1856 was fitted with a Fresnel lens. Built under the direction of the US Lighthouse Board, the new structure cost the government some $15,000. A description from that time shows where the money went: "The foundation of the tower is of concrete cement 2 feet thick, and 18 feet in diameter. The base is of hammered granite, laid in courses 2 feet thick to the height of 12 feet. The interior of the base forms a cistern, where water may be caught for household purposes. The column forming the tower is of brick laid in cement. The

Brant Point Light
Courtesy *Lighthouse Digest*

lamp is of cast iron, with twelve lights of plate glass. A circular iron stairway winds its spiral way up to a floor of iron, where rests the lantern, 58 feet above the foundation and 47 feet above the ground."

The still-standing 1901 tower is a white cylindrical structure of wood with a wooden bridge linking it to shore. The station's classic Fresnel lens has given way to a modern optic producing a fixed red light ordinarily visible for about 10 miles. ::

Bremerhaven Light

Location: Bremerhaven, Germany
Established: 1854
Tower height: 125 feet
Elevation of focal plane: 120 feet
Optic: Modern
Status: Active (automated in 1962)

The northwest coast of Germany is home to one of the world's more fanciful light towers. Bremerhaven Light, built by noted architect Simon Loschen, is a neo-Gothic brick tower meant to resemble a church. However, more imaginative observers might see in it an illustration from a volume of Grimm's fairy tales, perhaps the tower where Rapunzel did her spinning. This remarkable building is only one of a dozen light towers in and around Bremerhaven, which some consider a city of lighthouses.

Despite its appearance Bremerhaven Light (below) has been a hardworking navigational aid for a century and a half. Originally its beacon was produced by an array of mirrors and lamps fueled by rapeseed oil. The light was later powered by natural gas and, since 1925, by electricity. A decorative iron crane that extends from the top level of the tower was once used to hoist storm-warning markers. **::**

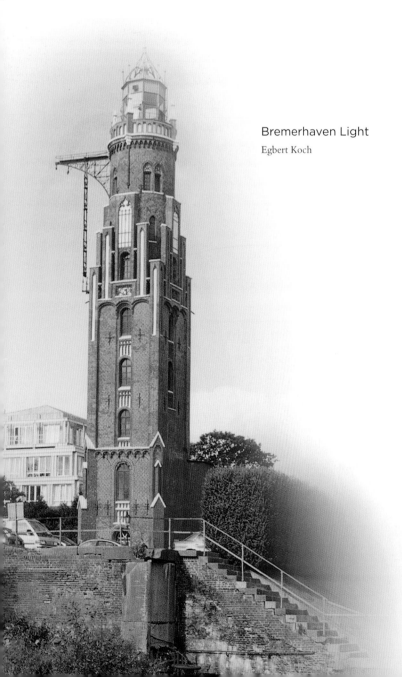

Bremerhaven Light
Egbert Koch

Buchan Ness Light

Location: Aberdeen, Scotland
Established: 1827
Tower height: 115 feet
Elevation of focal plane: 135 feet
Optic: Fresnel lens
Status: Active (automated in 1988)

Scotland's Northern Lighthouse Board engineer Robert Stevenson designed Buchan Ness Light, which was built by contractor John Gibbs in 1827. Hand-painted red and white bands added in 1907 make this tower a distinctive seamark. The station's flashing light is unusually powerful and has a range of up to 28 miles.

Buchan Ness Light was the victim of an unintentional attack in World War II, when a mine broke free, drifted ashore, and blew up only 50 yards from the tower. Fortunately, the explosion injured no one but shattered many panes of glass in the lantern and collapsed the ceiling in the assistant keeper's residence. **::**

Cabo de Mayor Light

Location: Near Santander, Spain
Established: 1839
Tower height: 98 feet
Elevation of focal plane: 299 feet
Optic: Fresnel lens
Status: Active

The magnificent Cabo de Mayor Light marks the entrance to the Spanish port of Santander and dominates a line of impressive cliffs overlooking the Cantabrian Sea. The station's original optic contained an amazing array of eight lenses and more than 100 mirrors. The existing bivalve prismatic optic floats in a tank of mercury—one of the few mechanisms of this type still in use. The bottle-green revolving lens produces a pair of white flashes every ten seconds, and its powerful signal can be seen from a distance of 21 miles. The land and seashore

Designed by Robert Stevenson, the Buchan Ness Light (above) has withstood storms and wars since 1827.
Courtesy Harbour Lights

Many Spanish lighthouses such as the one at Cabo de Mayor (right) still have their original Fresnel lenses (below) as well as the full-time keepers needed to properly maintain them.

Photos by Henry Gonzales

surrounding the station is beautiful and includes the popular El Sardinero beaches. The spectacular cliffs above the beaches have a dark history: Dozens of partisans were thrown to their deaths from these heights during the Spanish Civil War. **::**

Cabo Villano Light

Courtesy Lighthouse Digest

Cabo Villano Light

Location: Near Camariñas, Spain
Established: 1896
Tower height: 79 feet
Elevation of focal plane: 341 feet
Optic: Fresnel lens
Status: Active

Strewn with ship-killing rocks, the Finisterre region of Galicia in northwestern Spain long ago came to be called the Death Coast. Fortunately, lighthouses such as this one near Camariñas have considerably brightened the reputation of these shores. The octagonal stone Cabo Villano tower holds aloft an extraordinary lantern. Glassed from the floor all the way to the weather vane at the top, it looks something like an enormous incandescent light bulb. A large Fresnel lens inside the bulb produces a lightning-like beacon visible for 27 nautical miles. An extensive covered stairway links the tower to the station's sizable housing and work complex. **::**

Cana Island Light

Location: Baileys Harbor, Wisconsin
Established: 1870
Tower height: 81 feet
Elevation of focal plane: 89 feet
Optic: Fresnel lens (third-order)
Status: Active (automated in 1945)

Wisconsin's Door County, situated between Green Bay and Lake Michigan, is reputed to have more lighthouses than any other county in the United States. One of these, Cana Island Light, guides vessels to the attractive lakeside community of Baileys Harbor. The yellow brick tower took such a pounding from lake storms that maritime officials managed to save the crumbling tower only by sheathing it in a protective cocoon of metal plates. The station's original third-order Fresnel lens, still in use after more than 140 years, adds to the historic quality and beauty of this Lake Michigan sentinel. **::**

Cana Island Light
Bruce Roberts

Cape Agulhas Light

Location: L'Agulhas, South Africa
Established: 1849
Tower height: 87 feet
Elevation of focal plane: 100 feet
Optic: Fresnel lens (first-order)
Status: Active (automated in 1988)

Located only a few steps from a cairn marking the southernmost point on the continent of Africa, Cape Agulhas Light is part of a South African national park. The station's powerful first-order flashing beacon first guided vessels around the Horn of Africa in 1849. The light station was deactivated in 1968, but it was automated and returned to active service twenty years later.

Said to have been inspired by the Pharos of Alexandria Egypt, the station features a stout limestone tower that rises through the roof of a rectangular keeper's residence. False towers, which serve as fireplace chimneys, rise from either end of the dwelling, adding interest to this unique structure. The residence now houses South Africa's only lighthouse museum. ::

Cape Agulhas Light
Courtesy Harbour Lights

Cape Ann Light (158)

Location: Thatcher Island, near Rockport, Massachusetts

Established: 1771

Tower height: 124 feet

Elevation of focal plane: 166 feet

Optic: Vega (solar-powered)

Status: Active (automated in 1980)

Thatcher Island takes its name from Anthony Thatcher, a Protestant cleric who shipwrecked here in 1635. Over the years, many other vessels followed Thatcher's onto the island's deadly rocks.

Recognizing the island as an impediment to safe navigation, the colony of Massachusetts built a lighthouse here in 1771. When the Revolutionary War broke out, local patriots stormed the island and removed the keeper, a well-known Tory. Later keepers had longer tenures on lonely Thatcher Island. For instance, Captain Joseph Sayward served here from 1792 to 1814, a twenty-two-year stretch, while his successor, Aaron Wheeler, remained on the island for twenty years.

Among the earliest twin-light navigational stations in North America, the Cape Ann station had two lights displayed from separate towers spaced about 300 feet apart. Thatcher Island's current pair of 124-foot granite towers date to 1861, when they replaced the colonial structures. The north tower was taken out of service after 1924, when the Lighthouse Service discontinued all its multiple-light beacons. Soon afterward, the first-order Fresnel lenses that once focused the twin beacons were removed. The light that guides vessels today is produced by a modern optic. Its flashing beacon can be seen from distances of about 19 nautical miles. ::

Only the southern tower at Cape Ann remains in service.
Bruce Roberts

Cape Bonavista Light

Location: Bonavista, Newfoundland

Established: 1843

Tower height: 36 feet

Elevation of focal plane: 166 feet

Optic: Lamp-and-reflector system

Status: Deactivated in 1966

Bright red and white stripes combine with a spectacular setting to make Newfoundland's Cape Bonavista Light one of the most visually impressive navigational stations in North America. An enormous birdcage-style lantern rises through the roof of the station's main building. When the lighthouse was completed in 1843, it was fitted with a large, sixteen-mirror lamp-and-reflector optic previously used at Scotland's Bell Rock Light. In 1966 the lighthouse was deactivated and its light moved to a nearby steel-skeleton tower. In more recent times, Canadian lighthouse preservationists have restored the structure to its original appearance and replaced its extraordinary lamp-and-reflector lighting system. ::

Cape Bonavista Light

Courtesy *Lighthouse Digest*

A 45-foot wooden tower stood here from 1797 until 1831, when it was replaced by a brick building of about the same height. Today's Cape Cod Light, with its 66-foot brick tower, dates to 1857. The first-order Fresnel lens placed in the lantern room at that time was replaced in 1901 by a similar lens and then in the 1950s by a rotating aeromarine beacon.

Cape Cod (Highland) Light

Location: Truro, Massachusetts

Established: 1797

Tower height: 66 feet

Elevation of focal plane: 183 feet

Optic: Aeromarine beacon

Status: Active (automated in 1987)

Although it was not built until after colonial times, few American lighthouses can lay claim to as much history as Cape Cod Light. Established in 1797 while John Adams was president, the station, also known as Highland Light, is now in its third century of guiding mariners. Its beacons shone through several major wars, including the War of 1812. Author and naturalist Henry David Thoreau, whose writings cast a light of a different kind, visited the station and swapped tales with its keeper.

Cape Cod (Highland) Light

Bruce Roberts

In the 1990s the old lighthouse became the object of a near-frantic rescue effort when rapid erosion of the Cape Cod cliffs threatened to undermine it. To save the tower, engineers lifted it onto rails with jacks and rolled it back approximately 500 feet from the precipice. The technique was similar to the one later used at Cape Hatteras. Funding for the $1.5 million Cape Cod Light relocation came from government agencies, private interests, and preservationist organizations. ::

Cape Disappointment Light

Location: Ilwaco, Washington

Established: 1856

Tower height: 53 feet

Elevation of focal plane: 220 feet

Optic: Aeromarine beacon

Status: Active (automated in 1962)

Of the numerous hazards facing mariners along the North American Pacific coast, few are more formidable than the extensive bar of the Columbia River. Near its mouth the Columbia deposits vast quantities of silt, sand, and gravel, creating shallows that can trap ships and hold them tight while towering waves pound them to pieces. Among the many vessels lost in this manner was the *Oriole*, which foundered here in 1853 while attempting to deliver materials for construction of the Cape Disappointment lighthouse. Loss of the *Oriole* and its valuable cargo delayed completion of the light station for almost three years.

Finally made operational late in 1856, the Cape Disappointment beacon has helped countless ships avoid the unhappy fate of the *Oriole*. Considered a light station of first importance, Cape Disappointment appropriately received a first-order Fresnel lens. The light atop its 53-foot brick tower still shines, but the station's huge lens long ago gave way to a more modest fourth-order Fresnel lens. The original lens is now on display at the nearby Lewis and Clark Interpretive Center. ::

Cape du Couedic Light

Location: Kangaroo Island, Australia

Established: 1906

Tower height: 84 feet

Elevation of focal plane: 339

Optic: Fresnel lens

Status: Active

Like a number of other Australian lighthouses, this one on Kangaroo Island off Australia's southern coast gets a significant boost from its site. Cape du Couedic's conical tower stands on high ground, which provides three-quarters of the beacon's substantial elevation. The lighthouse is located in Flinders Chase National Park, a scenic wonderland alive with exotic flora and fauna. ::

Cape Disappointment Light
Bruce Roberts

Cape du Couedic Light

Cape Elizabeth Light

Bruce Roberts

Cape Elizabeth Light

Location: Cape Elizabeth, Maine

Established: 1828

Tower height: 67 feet (east tower)

Elevation of focal plane: 129 feet

Optic: Modern

Status: Active (automated in 1963)

Originally known to New England mariners as "Two Lights," the Cape Elizabeth station once guided mariners with a pair of lights, one fixed and the other flashing. To make the lights distinct, especially when seen from a distance, the station was given two separate towers spaced about 300 yards apart. The government spent only $4,250 on the first Cape Elizabeth Lighthouse—a bargain since its rough-stone towers lasted almost half a century. They were replaced in 1874 by two cast-iron towers, one of which remains in use today.

Cape Elizabeth's west tower was retired in 1924 when the Lighthouse Service opted to stop using twin beacons. The east tower continued to serve mariners, its second-order Fresnel lens shining until 1994. A modern optic now focuses the flashing beacon, which can be seen for about 15 miles. As with many other historic lighthouses, the Coast Guard maintains the station's light while a preservation group takes care of the tower. The lighthouse is located in Two Lights State Park. ⠒

Cape Flattery Light

Location: Tatoosh Island, Washington

Established: 1857

Tower height: 65 feet

Elevation of focal plane: 165 feet

Optic: Modern

Status: Active (automated in 1977)

At the northwestern corner of Washington and the contiguous United States, Cape Flattery Light marks the entrance to the Strait of Juan de Fuca.

Washington's Cape Flattery Light

Bob and Sandra Shanklin

The Cape Florida Light (above) and Cape Hatteras Light (opposite page) no longer look as depicted here. The Cape Florida tower has been thoroughly restored and painted white, while the spiral-striped Cape Hatteras tower has been moved 1,600 feet inland.

Bruce Roberts

Historic as well as strategic, this is one of the oldest lighthouses in the West. At the time the sandstone and brick tower was completed in 1857, the Northwest was still mostly a raw frontier. Visitors to Tatoosh Island today will find little has changed—it's still every bit the wilderness it was when the lighthouse was built more than 150 years ago.

Until the Coast Guard automated the light in 1977, keepers worked and lived at Cape Flattery year-round. Among the most remote light stations in North America, it could be reached only by boat. Pounding surf and rocky cliffs made getting on and off the island or landing supplies extremely difficult and dangerous. Coast Guard navigation personnel now make periodic visits to the island by helicopter. ::

Cape Florida Light

Location: Key Biscayne, Florida
Established: 1825
Tower height: 95 feet
Elevation of focal plane: 100 feet
Optic: Modern
Status: Private aid to navigation

Cape Florida Light was established in 1825 to warn vessels away from the ship-killing Florida Reef and guide them into the relatively safe waters of the Florida Channel. This lighthouse has a remarkable and sometimes bloody past. During the Seminole Wars of the 1830s, its isolated location on Key Biscayne left the station vulnerable to attack. A Seminole raid in 1836 took the lives of the keeper's wife and children. Devastated by his loss, he abandoned his post and fled to the mainland.

Soon afterward, John Thompson agreed to keep the light, and he was on duty in July 1836, when Seminole warriors once more raided the lighthouse. Thompson and his assistant took refuge in the station's brick tower, but its thick walls provided little protection. The attackers set fire to the building, driving the men onto the lantern gallery where they made easy targets. Thompson's assistant was killed, and the keeper survived only by clinging to the red-hot metal lantern. Badly burned and nearly dead from thirst, Thompson eventually was rescued by crewmen from a US warship. Since the tower steps had burned away, the sailors had to fire a line up to the gallery with a musket and then lower Thompson to the ground in a basket.

Because of the danger of renewed violence, the ruined lighthouse was not rebuilt and placed back in service until 1846. Fitted with a second-order Fresnel lens, the new tower guided mariners until 1878 when it was once more taken out of service. The old tower stood empty and abandoned for a century, but in 1978, partly for historical reasons, Cape Florida Light's beacon was relit. In the late 1990s the deteriorating tower was carefully restored and painted. It now serves as a museum and a private aid to navigation.. ::

Cape Hatteras Light

Location: Bodie Island, North Carolina
Established: 1803
Tower height: 193 feet
Elevation of focal plane: 198 feet
Optic: Aeromarine beacon
Status: Active (automated in 1936)

Perhaps the most famous lighthouse in the world, the spiral-striped Cape Hatteras tower is considered by many a quintessentially American edifice. With its dramatic rescue from rampaging beach erosion in 1999, the massive brick cylinder has become a symbol of a worldwide effort to preserve historic structures. Now part of the popular Cape Hatteras National Seashore, the station attracts a steady stream of visitors who come to learn about maritime history and this nineteenth-century giant.

The federal government commissioned the first Cape Hatteras tower in 1803. Although one of the largest buildings of its era, the original 90-

foot tower—later raised to 150 feet—was never considered adequate by mariners. Vessels regularly slammed into the shoals south of Hatteras Island without ever having seen the light. Among the vessels lost off Hatteras Island was the Union ironclad *Monitor,* which foundered on the shoals only a few months after having fought the Confederate warship *Virginia* to a standoff in 1862.

Bruce Roberts

Following the war, the Lighthouse Board replaced the old tower with the current structure, which was completed in 1870 and fitted with a first-order Fresnel lens with a range of more than 20 miles. Almost from the first, the new tower was threatened by erosion. The Cape Hatteras shoreline has never been stable, and on several occasions

The Ghost Light of Delaware's Cape Henlopen ::

Some navigational lights are so historic they somehow seem to survive their own destruction. This appears to be the case at Delaware's Cape Henlopen where mariners and evening beachcombers occasionally report seeing a ghostly light shining from the sandy bluffs. Some believe it is the beacon of the Old Cape Henlopen Lighthouse destroyed by erosion 1926.

Built nearly a decade before the outbreak of the Revolutionary War, Cape Henlopen Light played a role in both the American struggle for independence and the War of 1812. British marines burned the station in 1777, and it was not repaired and put back into service until 1784. A generation afterward, a flotilla of British warships arrived to enforce a War of 1812 blockade of the US coast. This time the Americans extinguished the Cape Henlopen light themselves to make navigation as difficult as possible for the British. Although British ships blasted the nearby town of Lewes with cannon and musket fire, the lighthouse remained unscathed.

Cape Henlopen Light survived these and later wars, not to mention countless sea storms, but it was destined to fall under a relentless assault by erosion. As early as 1883, Delaware's sandy Cape Henlopen bluffs were crumbling away beneath the octagonal stone tower. Efforts to stabilize the bluff accomplished little, and by 1897 the sand surrounding the lighthouse was blowing away at an alarming rate. By the 1920s, there was little holding up the tower. Following a spring storm in 1926, the venerable structure collapsed. Even so, more than a few say its light shines on.

The Cape Henlopen Lighthouse (above) collapsed during the 1920s.
National Archives

since 1870 the Atlantic has pushed to within 200 feet of the tower's vulnerable foundation. Finally, during the 1990s, ocean waves unleashed an all-out assault on the lighthouse, washing toward the tower on three sides. Attempts to push back the tides by pumping sand onto the beach proved fruitless.

Concluding that the historic tower could be saved only by moving it, in 1999 the National Park Service undertook a $12 million project to transport the structure out of danger. Now positioned on a foundation more than 1,600 feet inland, the old sentinel has resumed its two-century-long task of guiding vessels safely past the cape and shoals beyond. ::

Cape Henry Light

Location: Virginia Beach, Virginia
Established: 1792
Tower height: 163 feet
Elevation of focal plane: 164 feet
Optic: Fresnel lens (first-order)
Status: Active

Cape Henry, located on the south side of the entrance to the Chesapeake Bay, is the site of not one but two historic light towers. Although no longer in use, the sandstone tower built in 1792, during George Washington's first term as president, still stands. Built in part with stone left over from an earlier colonial construction effort, the 90-foot,

Cape Henry Light
Bruce Roberts

Having incorporated special reinforcements in its design, builders declared the original Cape Hinchinbrook Light on Alaska's Hinchinbrook Island "earthquake proof," but a pair of powerful temblors in 1927 and 1928 proved them wrong, and the octagonal keeper's residence and tower had to be replaced. The existing Art Deco–style lighthouse, completed in 1934, looks nothing at all like its predecessor, but it serves the same function—to mark the entrance to Prince William Sound. ::

Cape Hinchinbrook Light
Bob and Sandra Shanklin

octagonal Old Cape Henry tower guided vessels in and out of the Chesapeake for the better part of a century.

When cracks in the old tower raised concerns that it might collapse, the Lighthouse Board ordered construction of a replacement tower. The newer masonry cylinder, covered by bolted iron plates, was placed in service late in 1881. Today, more than one and a quarter centuries after it was completed, this giant still marks the bay entrance with a flashing first-order beacon. Oddly, the early federal tower was never demolished, and despite the cracks that led to its retirement, it remains standing, a testament to the quality of eighteenth-century masonry. ::

Cape Hinchinbrook Light

Location: Hinchinbrook Island, Alaska

Established: 1910

Tower height: 67 feet

Elevation of focal plane: 235 feet

Optic: Modern (solar-powered)

Status: Active (automated in 1974)

Cape Lookout Light

Location: Cape Lookout, North Carolina

Established: 1812

Tower height: 169 feet

Elevation of focal plane: 156 feet

Optic: Aeromarine beacon

Status: Active (automated in 1950)

In the 1850s the Lighthouse Board became convinced that low, featureless landfalls such as the North Carolina Outer Banks could be marked effectively only by tall towers housing navigational lights shining 150 feet or more above the tides.

Cape Lookout
Bruce Roberts

Cape May Light

Location: Cape May, New Jersey
Established: 1824
Tower height: 157 feet
Elevation of focal plane: 175 feet
Optic: Aeromarine beacon
Status: Active (automated in 1946)

At least two earlier lighthouses helped mariners navigate waters near Cape May before the existing brick tower was built in 1859. The soaring tower and its powerful beacon mark the southern tip of New Jersey and the northern approach to the Delaware Bay. Exposed to open water on three sides, Cape May is exceptionally vulnerable to sea storms, but the tower's double walls, nearly 4 feet thick at the base, have remained sturdy for the better part of one and a half centuries.

In 1986 the tower and other station buildings were leased to the Mid-Atlantic Center for the Arts, which has assumed responsibility for a $2 million restoration project. The US Coast Guard maintains the light. In good weather, this flashing beacon can reach mariners as far as 24 miles away.

Today, the Cape May Lighthouse is maintained by a regional arts center.
Bruce Roberts

Consequently, the board decided to replace the 96-foot tower that had guarded the southern tip of the Outer Banks since 1812. A brick giant much like those later built at Cape Hatteras, Bodie Island, and Currituck Beach was completed in 1859. Painted with a distinctive black and white diamond pattern, the new tower displays a powerful first-order light with a focal plane of 156 feet. Produced by an aeromarine beacon, the light is visible from up to 19 miles at sea. ::

Located in a popular resort area, the lighthouse has attracted visitors for generations. Over the years, more than a few marriage proposals have been made—and no doubt accepted—in the lofty lantern room. **::**

Cape Neddick Light

Location: Near York, Maine

Established: 1879

Tower height: 41 feet

Elevation of focal plane: 88 feet

Optic: Fresnel lens (fourth-order)

Status: Active (automated in 1988)

Cape Neddick Light
Bruce Roberts

In the far southwestern corner of Maine, a small, rocky island known as the Nubble threatens vessels moving toward the harbor at the old colonial town of York. As early as 1837 government maritime authorities considered establishing a coastal light here, but no action was taken until more than sixty years later, when the Lighthouse Service constructed a cast-iron tower on the island's highest point and equipped it with a Fresnel lens. Service crews also built a comfortable and attractive Victorian-style residence for the keeper and his family. A covered walkway enabled keepers to reach the tower without braving Maine weather. Now owned by York Township, these interesting and historic

structures still stand, and the station continues to guide mariners with a flashing red signal produced by the station's original Fresnel lens. **::**

Cape Romain Light

Location: McClellanville, South Carolina

Established: 1812

Tower height: 150 feet

Elevation of focal plane: 161 feet

Optic: Fresnel lens (removed)

Status: Deactivated in 1947

Cape Romain Light has not served as an active aid to navigation for more than half a century, but the station's remarkable octagonal tower is maintained by the US Fish and Wildlife Service for historic reasons. Built with slave labor shortly before the Civil War, the brick tower developed a slight lean shortly after it was completed in 1857. Although the building has always been somewhat out of plumb, it remains sound, as does an earlier Cape Romain tower built in 1812. **::**

Bruce Roberts

Ruins of the original Cape Romain Lighthouse can still be seen along with the intact but no longer functional 1857 tower.

Cape San Blas Light

Location: Near Key West, Florida

Established: 1848

Tower height: 90 feet

Elevation of focal plane: 101 feet

Optic: Fresnel lens (third-order)

Status: Deactivated in 1996

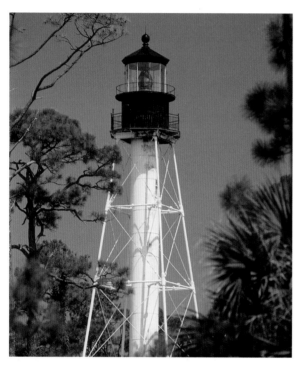

Cape San Blas Light

Bruce Roberts

The history of the hard-luck light station on Cape San Blas illustrates the difficulty of marking the shores of the Gulf of Mexico with navigational lights. The cape's first lighthouse, completed in 1848, stood for less than three years before a hurricane demolished it. A brick tower built in 1856 also gave way to a hurricane after only a few months of service. Inspectors who visited the area following the storm found a lagoon where the lighthouses had stood. A third brick tower completed in 1859 soon succumbed to a different sort of storm—the American Civil War. Confederate troops burned the tower, keeper's residence, and storage buildings.

The lighthouse was rebuilt after the war and placed back in service just in time to face a new assault, this time by the Gulf of Mexico itself. Erosion had swept away the beach in front of the lighthouse by 1881, and waves were lapping the tower walls. When jetties and sea walls failed to hold back the water, the Lighthouse Board gave up trying to save the tower and decided to build yet another one. This time the station received a steel-skeleton tower, one that could be taken apart and reassembled elsewhere if necessary. A third-order Fresnel lens focused the beacon until it was deactivated in 1996. ::

Cape St. George Light

Location: St. George Island, Florida

Established: 1833

Tower height: 70 feet

Elevation of focal plane: 72 feet

Optic: Fresnel lens (removed)

Status: Destroyed in 2005

Florida's extraordinary leaning lighthouse seems to have been saved—at least for now. The barrier

Cape St. George Light

Bruce Roberts

islands along the coast of the Gulf of Mexico are in constant motion, their sandy beaches washing away or taking on new shapes with each passing season. Cape St. George Light near Apalachicola, Florida, was never on stable ground, and the first tower built here in 1833 fell victim to hurricane floodtides after less than twenty years of service.

The tower, built in 1852, survived numerous powerful storms and even a cannonade by Confederate raiders. By the 1990s, however, beach erosion seemed about to accomplish what hurricanes and Civil War soldiers could not. Its foundation weakened, the old brick tower began to lean toward the Gulf, and in 1994 the Coast Guard deactivated the light. Despite frantic efforts to save the historic Cape St. George tower, it finally collapsed in October 2005. The lighthouse was restored in 2008. ::

Carysfort Reef Light
Bob and Sandra Shanklin

Carysfort Reef Light

Location: Near Key Largo, Florida
Established: 1852
Tower height: 120 feet
Elevation of focal plane: 100 feet
Optic: Modern (solar-powered)
Status: Active (automated in 1960)

Entire fleets have met their ruin on the jagged reefs and sandy shoals of the Florida Keys. To avoid these dangers, mariners needed advance warning of the sort that could be provided only by tall towers and bright beacons. In the 1850s the Lighthouse Board began marking the Keys with a string of offshore light towers. Because they would have to withstand onslaughts by gales and hurricanes as well as constant exposure to salt water, these could not be conventional stone or brick towers. A fresh approach was required, and for this the board turned to bright, young engineers such as I. W. P. Lewis and George Meade.

At Carysfort Reef not far from Key Largo, Meade supervised construction of an innovative steel-skeleton tower anchored to the sand and coral bottom with screw piles. Since the open walls of the tower offered little resistance to wind and water, the structure was very nearly hurricane-proof. In fact, Carysfort tower proved so durable that it still stands more than a century and a half after Meade's construction crew completed it. The Coast Guard refurbished the lighthouse in 1996. Today it draws power from batteries recharged by solar panels. Its flashing beacon is visible for up to 15 nautical miles. ::

Castro Urdiales Light

Location: Near Santander, Spain
Established: 1700s
Tower height: 66 feet
Elevation of focal plane: 161 feet
Optic: Revolving reflector
Status: Active

In the thirteenth century the famous crusading order known as the Knights Templars built a massive fortification on the Spanish coast between

Cantabria and the Basque country. Soldiers standing atop the castle's high walls could see the sails of enemy ships long before they reached land. About 500 years later the old crusader fort was put to a more friendly use—as the base for a masonry lighthouse. Having served mariners for more than two centuries, the light tower now seems almost as old as the castle beneath it. However, the station's lantern room contains an unusual revolving optic with reflectors that would have dazzled the knights who once defended this fortress. It produces a flashing light visible for about 20 nautical miles. **::**

Charleston Light

Location: Sullivans Island, South Carolina
Established: 1962
Tower height: 140 feet
Elevation of focal plane: 163 feet
Optic: Aeromarine beacon
Status: Active (automated in 1962)

The US Coast Guard established Charleston (Sullivans Island) Light in the early 1960s, after erosion forced abandonment of the historic lighthouse on Morris Island. One of the last true lighthouses built in the United States, this tower near the entrance to Charleston's busy harbor is different from its predecessors in many respects. It is built of reinforced concrete clad in aluminum, and its triangular shape and conveniences would have astounded the keepers of old-time light stations. For instance, an elevator links the ground floor with the lantern room nearly 140 feet above. The building even has air-conditioning. **::**

Spain's Castro Urdiales Light stands atop a medieval fortress.
Both photos by Henry Gonzales

Charleston Light
Bruce Roberts

Charlotte-Genesee Light

Location: Rochester, New York

Established: 1822

Tower height: 40 feet

Elevation of focal plane: 45 feet

Optic: Fresnel lens (removed)

Status: Deactivated

One of the oldest and most historic structures on the Great Lakes, the Charlotte-Genesee Lighthouse served Lake Ontario mariners for nearly sixty years. However, the venerable rubblestone tower stood empty and abandoned for generations after its light was deactivated in 1881. The lighthouse faced total extinction during the 1960s when the US Coast Guard planned to demolish it. A letter-writing campaign by high school students generated the public support needed to save it. A local preservation society now operates a museum in the former keeper's house. ::

Charlotte-Genesee Light

Bruce Roberts

The Chicago Harbor Lighthouse was built in 1893 at about the same time the remarkable Cleveland Lighthouse was demolished.

Bruce Roberts

Chicago Harbor Light

Location: Chicago, Illinois

Established: 1832

Tower height: 48 feet

Elevation of focal plane: 82 feet

Optic: Modern

Status: Active (automated in 1979)

A lighthouse marked the mouth of the Chicago River as early as 1832, and as Chicago grew, beacons shone out over Lake Michigan from several points along the shore or from piers along the waterfront of the rapidly expanding metropolis. When it was built in 1893, Chicago Harbor Light stood on land, but it was later moved to the end of a stone breakwater about a mile from shore. For many years, the tower held a third-order Fresnel lens that had been a popular attraction at the 1893 Chicago Columbian Exposition. That lens is now on display at Old Point Loma Light in San Diego, California, and a modern optic produces the Chicago Harbor beacon. Although the light is still maintained by the Coast Guard, the revered lighthouse is now owned by the City of Chicago, which has designated it an official city landmark. ::

Cleveland's Victorian Empress ::

Built in high Victorian style during the early 1870s, the Cleveland Lighthouse is counted among the most impressive structures that ever marked America's shores. Its octagonal brick tower rose from the corner of the brick residence, reminding some of a Middle Eastern minaret. The exotic tower and ornate residence dominated the waterfront. This remarkable edifice served as a lighthouse for little more than twenty years before its beacon was snuffed out and replaced by a small tower at the end of a nearby breakwater. To the regret of many, the original structures were eventually demolished.

National Archives

More than a century separates construction of Maryland's Concord Point Lighthouse (above) and Portugal's Contendas Lighthouse in the Azores (opposite), but both are important monuments to a rich worldwide maritime heritage.

Bruce Roberts

Concord Point Light

Location: Havre de Grace, Maryland
Established: 1827
Tower height: 32 feet
Elevation of focal plane: 35 feet
Optic: Fresnel lens (fifth-order)
Status: Private aid to navigation

Contractor John Donohoo built the modest stone Concord Point tower in 1827 for an equally modest fee of $3,500. He did his work well—the tower still stands. Although the US Coast Guard deactivated the light in 1975, it was relit, largely for historic reasons, and now serves as a private aid to navigation.

Concord Point Light is unusual in that all its keepers were members of the same family, the O'Neils. John O'Neil, a War of 1812 hero, earned the respect and appreciation of his entire nation by making—and surviving—an amazing one-man stand against a British invasion fleet. Four

Courtesy *Lighthouse Digest*

generations of O'Neils served as keepers here; the family relinquished the position only when the station became automated in 1920. **::**

Contendas Light

Location: Contendas, Azores
Established: 1934
Tower height: 43 feet
Elevation of focal plane: 173 feet
Optic: Fresnel lens (third-order)
Status: Active

The square-towered Contendas Light marks the southeast coast of Terceira Island in the Portuguese Azores. The tower rises from the center of a symmetrical dwelling and work complex that features four separate wings. The red metal lantern still contains the station's original third-order prismatic lens. **::**

Cordouan Light

Location: Near Verdon-sur-Mer, France
Established: 1611
Tower height: 197 feet
Elevation of focal plane: 223 feet
Optic: Fresnel lens (first-order)
Status: Active (automated in 1990)

It is widely believed that, during the ninth century, Louis the Pious, son of Charlemagne, built a lighthouse on the small island of Cordouan near the mouth of the Gironde River. The beacon guided freighters on their way to Bordeaux to take on loads of wine. It is not known how long this light served, if indeed it ever existed, but it was long gone by the fourteenth century, when Edward, the Black Prince of England, prevailed on local monks to maintain a light on the island. It consisted of an open fire built atop a stone tower.

The existing Cordouan Light dates back to 1611—about the time the Jamestown colony

The famed Cordouan Lighthouse (above) is linked to French royalty. Canada's Cove Island Light (below right) is considered an "Imperial" tower, hinting at a connection to the British crown.

Egbert Koch

Cove Island Light

Location: Near Tobermory, Ontario
Established: 1859
Tower height: 115 feet
Elevation of focal plane: 100 feet
Optic: Fresnel lens (second-order)
Status: Active (automated in 1991)

One of six so-called imperial towers erected along the Great Lakes under the authority of the British Board of Trade, this magnificent limestone structure was completed in 1859. It is the work of Scottish stonemason John Brown, who built several of the imperial towers in the Georgian Bay region. Quarrying the stone and building the tower and other station structures are said to have taken Brown nearly four years.

Cove Island Light

Bruce Roberts

was founded on the far side of the Atlantic. The Cordouan tower built at that time was the first ever to be built in open water. Designed by architect Louis de Foix, it was an ornate structure with a chapel and even an elaborate royal apartment, just in case the king should ever visit (apparently, however, no French monarch ever set foot in the place).

Extensively renovated and enlarged in the late eighteenth century, the station still stands and guides mariners. The Cordouan Lighthouse holds a significant place in modern lighthouse history because it was here that Augustin Fresnel tested the first of his lenses in 1823. At 223 feet in height, it is ranked among the tallest light towers in the world. ::

Cove Island Light marks the channel that links Lake Huron with Georgian Bay. Its stark white tower is impossible for mariners to miss during the daytime. At night, the station's beacon gets a hefty boost from its second-order Fresnel lens. A favorite landmark of recreational boaters who flock to the area in summer, the station is now part of Canada's Five Fathom Maritime Park. Although the light is now automated, it was maintained by resident keepers for more than 130 years. ::

Crisp Point Light
Bruce Roberts

Crisp Point Light

Location: Northwest of Paradise, Michigan
Established: 1904
Tower height: 58 feet
Elevation of focal plane: 58 feet
Optic: Fresnel lens (removed)
Status: Deactivated in 1947

Following many years of faithful service, the Crisp Point Light was deactivated shortly after World War II, and the property and structures were all but abandoned by the Coast Guard. Eventually the old tower fell into ruin and might have fallen into Lake Superior as well except for the tireless efforts of local preservationists who made a crusade of saving it. Once considered all but a lost cause, the tower now has been partially restored and protected from lake erosion. ::

Cudillero Light

Location: Northern coast of Spain
Established: 1858
Tower height: 25 feet
Elevation of focal plane: 99 feet
Optic: Fresnel lens
Status: Active

The sea cliffs below Spain's Cudillero Light extend like bony fingers into the Atlantic. The lighthouse itself has the look of a very old monastery chapel, and visitors might be led to believe that its precarious perch on the cliff tops is made possible only by prayer. Mariners, preferring not to rely exclusively on prayer, have looked to Cudillero Light for assistance for nearly one and a half centuries. The beacon is visible for 25 miles at sea and is often spotted before the cliffs themselves can be seen. ::

Cudillero Light
Bob and Sandra Shanklin

Currituck Beach Light
Bruce Roberts

Currituck Beach Light

Location: Corolla, North Carolina

Established: 1874

Tower height: 163 feet

Elevation of focal plane: 158 feet

Optic: Fresnel lens (first-order)

Status: Active (automated in 1939)

Near the northern end of the barrier islands known as the Outer Banks, Currituck Beach Light serves not only as a still-active aid to navigation but also as a popular tourist destination. Most visitors elect to pay a small fee and climb the 214 steps to the lantern room, where they can enjoy a remarkable view of the Atlantic Ocean and the broad North Carolina sounds. Until 1939, when the Coast Guard automated the light, Currituck Beach Light keepers made this same climb several times each evening.

Currituck Beach Light is one of several exceptionally tall towers built along the Outer Banks to warn mariners away from its deadly shallows. The walls of this redbrick tower are more than 5 feet thick and have withstood countless gales and more

than a few hurricanes. They were left unpainted to help mariners distinguish the tower from others to the north and south. The flashing beacon can be seen from vessels up to 18 miles from shore. **: :**

Curtis Island Light

Location: Camden, Maine

Established: 1835

Tower height: 25 feet

Elevation of focal plane: 52 feet

Optic: Modern (solar-powered)

Status: Active (automated in 1972)

Although it isn't a major coastal beacon and isn't easily seen from shore, Curtis Island Light is well known and loved by many because it serves the popular tourist community of Camden on Penobscot Bay. Passenger schooners and other pleasure craft sail past the lighthouse every day during the summer. The squat light tower, built in 1896, is attached to a modest dwelling on Curtis Island near the mouth of Camden's bustling harbor.

Cold blue water and wild scenery surround Maine's Curtis Island Light (above), while palms and lush tropical foliage all but envelop the Diamond Head tower (opposite left) near Honolulu. The two settings seem a universe apart, but both have been described as paradise.
Bruce Roberts

The little lighthouse replaced an earlier structure that had stood here for more than sixty years. The station's fourth-order Fresnel lens has been removed and put on display in the town library. A modern, solar-powered optic now produces Curtis Island's fixed green beacon. ::

Diamond Head Light

Location: Near Honolulu, Hawaii

Established: 1899

Tower height: 57 feet

Elevation of focal plane: 147 feet

Optic: Fresnel lens (third-order)

Status: Active (automated in 1924)

Standing beside an extinct volcano in the company of graceful palms, Diamond Head Light seems perfectly suited to Hawaii. Although it is part of an active Coast Guard base and, therefore, closed to the public, the bright white Diamond Head tower is one of the first buildings ship passengers are likely to see as their liners approach Honolulu. Thus it serves as something of a symbol for the island of Oahu. The Diamond Head beacon has pointed the way to Hawaii's capital city for more than a century, although the existing tower is not quite that old. It was built in 1917 after cracks undermined the foundation of the original tower. The station's original third-order Fresnel lens remains in use. The keeper's bungalow now provides quarters for the Coast Guard personnel. ::

Dondra Head Light

Location: Matara, Sri Lanka

Established: 1889

Tower height: 177 feet

Elevation of focal plane: 185 feet

Optic: Fresnel lens

Status: Active

Dondra Head Light marks the southernmost point of the island nation of Sri Lanka. Sir James

Diamond Head Light

Bob and Sandra Shanklin

Another lighthouse in paradise, the Dondra Head tower (above) in Sri Lanka raises its lantern above a forest of palms.

Courtesy *Lighthouse Digest*

Douglass, better known for his Trinity House light towers in England, designed this soaring brick and stone edifice on the Indian Ocean nearly half a world away from Great Britain. Still in operation after more than a century of service, the lighthouse is managed by the Sri Lanka Ports Authority.. ::

Dunkirk (Point Gratiot) Light

Location: Point Gratiot, New York
Established: 1829
Tower height: 61 feet
Elevation of focal plane: 81 feet
Optic: Fresnel lens (third-order)
Status: Active (automated in 1960)

Since it is relatively shallow, Lake Erie throws up huge waves in stormy weather, and shipwrecks on this lake are common. In the 1820s the US government established several key navigational lights along the lake to help mariners caught in storms find safety. Established in 1829, the Dunkirk or Point Gratiot Light became the site of early attempts to power a navigational beacon with natural gas. These efforts failed, leaving the station to rely on whale oil or similar fuels during much of its first century of operation.

Despite the powerful Dunkirk beacon, vessels continued to wreck in the waters off Point Gratiot. Loaded with nearly $200,000 worth of gold, silver, copper, and zinc, the freighter *Dean Richmond* came to grief near Dunkirk in 1893. Four years later, the *Idaho* met a similar fate. Laden with Christmas confections, the shattered *Idaho* spilled tons of candy into the lake, and for weeks afterward slabs of chocolate washed up on the shores of Point Gratiot.

Dunkirk Light's existing square rubblestone tower dates to 1857. The adjacent two-story brick keeper's residence, built in 1875, now serves as a museum. ::

Eagle Harbor Light

Location: Eagle Harbor, Michigan
Established: 1851
Tower height: 44 feet
Elevation of focal plane: 60 feet
Optic: Aeromarine beacon
Status: Active (automated in 1980)

The Dunkirk Light adds its luminance to a Lake Erie sunset.
Bruce Roberts

The Eagle Harbor Light on Michigan's Keweenaw Peninsula looks out toward Lake Superior.
Bruce Roberts

Staying Overnight at a Lighthouse ::

It's hard to imagine what life was like for the brave men and women who once lived and worked in lighthouses along America's coasts and around the world. However, you can sample the lighthouse keepers' lives, even if just overnight or for a long weekend. An increasing number of old lighthouses have been refurbished and opened to paying guests. Most still have operating maritime lights that are maintained by the Coast Guard, but the accommodations and meals are the responsibility of innkeepers who operate these lovely little inns either for profit or on behalf of a nonprofit preservation organization. The offerings nearly always include wonderful food, a peaceful setting far off the usual tourist beaten track, and of course, an extraordinary view. The following list includes some of the best currently available lighthouse B&Bs. Their websites offer stunning photographs, a list of amenities, contact information, directions, and assistance with making reservations.

Big Bay Lighthouse
Big Bay, MI
bigbaylighthouse.com

Heceta Head Lighthouse
Florence, OR
hecetalighthouse.com

Saugerties Lighthouse
Saugerties, NY
Saugertieslighthouse.com

Braddock Point Lighthouse
Hilton, NY
braddockpointlighthouse.com

Rose Island Lighthouse
Newport, RI
roseislandlighthouse.org

Two Harbors Lighthouse
Two Harbors, MI
Lighthousebb.org

East Brother Lighthouse
Richmond, CA
ebls.org

Sand Hills Lighthouse
Eagle Harbor, MI
sandhillslighthouseinn.com

The discovery of copper and iron ore in the hills of Michigan and Minnesota in the mid-nineteenth century brought a shipping boom to Lake Superior. Many freighters took on loads of ore at ports along the Keweenaw Peninsula. Eagle Harbor, near the outer end of the peninsula, became an important port and its lighthouse a key navigational marker. The existing brick keeper's dwelling and attached octagonal tower were built in 1871 and took the place of an earlier lighthouse, which had stood here since 1851. In 1968 the Coast Guard replaced the station's fourth-order Fresnel lens with an aeromarine beacon. ::

East Brother Light

Location: Near Richmond, California
Established: 1874
Tower height: 48 feet
Elevation of focal plane: 61 feet
Optic: Modern
Status: Active (automated in 1968)

Classical Victorian architecture distinguishes this still-active lighthouse, which also serves as a bed-and-breakfast. Established during the 1870s to guide vessels through the upper reaches of San Francisco Bay, East Brother Light is located off San Pablo

Holding its tower in what appears to be an intimate embrace, the ornate residence of California's East Brother Lighthouse (above) is nonetheless a separate structure. At England's famed Eddystone Lighthouse (right), the tower and residence were the same.
Bruce Roberts

Point on an island only about one-third acre in size. The station was scheduled for demolition in the late 1960s, but the combination tower and residence became the focus of an effective preservation effort. Proceeds from the bed-and-breakfast help maintain the property. Visitors are rewarded with a romantic view of the bay area and a glimpse of what life was like for nineteenth-century lighthouse keepers. ::

Eddystone Light

Location: Near Plymouth, England
Established: 1698
Tower height: 161 feet
Elevation of focal plane: 135 feet
Optic: Modern (solar-powered)
Status: Active (automated in 1982)

Rising from a wave-swept, open-water rock about a dozen miles west of Cornwall, Eddystone Light may be the world's best-known navigational marker. In a storm, the ocean seemingly overwhelms the tower, pounding its massive stone walls and throwing spray all the way to the lantern room more than 150 feet above the surface. But once the storm passes, the granite lighthouse invariably remains standing and continues to flash its warning signal.

The construction of the existing tower in 1882 still ranks among history's most impressive engineering achievements, but efforts to mark this exceptionally dangerous offshore obstacle date back to the seventeenth century. Henry Winstanley built the first lighthouse on the treacherous Eddystone Rocks in 1698. Five years later Winstanley was killed by a gale that crushed and washed away the structure while he was attempting to make repairs. A tower built in part of wood in 1709 guarded Eddystone for almost a half century. It was surprisingly resistant to storms but succumbed in 1755 to a fire that started in the lantern room and soon turned the tower into a gigantic torch.

The third Eddystone Light, completed four years later, was destined to make builder

Courtesy Library of Congress

John Smeaton almost as famous as the lighthouse itself. Determined to prove himself equal to the challenges of Eddystone, Smeaton constructed a monolithic edifice composed of huge, interlocking granite blocks. The harder the ocean pounded the stones, the more tightly the dovetailed blocks gripped one another. Completed in 1759, the Smeaton tower would still mark the Eddystone Rocks had it not been undermined by a subsurface cave-in in the late 1870s.

The builders of the current lighthouse used a technique similar to Smeaton's, and it has proven no less effective. When the new lighthouse was completed in the early 1880s, the Smeaton tower was dismantled stone by stone and rebuilt on shore as a monument to its designer.

Eddystone Light has employed a variety of lighting systems. The original 1698 station warned mariners with a light produced by as many as sixty candles. For nearly a century, the Eddystone beacon was focused by a first-order Fresnel lens. Today the light signal is produced by a modern solar-powered optic. ::

Eldred Rock Light

Location: Near Haines, Alaska
Established: 1905
Tower height: 56 feet
Elevation of focal plane: 91 feet
Optic: Modern (solar-powered)
Status: Active (automated in 1973)

The extraordinary appearance, long history, and spectacular setting of this light station make it one of America's foremost lighthouse treasures. Built in 1905, the original octagonal structure still stands and is the oldest lighthouse in Alaska. Despite its beauty and historic importance, however, the building faces an uncertain future. The Coast Guard automated the light more than thirty years ago and no longer needs the building. The Sheldon Museum in Haines is seeking title to the lighthouse and hopes to restore it.

Shining from a small tower on the roof, Eldred Rock's beacon remains in use. Mariners moving along the Inside Passage toward Haines and Skagway at the far northern end of the Alaska Panhandle are careful to heed its warning. They hope their vessels can avoid the fate of the *Clara Nevada,* a steamer lost near Eldred Rock in 1898. Several maritime disasters occurred during Alaska's gold rush years; this one claimed the lives of more than 100 passengers. ::

Eldred Rock Light
Bob and Sandra Shanklin

Estevan Point Light

Courtesy *Lighthouse Digest*

Estevan Point Light

Location: Estevan Point, British Columbia

Established: 1910

Tower height: 100 feet

Elevation of focal plane: 125 feet

Optic: Modern

Status: Active

With its extraordinary flying buttresses, the Estevan Point tower on Vancouver Island has a very modern, rocket-like appearance. The spreading buttresses help support a reinforced-concrete central cylinder enclosing the staircase leading to the lantern room. Canadian engineer William Anderson devised this highly unusual design to protect the structure from gales and earthquakes.

Although the story may be apocryphal, it is said the station came under fire from a Japanese submarine in 1942. Supposedly, some of the shells carried over the station and struck a nearby village

of Hesquiat Indians. Enraged tribesmen responded by organizing a war party of small powerboats and roaring off in pursuit of the sub. Had it not escaped under cover of a smokescreen, the Japanese boat might have become the only submarine in history to be attacked by Indians. ::

Fastnet Light

Location: County Cork, Ireland

Established: 1904

Tower height: 177 feet

Elevation of focal plane: 161 feet

Optic: Fresnel lens

Status: Active (automated in 1989)

Ireland's beautiful Fastnet Light represents a combination of grace and technological sophistication. Built with dovetailed granite blocks, the tapered tower reaches skyward from an exposed rock

Fastnet Light
Copyright Jean Guichard

off Ireland's far southwestern coast. William Douglass designed the tower, considered by many among the most beautiful in the world.

Adding to the superlatives than can be attached to this light station is its remarkable two-tiered rotating lens, designed by C. W. Scott, chief engineer for the Commissioners of Irish Lights. Each tier contains four enormous bull's-eye panels. Only the upper tier remains in use, emitting a flashing white beacon that can be seen for up to 27 miles at sea. ::

Fenwick Island Light

Location: Fenwick Island, Delaware
Established: 1858
Tower height: 84 feet
Elevation of focal plane: 83 feet
Optic: Fresnel lens (third-order)
Status: Active (automated in 1940)

Built only a few years before the Civil War, the Fenwick Island Lighthouse identifies an important landfall for mariners. It also marks the eastern end of an old colonial survey line that, symbolically at least,

Bruce Roberts

Fenwick Island Light

separated America's northern and southern states. Interestingly, Charles Mason and Jeremiah Dixon, whose "line" is celebrated in literature and song, are not responsible for the crown stone located in front of the lighthouse. Instead, the historic stone was placed by an earlier survey team that visited Fenwick Island in 1751.

Owned by the state of Delaware and leased to a local preservation group, the station has benefited from several major restoration projects and remains in excellent condition. Its occulting light has a limited range of only about 8 nautical miles. A small museum located in the base of the tower houses information concerning the light station's history. ::

Fidra Light

Location: Near North Berwick, Scotland
Established: 1885
Tower height: 51 feet
Elevation of focal plane: 112 feet
Optic: Modern
Status: Active (automated in 1970)

Said to have been the inspiration for Robert Louis Stevenson's classic *Treasure Island,* this nearly barren islet off the southeastern coast of Scotland likely conceals no chests of gold and silver, but mariners have long placed a high value on its navigational light. Built by David and Thomas Stevenson under the authority of the Northern Lighthouse Board, Fidra Light has guided vessels into the Firth of Forth since 1885 and is located just across from Yellowcraigs Beach, a popular tourist destination. The white brick tower displays a flashing light visible for about 24 miles at sea. ::

Finisterre Light

Location: Galicia, Spain
Established: 1853
Tower height: 56 feet
Elevation of focal plane: 143 feet
Optic: Fresnel lens
Status: Active

Still operated by a resident keeper, Finisterre Light guards a stretch of coast once thought to have been

Do visitors to Fidra Island encounter an old peg-legged pirate, a parrot, or a "dead man's chest"? Who knows, but the island is said to have served as inspiration for Robert Louis Stevenson's *Treasure Island.*
Shutterstock.com

On the far side of the Atlantic, a present-day view of Spain's Finisterre Light.

Henry Gonzales

the end of the world. Fog often gripped these lofty cliffs, and peering off into it, the ancients imagined that no dry and habitable land could possibly exist beyond this rugged and forbidding place. Of course, the Spanish later understood that there was a vast ocean out there and not a void, so they marked the Finisterre cliffs with a lighthouse. Focused by an unusually powerful Fresnel lens, its beacon reaches 25 miles. Large numbers of freighters moving north and south along the western Spanish coast rely on its guidance. ::

Fire Island Light

Location: Fire Island, New York
Established: 1827
Tower height: 168 feet
Elevation of focal plane: 167 feet
Optic: Aeromarine beacon
Status: Active (automated in 1986)

Long ago some romantically inclined person dubbed Fire Island Light, with its rapidly flashing light, the "Winking Woman." Indeed, the tall, gently tapered black and white tower has a graceful, almost feminine appearance. However, this was not the case in the late 1970s, when the abandoned tower

suffered greatly from neglect and decay. Having declared the structure unsafe and beyond repair, the US Coast Guard planned to demolish the tower in 1982, but a local preservation group came to the rescue. Now handsomely restored, the lighthouse is a key attraction of the Fire Island National Seashore.

The existing brick tower was built in 1858 to replace an earlier granite structure of only about half its height. The new tower was given a flared base to increase its stability. A first-order Fresnel lens focused the light produced by the station's whale-oil lamps. During the 1890s, a coal-fired power plant was added to the station, complete with a tramway to bring fuel from a nearby dock. The station was not electrified until 1939.

The Coast Guard deactivated Fire Island Light in 1974, but twelve years later, the Fire Island Preservation Society managed to restore the light. The beacon flashes white eight times a minute and

A historic image of New York's Fire Island Lighthouse.

Courtesy Library of Congress

Fire Island Lighthouse without its black and white stripes.

is visible for an impressive distance of 24 nautical miles. ::

Fisgard Light

Location: Victoria, British Columbia
Established: 1860
Tower height: 56 feet
Elevation of focal plane: 67 feet
Optic: Aeromarine beacon
Status: Active (automated in 1929)

Few cities are more conscious of their heritage than Victoria, British Columbia, and fittingly, this Canadian provincial capital is served by a grand old lighthouse. Built in 1860 on a small, rocky island at the entrance to Victoria's Esquimalt Harbor, the tower and attached two-story keeper's residence were the work of John Wright, an architect and contractor whose name is associated with a number of the province's major government buildings. Wright worked with brick, granite, and heavy timbers to construct edifices intended to last. Designed to withstand punishing weather, the Fisgard Lighthouse looks very much today as it did in the nineteenth century.

The station's first keeper was a young Englishman named George Davies, who arrived in Victoria from Britain in 1860 after a six-month voyage that took him halfway around the world. Davies brought with him the lamps and machinery necessary to outfit the Fisgard tower. In its early years the station employed a lamp-and-reflector system to produce its beacon. The lamps burned vegetable or dogfish oils. A far more efficient fourth-order Fresnel lens replaced the reflector system in the 1880s. Today, an aeromarine beacon provides the light. ::

Fisgard Light
Bruce Roberts

Flügge Light

Location: Fehmarn Island, Germany

Established: 1916

Tower height: 121 feet

Elevation of focal plane: 126 feet

Optic: Modern

Status: Active

Built at the height of World War I, the octagonal Flügge tower anchors the southwest corner of Fehmarn Island just off Germany's Baltic coast. Distinctive red and white bands set this tower apart from others along the Baltic, as does the unusual double cast-iron gallery near the top. The beacon is maintained by Germany's Ministry of Transportation. ::

Courtesy *Lighthouse Digest*

Flügge Light

Courtesy *Lighthouse Digest*

Gabo Island Light

Location: Gabo Island, Australia

Established: 1862

Tower height: 85 feet

Elevation of focal plane: 180 feet

Optic: Fresnel lens

Status: Active (automated in 1993)

The stark white tower of Gabo Island Light marks the entrance of Bass Strait off the east coast of Victoria. As with many Australian lights, the tower provides less than half the elevation of the beacon. The light flashes white every twenty seconds and is visible for a distance of 16 nautical miles. Gabo Island also hosts the largest colony of "little" penguins in the world. ::

Gibbs Hill Light

Location: Hamilton, Bermuda

Established: 1846

Tower height: 117 feet

Elevation of focal plane: 362 feet

Optic: Fresnel lens (first-order)

Status: Active (automated in 1964)

One of the oldest cast-iron light towers in the world, Gibbs Hill Light has been warning mariners away from the dangerous reefs just west of Bermuda since 1846. Nearly forty large vessels were lost on these reefs during the decade before the lighthouse was completed. Since that time, the powerful Gibbs Hill beacon has no doubt saved countless other ships from a similar fate.

From its perch on one of Bermuda's highest points, the light station casts a light that is visible from as far as 40 miles away. In fact, it has been seen by airplane pilots at distances greater than 100 miles. The light signal is produced by a huge Fresnel prismatic lens that floats on a tank containing 1,200 pounds of mercury.

Originally the clockwork mechanism that drove the revolving lens was powered by weights that had to be pulled back to the top of the tower repeatedly during the night by a keeper. Reaching the top of the tower was no small task, as it required a climb of 185 steps. Now driven by automated machinery, the optic no longer requires a full-time attendant. Instead of a keeper, the station's old residence now houses a gift shop and tearoom for tourists. ::

Nearly half a world apart are Australia's Gabo Island Light (opposite page, top right) and the Gibbs Hill Light (right) in Bermuda.

Henry Gonzales

Godrevy Light clings to rocks off the southwestern coast of England.

Godrevy Light

Location: Off the coast of Cornwall, England

Established: 1859

Tower height: 85 feet

Elevation of focal plane: 121 feet

Optic: Fresnel lens (second-order)

Status: Active (automated in 1939)

The Godrevy Light station consists of a stark white hexagonal tower surrounded by a wall that gives it an appearance something like that of an ancient fortress. However, nature has provided this remote island with more than adequate defenses. The station's keepers could reach the place only by means of a primitive chairlift. Today the light is powered by solar panels. When maintenance is necessary, the station is reached by helicopter. ::

Goulphar Light

Copyright Jean Guichard

Goulphar Light

Location: Belle-Ile, France

Established: 1836

Tower height: 171 feet

Elevation of focal plane: 285 feet

Optic: Fresnel lens

Status: Active

The magnificent Phare de Goulphar on Belle-Ile is noteworthy for historical and architectural reasons as well as for the extraordinary power of its beacon. The light station's massive stone cylinder tower dates back to the 1830s, but as early as the tenth century, attempts were made to put a beacon on Belle-Ile, a prominent island landfall off the southern coast of Brittany.

Plans for the existing structure were drawn up in the 1820s by Beautemps Beaupré under the watchful eye of Augustin Fresnel, but construction did not begin immediately. In 1827, while preparations for the project were still being made, Fresnel succumbed to a long illness, probably tuberculosis. His death and the chaos of the 1830 revolution in France delayed completion of the light station for almost a decade. When the tower was at last finished in 1836, however, it ranked among the world's finest lighthouses. It still does. The station's double-walled granite tower has weathered countless gales and likely could stand up to any storm. Its distinctive red metal lantern houses a double Fresnel lens that produces a flashing light visible from as far away as 26 miles at sea. The lighthouse and its important beacon remain in the care of full-time keepers. ::

Grand Haven Pier Lights

Location: Grand Haven, Michigan

Established: 1905

Tower heights: 51 feet (inner tower), 36 feet (outer tower)

Elevation of focal planes: 52 (inner tower) 42 feet (outer tower)

Optic: Modern

Status: Active (automated in 1969)

Distinctive red sentinels have marked the approach to Grand Haven on Lake Michigan for more than a

Grand Haven Pier Lights
Bruce Roberts

Grosse Point Light
Bruce Roberts

century. They stand several hundred feet apart on a long concrete pier near the entrance to the harbor. Like other range lights, the two function in tandem, and navigators in safe water will see the beacons aligned vertically, one atop the other. The outer tower is rectangular, and the inner is cylindrical. An elevated walkway links the towers to shore. ::

Grosse Point Light

Location: Evanston, Illinois
Established: 1873
Tower height: 119 feet
Elevation of focal plane: 121 feet
Optic: Fresnel lens (second-order)
Status: Private aid to navigation

When Grosse Point Light was built in 1873, the Lighthouse Board assigned it a second-order Fresnel lens, the largest and most powerful optic ever used on the Great Lakes. Maritime authorities felt the station merited this impressive lens because the Evanston light pointed the way to Chicago. Although it was decommissioned by the Lighthouse Service in 1935, the Grosse Point beacon eventually was reestablished as a private aid to navigation. The light is still focused by the station's original

lens, which remains the largest on the lakes. The handsome tower and keeper's residence now serve as the primary attractions of an Evanston city park and museum complex. ::

Hartland Point Light

Location: Hartland, England
Established: 1874
Tower height: 59 feet
Elevation of focal plane: 120 feet
Optic: Fresnel lens
Status: Active (automated in 1984)

Vessels approaching the Bristol Channel have long depended on the bright beacon of Hartland Point Light, built by noted Trinity House engineer James Douglass. The station clings to the tip of the rugged point, and continuous pounding by the sea has caused the rocks along the point to crumble, threatening to undercut the station. A seawall in place since 1925 protects the rock face immediately

Designed by Sir James Douglass during the 1870s, England's Hartland Point Light gets much of its 120-foot elevation from seaside cliffs.

Shutterstock.com

below the lighthouse. The station remains active, displaying a flashing white light visible for about 25 nautical miles. ::

Heceta Head Light

Location: Near Florence, Oregon

Established: 1894

Tower height: 58 feet

Elevation of focal plane: 205 feet

Optic: Fresnel lens (first-order)

Status: Active (automated in 1963)

Shining seaward from the side of a cliff overlooking the Pacific, the Heceta Head beacon warns ships away from rocks and a deadly labyrinth of

subsurface mountain peaks along the central Oregon coast. Spanish explorer Don Bruno de Heceta noted these hazards as early as 1755 when he passed this way. Even though this considerable threat to shipping had been known for more than a century, the rugged terrain discouraged early attempts to build a lighthouse here. The US Lighthouse Board made no effort to mark this dangerous stretch of coast until the nineteenth century was almost at an end. When Heceta Head Light was finally built in the 1890s, construction crews had to bring materials ashore at a distant landing and then laboriously haul them up the precipitous cliffs. Completed in 1894, the 56-foot Heceta Head tower, two-story dwelling, and

Spectacular view of Heceta Head at dusk (below). The station's twin storage buildings (above).

Photos by Bruce Roberts

Highlands (Navesink) Light

Location: Highlands, New Jersey
Established: 1828
Tower height: 73 feet
Elevation of focal plane: 246 feet
Optic: Fresnel lens (sixth-order)
Status: Private aid to navigation

In 1828 the US government established a twin-light navigational beacon atop the Navesink Highlands in New Jersey to point the way to New York Harbor. The lights shone out from a pair of rubblestone towers spaced about 320 feet apart. During the Civil War, these structures were torn down and replaced by a long brownstone building with a pair of turret-like towers that would have looked at home on a medieval fortress. The octagonal north tower was fitted with a first-order Fresnel lens while the square south tower received a rotating second-order Fresnel.

Over the years Highlands Light has achieved a significant number of historic firsts. In 1841 it became the first US light station to employ a Fresnel lens. In 1898 Highlands became the first light station to power a major navigational beacon

other structures cost the government more than $180,000—a breathtaking sum at that time.

Most would now agree the lighthouse has proven well worth its hefty price. After more than a century of service, Heceta Head remains in operation, warning vessels far out at sea with its first-order light. The station also serves as a charming bed-and-breakfast, where visitors can enjoy the view of a lifetime. ::

Highlands (Navesink) Light
Bruce Roberts

colored station might have been demolished except for determined efforts by preservationists to save it. The Coast Guard planned to abandon the station in the 1970s but relented after the citizens of Holland mounted a vigorous petition drive. The lighthouse is now owned by a local historical commission, while its light is maintained by the Coast Guard. The lighthouse stands on a pier near the harbor entrance. **::**

with electricity. Also in 1898 Highlands was the first station to be fitted with a hyper-radial lens (much larger than a standard first-order lens). In 1899 Guglielmo Marconi used the station grounds for one of his first experimental wireless broadcasts—a report on the America's Cup races.

Highlands Light is now used primarily as a museum. The north tower has a small Fresnel lens that serves as a private aid to navigation. **::**

Holland Harbor Light

Location: Holland, Michigan

Established: 1872

Tower height: 32 feet

Elevation of focal plane: 52 feet

Optic: Fresnel lens (sixth-order)

Status: Active (automated in 1936)

Known affectionately to mariners and Holland, Michigan, residents alike as "Big Red," this brightly

Holland Harbor Light
Bruce Roberts

Ireland's centuries-old Hook Head Light with its bold black and white bands.

Kathy Finnegan photo, courtesy *Lighthouse Digest*

it over the cliffs at night to warn mariners. It is said this practice was continued by local monks right on up until the twelfth century.

The church Dubhan built in nearby Churchtown still stands, but the existing Hook Head Light tower is of more "recent" vintage—it dates to 1172. The hulking stone base of the structure was the work of Normans who, having conquered England just a few years earlier, had pushed on to Ireland. It is said the invading Norman warriors were told to land either on the hook or a nearby point known as the crook. Having made landfall "by hook or by crook," the Normans conquered once again and built the tower. The tower served as a battlement, watchtower, and dungeon, as well as a navigational marker. With walls 80 feet tall and 10 feet thick, the tower was capable of standing up to any assault whether by well-armed soldiers or howling gales. The old Norman tower still serves as the lower section of the lighthouse. The short upper section and lantern room were placed here in the 1670s and substantially renovated in 1859. The flashing white light can be seen for up to 23 miles at sea. ::

Hook Head Light

Location: Near Churchtown, Ireland
Established: 1172
Tower height: 118 feet
Elevation of focal plane: 151 feet
Optic: Fresnel lens (first-order)
Status: Active (automated in 1996)

The story of the light at Hook Head goes back to about AD 500, not many years after the fall of the Roman Empire. According to legend, a light was established by a Welsh monk named Dubhan, who was horrified by the bodies of drowned mariners he often found on this jutting "hook" of Irish rock. Dubhan built fires in a large iron basket and hung

Isle au Haut Light

Location: Isle au Haut, Maine
Established: 1907
Tower height: 40 feet
Elevation of focal plane: 48 feet
Optic: Modern (solar-powered)
Status: Active (automated in 1934)

The Isle au Haut tower is a modest brick cylinder that stands at water's edge on rock-strewn Point Robinson, its massive granite base awash at high tide. An elevated walkway links the tower to dry land, where its two-and-a-half-story Victorian keeper's residence has been converted into a popular bed-and-breakfast. The station's solar-powered modern optic still flashes, serving local fishermen as well as

Now available for tourist rentals, Maine's Isle au Haut Lighthouse (below) is a refuge for city-weary tourists.

Bruce Roberts

the ferries bringing visitors to this island, much of it now included in Acadia National Park.

The famous French explorer Samuel de Champlain gave Isle au Haut, "high island," its name. When he arrived in 1604, no one was living there. The island is sparsely populated to this day, with only a few dozen hardy Mainers living here year-round. ::

Kalaupapa Light

Location: Molokai Island, Hawaii

Established: 1908

Tower height: 138 feet

Elevation of focal plane: 213 feet

Optic: Aeromarine beacon

Status: Active (automated in 1970)

A wall of soaring cliffs separates the Kalaupapa Peninsula from the rest of Molokai Island, making it remote even by Hawaiian standards. Once the site of a notorious leper colony, the peninsula was long considered a dark and forbidding place, especially by mariners who could find no safe anchorage along its rugged shores. To warn vessels to keep their distance, the US government placed a light station here in 1908. The 138-foot tower is Hawaii's tallest. Until the station was automated in 1970, a second-order Fresnel lens focused its light, but an aeromarine optic now produces the beacon.

Although the leper colony closed years ago, tragic stories of Hawaiians whose bodies were wracked and lives wrecked by Hansen's disease (leprosy) still haunt this place. The old colony, the lighthouse, and most of the peninsula are now

Kalaupapa Light
Bob and Sandra Shanklin

included in the Kalaupapa National Historical Park. Visitors can reach the park by climbing down the 2,000-foot cliffs on foot or on mules. ::

Kap Arkona Light
Egbert Koch

Kap Arkona Light

Location: Rügen Island, Germany
Established: 1827
Tower height: 115 feet
Elevation of focal plane: 245 feet
Optic: Fresnel lens
Status: Active

Kap (Cape) Arkona extends into the Baltic Sea from the northern end of Germany's Rügen Island. Beginning in 1827, a beacon shining from atop a 75-foot square brick tower guided vessels safely around the cape. Increased maritime traffic along the northern coast of Germany at the turn of the twentieth century led maritime authorities to order construction of a taller tower at Kap Arkona. That tower, completed in 1902, is a conical structure crowned by a red lantern with two galleries. The optical system consists of three separate prismatic lenses on a revolving base. The beacon has a range of up to 24 miles. The original square tower still stands and is now used as a maritime museum. ::

station continues to stand up to the Atlantic's most destructive storms.

The Kéréon station was privately financed by the Kéréon family, which built the tower to honor an ancestor guillotined during the French Revolution. The tower's rugged gray granite exterior stands in sharp contrast to the comfortable, somewhat luxurious keeper's residences and workspaces it encloses. The pleasant surroundings rewarded keepers who had to remain on duty here even during fierce Atlantic storms. Getting on and off the station was no simple matter and had to be accomplished by winch or helicopter. In 2004 the lighthouse was finally automated, but it continues to do its lifesaving work of guiding mariners. The light is powered by a small windmill atop the lantern. Kéréon's red and white beacon is visible from up to 17 nautical miles. **::**

Kéréon Light

Copyright Jean Guichard

Kéréon Light

Location: Near Ile d'Ouessant, France

Established: 1916

Tower height: 157 feet

Elevation of focal plane: 144 feet

Optic: Fresnel lens

Status: Active

The Kéréon light station marks a particularly dangerous reef called Mentensel, a Gaelic word meaning "aggressive stone." Kéréon also marks an important sea channel off Ile d'Ouessant, an island off the rugged west coast of Brittany. Like the nearby La Jument lighthouse, the Kéréon tower often seems caught in the ocean's powerful grip, at the mercy of huge, storm-driven waves, but this

Kilauea Point Light

Location: Kauai Island, Hawaii

Established: 1913

Tower height: 52 feet

Elevation of focal plane: 216 feet

Optic: Fresnel lens (second-order)

Status: Deactivated in 1976

Now the centerpiece of a wildlife sanctuary teeming with seabirds, Kilauea Point Light surely ranks among the most beautiful man-made structures in a state renowned for its impressive natural beauty. The station marks the northernmost point in the main Hawaiian Island chain. The beacon emanating from this rugged precipice on Kauai is often the first one seen by vessels and aircraft approaching from the US mainland.

In 1927 the bright flash of Kilauea Point Light caught the eye of adventuring pilot Lester "Lone Eagle" Maitland, saving him from becoming hopelessly lost over the Pacific. Maitland and copilot Albert Hegenberger were attempting to make the first flight from the North American mainland to

Kilauea Point Light on Hawaii's Kauai Island
Bob and Sandra Shanklin

Now home to a local yacht club, this graceful light station with its octagonal tower still functions as an active aid to navigation on Lake Huron, serving as a rear range light in tandem with a second beacon about a quarter mile away. Legend has it that a Scottish piper once guided vessels into the harbor during periods of fog. In keeping with the legend, a piper plays in the lighthouse gallery at sunset during the summer. Unlike the piper, the light puts on a show all year long, guiding mariners with red and white flashes visible for about 16 miles. **::**

Kincardine Light
Bruce Roberts

the Hawaiian Islands. Except for the Kilauea Point beacon, their record-setting flight would have ended in disaster.

Today's Kilauea Point Light is not the same one that once guided Maitland and other Pacific travelers. The light in the station's handsome cylindrical tower was snuffed out in 1976 and replaced by a smaller automated beacon shining from a nearby metal tower. However, the original clamshell Fresnel lens remains in the tower, where it now delights sanctuary visitors. **::**

Kincardine Light

Location: Kincardine, Ontario
Established: 1881
Tower height: 63 feet
Elevation of focal plane: 80 feet
Optic: Fresnel lens
Status: Active (automated in 1963)

Kinnaird Head Light

Location: Fraserburgh, Scotland
Established: 1827
Tower height: 33 feet
Elevation of focal plane: 82 feet
Optic: Fresnel lens
Status: Deactivated in 1991

Set atop the corner turret of a sixteenth-century castle, Kinnaird Head Light is the work of Thomas Smith, an early Northern Lighthouse Board engineer and stepfather of Robert Stevenson. This lighthouse was the first one built under the authority of the

The twin towers of Kinnaird Head Light in Scotland
Courtesy Harbour Lights

board, which eventually established hundreds of navigational lights in Scotland. The station's original optic was an extraordinary device featuring an array of seventeen silvered glass reflectors. Thought to be one of the best lighthouse optics of its day, it had a range of up to 14 miles.

The Kinnaird Head Light marked a promontory long known to mariners. Early Greco/Egyptian and Roman travelers mentioned these heights when writing about the British Isles, most likely because early seamen used them as a seamark. A cherished local legend tells of a young woman leaping to her death off the Kinnaird Head cliffs. Her motive, of course, was love, and it is said the ghost of her lover often plays the pipes down along the shore.

Deactivated in 1991 and replaced by a nearby automated beacon, the old Kinnaird Head Lighthouse now serves as home to the Museum of Scottish Lighthouses. Housing one of the world's largest collections of Fresnel lenses and other lighthouse equipment, the museum retraces the dramatic history of Scotland's extraordinary maritime beacons. ⁞⁞

Kvitsoy Light

Location: Kvitsoy, Norway
Established: 1700
Tower height: 90 feet
Elevation of focal plane: 148 feet
Optic: Fresnel (second-order)
Status: Active (automated in 1969)

The light station at Kvitsoy began as a private enterprise in 1700, when the King of Norway granted permission for a navigational beacon here. Contributions from passing seamen were expected to support the station, but they were rarely sufficient to cover costs. Perhaps mariners objected

Kvitsoy Light
Courtesy Harbour Lights

La Corbière Light

Location: Jersey, Channel Islands (United Kingdom)
Established: 1874
Tower height: 62 feet
Elevation of focal plane: 119 feet
Optic: Fresnel lens
Status: Active (automated in 1976)

Located off the southwest tip of Jersey in the Channel Islands, La Corbière is the first British lighthouse to be built entirely of concrete. Like other aids to navigation in these islands, which are much closer to France than to England, the station is maintained by Trinity House. It displays a white light to seaward and a red light toward land. The white signal can be seen for about 18 miles.

La Corbière Light is located in a district of Jersey known as La Moye, or "stony heaps." A quick look at the area around the tower makes it easy to understand how the land hereabouts came to be called that. Victor Hugo, the nineteenth-century author of *Les Miserables* and other classics of French literature, was no less impressed with the local scenery than visitors are today. He once referred to La Corbière Light as "the shepherd of the waves."

According to legend, local pirates—sometimes called wreckers—long ago lured a vessel onto the rocks where La Corbière Light now stands.

to the primitive nature of the light, which at first was nothing more than a blazing basket of coal hoisted skyward on a long pole attached to a lever. The massive hexagonal tower that marks Kvitsoy today was built by the Norwegian government in 1829. Even after 1829, the light was still produced by burning coal, but an oil lamp was added in 1859, when a thorough renovation nearly doubled the height of the tower. Today the tower is part of a protected historic site. ::

La Corbière Light
Courtesy *Lighthouse Digest*

The wreckers stood by and allowed the ship's crew to drown. Before he died, the ship's master placed the following curse on the wreckers: "Doomed by the same cruel death to die, I summon ye to meet me within a year below the waters of this bay." Exactly one year later, the wreckers held a feast to celebrate their continuing success. The legend holds that a storm drove a freak tide into the bay and drowned the pirates. Far more fortunate were those onboard the French vessel *Saint-Malo,* which struck a submerged rock and foundered near the lighthouse in 1995. Thanks to a dramatic rescue effort mounted by locals and the crews of nearby vessels, all 307 passengers and crew were rescued. **::**

La Jument Light

Location: Near Ouessant, France
Established: 1911
Tower height: 154 feet
Elevation of focal plane: 135 feet
Optic: Fresnel lens
Status: Active (automated in 1991)

Although less than a century old—hardly venerable by European standards—the gray stone La Jument tower off the coast of Brittany has become an icon for lighthouse lovers all over the world. In fact, its image can be seen on the walls of business offices, government buildings, and homes everywhere. Its considerable fame dates to December 21, 1989, when a mighty sea storm bore down on the coast of Brittany. While the storm raged and huge waves engulfed the tower, a young photographer named Jean Guichard snapped pictures of the station

Although both seem old to us today, Europe's La Laterna (right) and La Jument (next page) towers were built almost 800 years apart. Italy's La Laterna may have inspired Columbus to dream of crossing the Atlantic. Nowadays, La Jument Light in western France calls mariners home from that same great ocean.

Audrey B. Conner

from a helicopter. The dramatic images Guichard captured on film that day are now seen on posters and framed prints worldwide. **::**

La Laterna

Location: Genoa, Italy
Established: 1128
Tower height: 249 feet
Elevation of focal plane: 383 feet
Optic: Fresnel lens (second-order)
Status: Active (automated in 1991)

No list of the world's most important lighthouses would be complete without La Laterna, the magnificent square tower that guards the promontory of San Benigno in Genoa, Italy's old royal capital. Rising nearly twenty-five stories into the blue Mediterranean sky, La Laterna is the tallest masonry light tower in the world as well as one of the oldest. The existing structure dates to 1543, but

the light station itself was much older, established in 1128. Frequently damaged by warfare, the lighthouse had to be repaired and rebuilt several times. Antonio Columbo, the uncle of Christopher Columbus, once served as keeper of this light. Some believe Columbo ignited a passion for the sea and exploration in his nephew. ⠃

La Vieille Light

Location: Brittany, France
Established: 1887
Tower height: 88 feet

Elevation of focal plane: 108 feet
Optic: Fresnel lens
Status: Active (automated in 1995)

The La Vieille light station looks very much like a chess rook or castle, but this rook plays on a particularly violent chessboard—the tossing seas off the far west coast of Brittany. La Vieille has stood solid and unmoving since 1887 and remains a mainstay in the defensive wall of navigational lights that mark the Atlantic coast of France. La Vieille displays red, white, and green lights that flash every twelve seconds and are visible for up to 19 miles. ⠃

In sharp contrast to its venerable neighbor, a more brightly colored modern maritime beacon rises from the waves not far from La Vieille. The offshore towers at La Jument (opposite page) in Western France reflect the castle-turret architecture typical of nineteenth-century French lighthouses. Frequently besieged by Atlantic storms, these structures are fortresses in a very real sense.

Les Pierres Noires Light

Location: Brittany, France

Established: 1872

Tower height: 91 feet

Elevation of focal plane: 98 feet

Optic: Fresnel lens

Status: Active (automated in 1992)

The waters surrounding Les Pierres Noires Light off the west coast of Brittany are cold, but much of the time they appear to boil. Waves erupt when they smash into these rock-strewn shallows, sending up massive sprays of white foam. For more than 140 years, the light station at Les Pierres Noires has warned mariners to keep well away. During much of that time, keepers could maintain this important light only by living and working in the isolated, sea-besieged stone tower. Now automated, the beacon at Les Pierres Noires displays a red flash every five seconds. The station serves not only as a navigational beacon but as a popular maritime museum. ⸬

Les Pierres Noires Light

Copyright Jean Guichard

Lindesnes Light

Location: Lindesnes, Norway

Established: 1655

Tower height: 52 feet

Elevation of focal plane: 164 feet

Optic: Fresnel lens

Status: Active

Perhaps the oldest light station in Scandinavia is the one at Lindesnes on Norway's southernmost point to the southwest of Kristiansand. The station dates to 1655, when a wooden tower was erected to guide vessels in from the stormy North Sea. Several different towers, including the original wooden one,

Lindesnes Light

Courtesy Harbour Lights

have served Lindesnes. The existing red and white iron tower has been in place since 1915. Because of its highly strategic location, German forces fortified Lindesnes during World War II. ::

Little River Light

Location: Near Cutler, Maine
Established: 1847
Tower height: 41 feet
Elevation of focal plane: 56 feet
Optic: Fresnel lens (fifth-order)
Status: Reactivated in 2001

Although never a major coastal light station, Little River Light has an inspiring story to tell. Now something of a poster child for the preservation movement, it stands as evidence that even long-forgotten lighthouses may be saved by friendly, helping hands.

In 1847 maritime authorities ordered construction of a stone tower and attached stone dwelling on a small island near the harbor entrance of Cutler, a fishing village in far eastern Maine. In 1876 the station received a new cast-iron tower, and a few years later, a Victorian keeper's residence was added. These structures remained in use until 1975, when the old light station was shut down and boarded up by the Coast Guard.

The government offered the station property and buildings for sale, but there were no takers. After guiding Maine fishermen for more than a century, the old lighthouse was deemed useless. Twenty-five years of neglect took a heavy toll on the station, but in 2000 its cast-iron tower, wooden keeper's dwelling, stone oil house, and wooden boathouse came under the protective wing of the American Lighthouse Foundation headquartered in Wells, Maine. At first the foundation only leased the property, but eventually it acquired the station under the National Historic Lighthouse Preservation Act. Several years of fund-raising and hard work by

Recently the object of a vigorous preservation effort, the Little River Lighthouse (above) has a distinctly rural, woodsy appearance.
Bob and Sandra Shanklin

foundation members not only halted deterioration of the buildings but also made it possible to relight the station's beacon. ::

Lizard Light

Location: Near Plymouth, England
Established: 1619
Tower height: 62 feet
Elevation of focal plane: 230 feet
Optic: Fresnel lens
Status: Active (automated in 1998)

The distinctive twin octagonal towers of Lizard Light mark a key landfall in southwest England and help guide mariners along the British side of the English Channel. The existing station has served mariners for about two centuries, but there was a lighthouse in this strategic place as early as 1619. The first tower was built by Sir John Killigrew, over the objections of locals said to have made a good living off the spoils of shipwrecks. Fearing the light would prove as useful to pirates and invading enemies as

This antique image depicts one of many maritime sentinels that once helped the Lizard and Longships Lights guard the southwest coast of England.

to well-meaning English seamen, even the British crown resisted construction of a navigational tower at Lizard Point. Killigrew received a patent from King James I only after agreeing to extinguish the light whenever enemy ships approached, but he need not have made the promise. The high cost of maintaining the light quickly bankrupted Killigrew, and his tower was soon demolished.

A much later private patent holder named Thomas Fonnereau built a second lighthouse here in 1751. Twenty years later Fonnereau sold the station to Trinity House, which has maintained it ever since. A Gothic-style nineteenth-century renovation left the station with the rather austere appearance of a rural British prep school, and it has changed little since. Automated in 1998, the Lizard Light now displays a single flashing white signal visible for up to 26 nautical miles. Ships use the light as a point of reference for timing transatlantic crossings. ::

Longships Light

Location: Penzance, England
Established: 1795
Tower height: 115 feet
Elevation of focal plane: 115 feet
Optic: Fresnel lens
Status: Active (automated in 1988)

Situated about a mile west of Land's End, the extreme southwestern point of the British mainland, Longships Light stands guard over one of the Atlantic's wildest and most violent spectacles. Here waves sweep in from three directions, producing what author John Ruskin described as "a rushing, writhing, tortured . . . anarchy of enormous power."

Mariners blundering into this maelstrom could not hope to survive, and many ships and seamen have been lost here. To warn them away, Trinity House had architect Samuel Wyatt design a three-story stone tower, which was erected on a large rock known as Carn Bras in 1795. Early keepers are said to have endured a primitive lifestyle, and some actually cooked their meals on the station's lamps.

A more modern and better-equipped tower was completed in 1875 by noted lighthouse builder Sir James Douglass. The Longships beacon, automated in 1988, continues to guide mariners with a fixed white light visible for about 14 miles. **::**

Los Angeles Harbor Light

Location: San Pedro, California
Established: 1913
Tower height: 69 feet
Elevation of focal plane: 73 feet
Optic: Aeromarine beacon (solar-powered)
Status: Active (automated in 1972)

Located at the far end of a breakwater near the entrance to the bustling harbor at San Pedro, California, Los Angeles Harbor Light holds the dubious distinction of having been rammed by a battleship. The tower survived that incident, as well as a number of earthquakes and furious Pacific storms. The station's steel and concrete cylinder tower is painted with black vertical stripes, giving it a unique design and appearance. From the first, the station was equipped with a powerful foghorn, and over the years sleepless San Pedro residents gave it colorful names, such as "Moaning Maggie" and "Blatting Bettie." **::**

Lundy North Light

Location: Lundy Island, England
Established: 1897
Tower height: 56 feet
Elevation of focal plane: 165 feet
Optic: Modern
Status: Active (automated in 1994)

For more than a century, the Lundy Lights (North and South) have guided vessels into the Bristol Channel of western England. The rugged granite mass of Lundy Island is surrounded by threatening reefs and dangerous rocks that have been claiming ships for centuries. The more substantial of the two stations is Lundy North Light, established shortly

Shown in the last light of a late summer's day, the Los Angeles Harbor Light guides vessels into port at San Pedro. Located near the end of a long pier, the tower is very exposed and has been struck by more than one large ship.
Bruce Roberts

Lundy North Light
Courtesy *Lighthouse Digest*

Francis Greenway, who was responsible for many of Sydney's most beautiful early buildings.

Greenway warned his superiors that the sandstone used to construct the tower would not stand up to weathering, and this proved to be the case. Within a few years, the tower walls began to crumble. Iron bands were placed around the cylindrical structure to hold the walls together, but this only slowed their deterioration. Fearing the old tower would collapse, the government had it completely rebuilt. The new lighthouse, built in 1883, was a near exact copy of the original, except that far better materials were used in its construction.

With its sixteen-sided Chance Brothers lens, the station displayed a beacon that could be seen for up to 25 nautical miles. The Macquarie Light also made early use of electric lighting; a coal-gas engine drove a pair of magnetos that produced electricity for the light.

Among the best known and loved lighthouses in Australia, the Macquarie light station remains in operation, its powerful light still guiding vessels into Sydney's bustling harbor. The structure itself

before the turn of the twentieth century. It features a conical tower attached to the station residences.

An earlier light station located on nearby Chapel Hill often created confusion for mariners, who mistook its double beacon for a single light. Just such a navigator's error led to tragedy in 1819, when the master of the French passenger vessel La Jeune misread the lights and crashed into the Lundy rocks, resulting in the loss of thirteen lives. ::

Macquarie Light

Location: Sydney, Australia
Established: 1818
Tower height: 79 feet
Elevation of focal plane: 344 feet
Optic: Fresnel lens (first-order)
Status: Active (automated in 1976)

The history of Macquarie Light is bound closely to that of the nation it serves. The first light on this strategic headland near Sydney was a wood- and coal-fired beacon maintained by convicts deported to Australia by British penal authorities. First displayed in 1793, the simple lantern light was replaced by a true lighthouse in 1818. Its sandstone tower was the work of convict architect

Macquarie Light
Courtesy Harbour Lights

and the city of Honolulu. The station's enormous lens completely fills the lantern and dominates the diminutive tower. Weighing several tons, it focuses a beacon that is visible for up to 28 miles. Although the tower is relatively modest in height, it is perched on a lava cliff, which boosts the beacon to a whopping elevation of 420 feet. ::

Still functional, a giant, hyper-radial lens all but fills the lantern at Oahu's Makapuu Point (above), but the much smaller third-order Fresnel that once brightened Marblehead (below) in Ohio has been replaced by a modern optic.

Bob and Sandra Shanklin

Marblehead Light

Location: Marblehead, Ohio
Established: 1821
Tower height: 65 feet
Elevation of focal plane: 67 feet
Optic: Modern
Status: Active (automated in 1958)

During the War of 1812, Commodore (then Lieutenant) Oliver Hazard Perry won a resounding victory over the British Great Lakes fleet in the open waters of Lake Erie a few miles north of Marblehead, Ohio. Following the battle, Perry sent ashore his famous message: "We have met the enemy, and they are ours." A few years after the battle, which helped the United States retain control of its Great Lakes

is considered a historic architectural marvel. A colorful bust of Queen Victoria greets visitors at the door. ::

Makapuu Point Light

Location: Oahu, Hawaii
Established: 1909
Tower height: 46 feet
Elevation of focal plane: 420 feet
Optic: Fresnel lens (hyper–radial)
Status: Active (automated in 1974)

With the most powerful Fresnel lens in the United States, Makapuu Point Light at the eastern tip of Oahu signals vessels approaching the island of Oahu

Marblehead Light

Bruce Roberts

territories, federal maritime authorities established a light station at Marblehead.

Now the oldest continuously operational lighthouse on the lake, Marblehead Light serves both as an active aid to navigation and a notable historic attraction. The original limestone tower remains in excellent condition, as does the wooden keeper's residence, built in 1880. The latter now houses a museum. Replaced by a modern optic some years ago, the station's old prismatic lens is now on display in a nearby Coast Guard station. The Marblehead beacon flashes green every six seconds and can be seen for about 11 miles. ::

The red walls of the Marquette Harbor Light are so eye-catching that the station may do a better job of guiding mariners during the day than at night.

Bruce Roberts

Marquette Harbor Light

Location: Marquette, Michigan
Established: 1866
Tower height: 40 feet
Elevation of focal plane: 77 feet
Optic: Aeromarine beacon
Status: Active

Painted bright red for easy visibility, the square brick tower and attached two-story keeper's dwelling that make up the Marquette Harbor Light have dominated the waterside entrance to Marquette, Michigan, since 1866. Coast Guard personnel still live in the keeper's house. The fourth-order Fresnel lens that once served here is now on display at the nearby Marquette Maritime Museum. ::

Matinicus Rock Light

Location: Penobscot Bay, Maine
Established: 1827
Tower height: 48 feet
Elevation of focal plane: 90 feet
Optic: Modern (solar-powered)
Status: Active (automated in 1988)

No lighthouse keepers faced weather more extreme, privations more taxing, or loneliness more profound than those who served at Matinicus Rock. But the historic station came to be known as much for the daring exploits of keeper's daughter Abbie Burgess as for its isolation.

In 1827 federal lighthouse authorities ordered construction of two wooden towers on Matinicus Rock. They displayed a double beacon, a characteristic that helped mariners distinguish this light station from others closer to shore. These early towers survived the fierce Atlantic weather for more than twenty years, but they were replaced by granite towers in 1848. The new towers stood 60 yards apart and, like their predecessors, displayed two lights that appeared close together when seen from a distance.

The storm-dashed Matinicus Rock Light in Maine is one of the most remote light stations in North America. Keepers and their families were often marooned on the rock for weeks by foul weather.
Shutterstock.com

Dissatisfied with the performance of the station—it had been equipped with inefficient lamp-and-reflector beacons—the Lighthouse Board ordered the towers torn down and rebuilt once again in 1857, this time to be outfitted with third-order Fresnel lenses. Constructed of massive, carefully shaped granite blocks, these structures proved a match for the heavy seas that sweep over Matinicus Rock during storms.

Although the south tower still stands, it was taken out of service in 1924 when the Lighthouse Service stopped using multiple beacons. Eventually its lantern was removed. The north tower remains in service, warning mariners with a flashing light visible for 20 miles. The tower's Fresnel lens has been replaced by a modern optic, and the original lens is on display at the Maine Lighthouse Museum in Rockland. ::

Mersey Bluff Light

Location: Tasmania, Australia
Established: 1889
Tower height: 120 feet
Elevation of focal plane: 45 feet
Optic: Fresnel lens
Status: Active (automated in 1920)

Shipwrecks were once common near the mouth of Tasmania's Mersey River, but Mersey Bluff Light all but eliminated them. The station displays both

Mersey Bluff Light

Courtesy *Lighthouse Digest*

dwelling. The lighthouse had not been in operation for long before maritime officials learned, to their dismay, that it had been built in the wrong place—in fact, on the wrong island altogether. The station was meant for a site farther south, on nearby Long Island. The Lighthouse Board decided that mariners could make good use of the station where it stood, and its beacon still shines today after more than 160 years of service.

The light remains in use, but the original structures were replaced in 1880, when Michigan Island station received a new and much taller tower, an iron-skeleton structure relocated here from Delaware. This whitewashed iron giant stands on six legs. A small entrance building provides access

white and red warning lights with a range of up to 17 miles. A pair of distinctive vertical red stripes makes this tower an excellent daymark as well.

Michigan Island Light

Location: Apostle Islands, Wisconsin
Established: 1857
Tower height: 118 feet
Elevation of focal plane: 170 feet
Optic: Modern
Status: Active (automated in 1943)

The oldest of six light stations in Wisconsin's Apostle Islands, Michigan Island Light was established not long after the Soo Locks opened Lake Superior to shipping from the other Great Lakes. The Michigan Island station originally consisted of a modest masonry tower and attached

Michigan Island Light

Bruce Roberts

to a stairway that spirals through an enclosed metal cylinder to the lantern room.

To the delight of travelers who flock to the Apostle Islands National Lakeshore during the summer, the 1857 tower and dwelling, although long abandoned, remain standing. The third-order Fresnel lens that focused the station's beacon for many years is now on display at a visitor center in Bayfield, Wisconsin. ⠒⠒

Minot's Ledge Light

Location: Near Cohasset, Massachusetts
Established: 1850
Tower height: 114 feet
Elevation of focal plane: 85 feet
Optic: Modern
Status: Active (automated in 1947)

A deadly obstacle lurking just below the surface near the southern rim of Boston Bay, Minot's Ledge had been destroying ships and lives for centuries before any serious attempt was made to mark it. In 1847 a young lighthouse inspector named I. W. P. Lewis proposed a bold plan to build a lighthouse directly over the ledge. Lewis believed that an open-walled, iron-skeleton structure could stand the stress of slaps from high waves generated by storms. The plan was adopted and the tower completed in 1850. Unfortunately, the following year an April gale proved Lewis to have been tragically mistaken. Unable to withstand the constant pounding by the gale's towering waves, the tower collapsed, dragging two assistant keepers to their deaths.

During the 1850s Minot's Ledge was carefully guarded by a lightship while plans for a new lighthouse were drawn up by Lighthouse Board engineers. In 1855 work began on a second tower, this time a stone edifice rather than a metal one. Completed in 1860, the tower consisted of massive granite blocks shaped and assembled in a way that made the structure all but impervious to storms. Although the lighthouse cost the government

Minot's Ledge Light
Bruce Roberts

$330,000, a titanic sum in the 1850s, the money was well spent. The strategy of building the open-water tower with stone proved so successful that the lighthouse still stands after more than 150 years of battering by waves. Although the station's Fresnel lens has been replaced by a modern optic, the beacon retains its familiar one-four-three flashing characteristic that long ago caused romantics to call it the I-LOVE-YOU light. Its light can be seen for about 15 miles.

The second-order lens that once graced the Minot's Ledge tower is now housed in a replica of the lantern room on nearby Government Island. The replica was built with granite blocks removed from the lighthouse during a 1987 renovation. Visitors can also see the station's old fog bell. ⠒⠒

Montauk Point Light

Location: Montauk, New York
Established: 1796
Tower height: 110 feet
Elevation of focal plane: 168 feet
Optic: Aeromarine beacon
Status: Active (automated in 1987)

Now in its third century of service to mariners, Montauk Point Light and its flashing white beacon mark the far end of Long Island, warning vessels away from a beach where stranded ships have been known to "melt away like butter."

During the late nineteenth and early twentieth centuries, the Montauk light (below) welcomed countless immigrants to America—its light was often the first sight they saw of their new homeland as they approached the coast of New York.

With its 6-foot-thick walls and solid 13-foot-deep foundation, Montauk Point Light's tower is not particularly vulnerable to high winds or storms, but erosion poses a significant threat. The tower stands on a high, sandy bank, carefully terraced and planted in a thick carpet of grass to keep it from crumbling away. Now owned and maintained by the Montauk Point Historical Society, the large, two-story keeper's residence now houses a fine museum featuring an excellent display of lighthouse optics, including the third-order clamshell Fresnel lens that focused the Montauk Point beacon from 1904 to 1987. The aeromarine optic now in the tower produces a powerful light visible for up to 19 nautical miles. In 2012, the lighthouse was designated a National Historic Landmark. **::**

Morris Island Light

Location: Charleston, South Carolina
Established: 1767
Tower height: 161 feet
Elevation of focal plane: 158 feet
Optic: Fresnel lens (removed)
Status: Deactivated in 1962

Settled in the seventeenth century, in part by French Huguenots, the city of Charleston, South Carolina, became home to one of the first navigational lights in North America. As early as 1673, some say, residents lit pitch fires at night near the mouth of the harbor to aid navigation. In 1767 the colony of South Carolina built an octagonal brick light tower on Morris Island, near the entrance to the city's harbor. It was among the colonial lighthouses turned over to the federal government in the 1790s, and in 1800 a $5,000 congressional appropriation funded renovation of the 102-foot tower. Beginning in 1858, a first-order Fresnel lens focused the station's flashing light.

At the beginning of the Civil War, Confederate authorities in Charleston seized the federally owned Morris Island lighthouse, along

Bruce Roberts

Morris Island • South Carolina

The Montauk Point Light (opposite page) and the old Morris Tower (left) towers are monuments to US maritime history. Both have stood up to more than two centuries of storm winds and decay.

Courtesy Harbour Lights

with several lighthouse tenders, the Rattlesnake Shoal lightship, and a substantial quantity of lighthouse-related supplies and equipment. The lighthouse inspector in Charleston reported to his superiors in Washington that the Governor of South Carolina had "requested" he leave the state. The light at Morris Island soon went dark and remained that way until after the war.

Severely damaged during the war, the lighthouse was rebuilt and relit in 1876 at a cost of nearly $150,000. The new, 150-foot brick tower stood atop a concrete foundation supported by piles driven some 50 feet into the mud. The structure survived an 1886 earthquake that destroyed much of the city and stood up to decades of hurricanes, cyclones, and the permanent flooding of Morris Island.

Morris Island Light also survived decades of near total neglect following its deactivation by the Coast Guard in 1962. But by the late twentieth century, its fate hung in the balance as preservationists fought desperately to reclaim the station from the destructive power of weather and erosion. A private group called Save the Lighthouse, Inc. launched a fund-raising drive to rescue it, and this effort appears to have succeeded. A concrete barrier has halted the erosion, and the old tower appears stable for the moment. Friends of the lighthouse emphasize its historic importance by pointing to the copper plate on the tower cornerstone. It reads: "Laid on the 30th of May 1767 in the seventh year of his majesty's reign, George III." **::**

Mount Desert Rock Light

Location: Near Mount Desert Island, Maine
Established: 1830
Tower height: 58 feet
Elevation of focal plane: 75 feet
Optic: Modern (solar-powered)
Status: Active (automated in 1977)

Since the late 1970s students and faculty from Maine's College of the Atlantic have used Mount Desert Rock as a whale-watching station. The college picked a good spot for the station, which is located in an environment more conducive to the survival of whales than of people. Located about 20 miles offshore near the entrance to Frenchmans Bay, Mount Desert Rock is a barren ocean ledge little more than 600 yards long and rising only 20 feet above high water. Constantly battered by waves and swept by storms, it offers precious little shelter to either plants or people. Even so, this inhospitable place served as home for lighthouse keepers and their families for almost 150 years.

To warn ships away from Mount Desert Rock, the US government established a light station here in 1830. It consisted of a small two-story wooden cottage with a lantern on its roof. The station's beacon, produced by an inefficient lamp-and-reflector system, proved so ineffective that navigators on nearby ships often could not see it at all. In response to complaints by mariners, the Lighthouse Board upgraded the station in 1857, giving it a third-order Fresnel lens and a sturdy granite tower tall enough to raise the focal plane of the light 75 feet above the Atlantic waves. From this height the beacon could be seen from as far as 20 miles away.

These improvements made local navigation much safer but did little to make life more comfortable for those assigned to keep the light. Keeper families often remained for months, if not years, on the Mount Desert Rock, where existence was hard and lonely. The rock supported little plant life, so friendly springtime visitors often brought baskets of soil so the keeper could create miniature gardens in the cracks and crevasses between the island boulders.

A notable wreck took place in 1902, when the ocean tug *Astral* slammed into the rock. Blinded by a fierce winter storm, the master of the tug had not seen the light. Fighting through high

The old photograph (below) taken on Mount Desert Rock off the coast of Maine shows the station's keeper, assistants, and their families standing beside the tower and residence. Dressed in their Sunday best, the island residents may have used the opportunity to wash some of their work clothes—notice the laundry hung on the right.
National Archives

waves and freezing spray, the Mount Desert Rock keeper and his wife managed to save all but one of the crew.

The last keepers left Mount Desert Rock in 1977 when the light was automated. In 1998 the structure was transferred to the College of the Atlantic for use as a research station for studying whales. The light remains active, however, flashing a white signal every fifteen seconds. ::

Needles Light

Location: Near the of Isle of Wight, England

Established: 1786

Tower height: 100 feet

Elevation of focal plane: 85 feet

Optic: Modern

Status: Active (automated in 1994)

Ships approaching the Isle of Wight from the west pass a line of prickly rocks—the Needles—rising from the sea just below a soaring cliff of chalk. If the dominant cliffs catch the navigator's eye rather than the rocks—and this can easily happen in moonlight—the result could be calamitous. Trinity House built a lighthouse here in 1786, but since it was located on top of the cliffs, it was of little use to mariners who hoped to avoid the ship-killing rocks far below. Making matters worse, low-lying clouds and fog frequently obscured the light.

Decades passed and more than a few ships were lost on the Needles before Trinity House acted to improve the situation. In 1859 noted Trinity House engineer James Walker designed a new Needles lighthouse. Built at a cost of £20,000, its cylindrical granite tower rose from the far, seaward end of the Needles, a position that allowed it to guide vessels safely around the hazard. The last full-time keepers left the station in 1994, but its red, green, and white light signals continue to warn mariners. ::

Antique image of keepers' dwellings, near the Needles Light in Great Britain.

New London Harbor Light

Location: New London, Connecticut

Established: 1760

Tower height: 89 feet

Elevation of focal plane: 90 feet

Optic: Fresnel lens (fourth-order)

Status: Active (automated in 1912)

In 1760 funds raised by means of a public lottery paid for construction of a 62-foot navigational tower of hammer-dressed stone near the mouth of Connecticut's Thames River. At that time, only three other lighthouses (Boston Harbor Light, Brant Point Light in Massachusetts, and Beavertail Light in Rhode Island) existed in what would later become the United States. Fitted with oil lamps, the New London tower guided vessels in and out of the city's harbor for forty years.

Eventually, the tower became federal property, and when broad cracks appeared in its masonry, Congress appropriated $15,700 for a replacement. The new lighthouse, completed in 1800, consisted of an 89-foot-high octagonal stone tower with an adjacent keeper's dwelling and an oil storage vault.

New London Harbor Light
Bruce Roberts

An 1838 government report described the station as "of great importance as a leading light for vessels going in and out of the harbor of New London, which, on account of its position and security, is much resorted to during the heavy gales of winter."

In 1857 a fourth-order Fresnel lens took the place of the station's old-fashioned lamp-and-reflector system. This lens remains in the tower, guiding vessels with an alternating beacon that shines six seconds of white light followed by six seconds of darkness. ::

Nobska Point Light

Location: Woods Hole, Massachusetts
Established: 1829
Tower height: 40 feet
Elevation of focal plane: 87 feet
Optic: Fresnel (fourth-order)
Status: Active (automated in 1958)

For nearly a half century, a simple stone cottage with a rooftop lantern marked Nobska Point near the well-known Cape Cod village of Woods Hole. In 1876 a much sturdier and far more up-to-date steel cylinder tower took the place of the original light station. The tower still serves ships, ferries, and fishing boats plying the broad channel separating the cape from Martha's Vineyard. The tower's original fourth-order Fresnel lens still focuses the station's red and white beacon. ::

Nobska Point Light
Bruce Roberts

North Point Light

Location: Milwaukee, Wisconsin
Established: 1855
Tower height: 74 feet
Elevation of focal plane: 154 feet
Optic: Fresnal lens (removed)
Status: Decomissioned

Milwaukee's unusual North Point tower consists of two separate structures set one on top of the other. The first, an octagonal, cast-iron tower of relatively modest height, was built in 1888 to replace an earlier lighthouse that had been undercut by erosion. About twenty-five years later, the US Bureau of Lighthouses decided to increase the height of the tower in order to raise its beacon above the

spreading limbs of trees along the waterfront. This was done by setting the old tower on top of a newly constructed octagonal base.

Decomissioned in 1994, the lighthouse is now part of a Milwaukee City Park. A local preservation group has restored the old 1855 keeper's residence and turned it into exhibit space for maritime artifacts, including the fourth-order Fresnel lens that served here for many years. ::

More than a few light towers are octagonal. See, for instance, the eighteenth-century New London Harbor Light (opposite page upper) and nineteenth-century North Point Light (above). However, most are cylindrical like the cast-iron Nobska Point tower (opposite page right) and the stone Nottawasaga Island tower (below).

Bob and Sandra Shanklin

Nottawasaga Island Light

Location: Near Clearwater, Ontario
Established: 1858
Tower height: 84 feet
Elevation of focal plane: 90 feet
Optic: Fresnel lens (second-order)
Status: Active (automated in 1960)

Mariners braving the waters of Canada's Georgian Bay must take care to avoid the small but hazardous Nottawasaga Island, which is so low-lying that it is barely visible even from a short distance. To help mariners avoid it, maritime authorities established a substantial light station here in 1858. Like several other impressive "imperial towers" built at about that time in the Great Lakes region of Canada, Nottawasaga Island Light still stands and remains in use.

Bruce Roberts

The massive limestone tower places its second-order beacon nearly 90 feet above the lake's aquamarine waters, enabling it to warn mariners at considerable distances. While ships must keep well away, birds have no reason to avoid the island, and egrets, herons, and cormorants flock here in great numbers. The island is now a bird sanctuary. ::

Old Point Comfort Light
Bruce Roberts

Owls Head Light
Courtesy *Lighthouse Digest*

Old Point Comfort Light

Location: Fort Monroe, Virginia

Established: 1802

Tower height: 58 feet

Elevation of focal plane: 54 feet

Optic: Fresnel lens (fourth-order)

Status: Active

One of the oldest and most historic light stations on the Chesapeake Bay or, for that matter, in the entire United States, Old Point Comfort Light was built in 1802 during the presidential administration of Thomas Jefferson. In the War of 1812, British troops overwhelmed Fort Monroe and used the lighthouse as a watchtower. Several Civil War engagements were fought within sight of the tower, including the 1862 slugfest between the ironclad warships *Virginia* and *Monitor*. Not far from the lighthouse is the cell where federal authorities imprisoned Confederate President Jefferson Davis. Still located on an active military base, the octagonal sandstone tower continues to guide shipping. Its 150-year-old Fresnel lens flashes a red and white light at twelve-second intervals. ::

Owls Head Light

Location: Near Rockland, Maine

Established: 1825

Tower height: 25 feet

Elevation of focal plane: 100 feet

Optic: Fresnel lens (fourth-order)

Status: Active (automated in 1989)

Waves and weather have sculpted the cliffs at Owls Head into fantastic shapes, including one prominent rock formation said to look something like an owl. More likely to catch the eye, however, are the bright white walls of Owls Head Light, which has marked this promontory and pointed the way to Rockland Harbor since 1825. Although the squat, cylindrical tower stands only 25 feet tall, the elevation of the site raises the light's focal plane to the serviceable height of approximately 100 feet. The station's fourth-order Fresnel lens focuses a beacon visible from many miles out to sea.

Many delightful stories circulate about Owls Head and its lighthouse. According to one often repeated legend—which has some basis in fact—a pair of young lovers ran their boat aground here during an early twentieth-century blizzard. According to the tale, by the time rescuers arrived, the two were locked into a rigid embrace by a solid block of ice. They were thawed out and were later married in a nearby church. Another story recalls a foggy evening when the Owls Head keeper's dog saved a ship by warning it away from the rocks with its loud barking. It's also said the keeper trained the dog to pull on the fog bell rope whenever a vessel approached. ∷

Peggy's Cove Light

Location: Peggy's Cove, Nova Scotia
Established: 1868
Tower height: 37 feet
Elevation of focal plane: 50 feet
Optic: Modern
Status: Active (automated in 1972)

The picturesque fishing village of Peggy's Cove, Nova Scotia, has only about fifty year-round residents, but during the summer, its population swells with tourists. Many come just to see and photograph the lovely little lighthouse that marks the local harbor and is counted by some among the most beautiful structures in North America. Although its size is not impressive compared to that of Canada's soaring imperial towers on the Great

Nineteenth-century navigational towers at Old Point Comfort (opposite page upper) in Virginia, Owls Head (opposite page lower) in Maine, and Peggy's Cove (left) in Nova Scotia bring history as well as light into focus. During the summer tourist season, the Peggy's Cove Lighthouse doubles as a post office.
Courtesy *Lighthouse Digest*

Lakes, Peggy's Cove lighthouse can claim a setting second to none. Rising from a rugged, granite outcropping, and capped by a red iron lantern, the octagonal, white tower is framed by seemingly endless expanses of ocean and sky. The station has another distinction—it doubles as a post office. Since 1972 visitors have been able to mail cards from a desk on the lower level. **::**

Pemaquid Point Light

Location: Damariscotta/Pemaquid Point, Maine
Established: 1827
Tower height: 38 feet
Elevation of focal plane: 79 feet
Optic: Fresnel lens (fourth-order)
Status: Active (automated in 1934)

The fantastical, wave-like rock formations along the shore of Pemaquid Point represent an alarming threat to vessels moving through the waters off Damariscotta. Pemaquid Point Light has been

warning mariners to keep their distance since 1827. Although two earlier towers succumbed to Maine's harsh weather, the station's third tower, built in 1857, still stands. A conical, white rubblestone structure with a black iron lantern, the tower contains its original fourth-order Fresnel lens. The station's wood-frame keeper's residence, also built in 1857, now houses a museum celebrating the local lobster and fishing industries. **::**

Pensacola Light

Location: Pensacola, Florida
Established: 1824
Tower height: 150 feet
Elevation of focal plane: 191 feet
Optic: Fresnel lens (first-order)
Status: Active (automated in 1965)

Pensacola Light (above)
Bruce Roberts

Pemaquid Point Light (left)
Bruce Roberts

The Petit Manan Lighthouse (above) near Machias, Maine, lost its old Fresnel lens in 1972, but the Pemaquid Point Light (opposite page left) still makes use of its century-old optic. So does the soaring tower (opposite page right) at Pensacola, where Fresnel technology originally developed to guide wooden ships now helps ultramodern US warships find their way to harbor.

Bob and Sandra Shanklin

Pensacola has served as a key base for the US Navy for the better part of two centuries. To guide warships in and out of Pensacola's well-protected anchorage, the government established a light station in 1824, just three years after the United States acquired Florida from the Spanish. A 45-foot tower built by Winslow Lewis for $5,725 served the station less than adequately, according to naval officers who often watched in vain for its weak beacon.

The situation improved dramatically after 1858, when the existing brick tower was constructed. Equipped with a powerful first-order Fresnel lens, the new tower had a focal point more than 190 feet above the waters of the Gulf of Mexico, making the light visible in fair weather at distances up to 25 miles. Having survived countless gales as well as a determined Union cannonade during the Civil War, the historic tower remains active and still uses its nineteenth-century lens. ::

Petit Manan Light

Location: Near Milbridge, Maine
Established: 1817
Tower height: 119 feet
Elevation of focal plane: 123 feet
Optic: Modern
Status: Active (automated in 1972)

The deadly rocks off Petit Manan Island have threatened mariners for centuries. Schooners and other vessels that kept close to the coast were especially vulnerable, for they had to make sudden course changes to avoid crushing their hulls on the shoals. More than a few shipmasters failed to recognize the danger in time and met with disaster. A stone lighthouse built in 1817 did little to assist mariners. The tower was too short and its lamp-and-reflector beacon far too weak to provide mariners with adequate warning.

In the 1850s, the Lighthouse Board sought to improve the situation and ordered construction of a granite tower able to place the focal plane of its light more than 120 feet above the seas around Petit Manan. Equipped with a second-order Fresnel lens, the new lighthouse produced a flashing light that could be seen over a distance of up to 25 nautical miles. The Coast Guard automated the station in 1972, replacing the Fresnel lens with a modern optic of similar strength. The light flashes white once every ten seconds. ::

Pigeon Point Light

Location: Pescadero, California
Established: 1872
Tower height: 115 feet
Elevation of focal plane: 160 feet
Optic: Aeromarine beacon
Status: Active (automated in 1974)

Pigeon Point takes its name from the Yankee clipper *Pigeon*, which wrecked here in 1853. Had Pigeon Point Light been in operation at that time, the hapless vessel might have survived. The station's flashing beacon became active about twenty years after the *Pigeon*'s demise, and since that time has helped countless other ships avoid the dangerous rocks that litter these shores.

Many lighthouses on the West Coast depend on the terrain to provide most of their elevation, but not this one. Pigeon Point station's brick tower soars 115 feet, enough to place the focal plane of its beacon 160 feet over the Pacific. In fair weather, the flashing light reaches mariners more than 17 miles away. Motorists driving along California Highway 1 watch for it and can see it long before they reach Pigeon Point. Although the light is produced by a modern optic, the station's old Fresnel lens remains in place and is lit up once a year for historical reasons. ::

Bruce Roberts

The light station at Pigeon Point (opposite page) dates to the 1870s. That may seem quite old, but by lighthouse standards it's only about average. The Plymouth (Gurnet) Light (left) in Massachusetts has guided mariners since 1769.

Courtesy *Lighthouse Digest*

Plymouth (Gurnet) Light

Location: Plymouth, Massachusetts

Established: 1769

Tower height: 34 feet

Elevation of focal plane: 102 feet

Optic: Modern (solar-powered)

Status: Active (automated in 1986)

When the Pilgrims arrived at Plymouth in 1620, they had to sail around a long sandy peninsula, which they called the Gurnet, after a fish often caught along the coast of their native England. More than a century later, the Massachusetts legislature chose the Gurnet as the site for one of North America's first lighthouses. Built in 1769 at a cost of £660, the original Gurnet Lighthouse was thirty feet long and twenty feet high, with a lantern at each end. Its display of two lights made it easy to distinguish this peninsula beacon from other lights along the Massachusetts coast.

The station stood on land owned by John Thomas, and he agreed to tend the light in exchange for a salary of £200 a year. When Thomas died in 1776, his wife, Hannah, took over the task, becoming America's first female lighthouse keeper. In 1790 Hannah Thomas passed the job along to her son John, who kept the light until 1812.

Struck by British cannon fire during the Revolutionary War, the lighthouse was repaired and remained in use until 1801, when it was destroyed by fire. The structure was rebuilt later that year and again in 1842, when a pair of octagonal towers were completed. In 1924 the US Bureau of Lighthouses converted all multiple-light stations to single lights, and one of the Plymouth towers was dismantled. The other remains in service; its modern flashing beacon is visible for about 16 miles. **::**

Point Arena Light

Location: Point Arena, California

Established: 1870

Tower height: 115 feet

Elevation of focal plane: 155 feet

Optic: Aeromarine beacon

Status: Active (automated in 1977)

One of California's notorious geological faults cuts through the rocks beneath Point Arena. The plates on either side of the fault slipped in 1906, generating an earthquake so powerful that it leveled much of San Francisco about a hundred miles to the south. The massive quake also destroyed the brick-and-mortar lighthouse that had marked Point

Point Arena Light

Arena since 1870. Shattered remains of the station's first-order Fresnel lens littered the tower ruins.

Within two years, government crews built a new tower, using reinforced concrete to help it withstand future temblors. The replacement Fresnel lens installed at that time remains in the tower but is no longer in service. Since 1977 an automated aeromarine beacon has been used to warn mariners away from Point Arena's jagged rocks. A museum in the station's fog-signal building holds exhibits of lighthouse equipment, photographs, art, and local wildlife. ::

Point Bonita Light

Location: San Francisco, California
Established: 1855
Tower height: 33 feet
Elevation of focal plane: 140 feet
Optic: Fresnel lens (second-order)
Status: Active (automated in 1980)

In 1854 a clipper ship—ironically named the *San Francisco*—struck rocks and sank off Point Bonita, just west of the Golden Gate Strait. This wreck and similar calamities sparked a public outcry and demands for a light station to warn mariners and mark the entrance to the strait. In the spring of 1855, government contractors completed a 56-foot brick tower and adjacent Cape Cod–style residence at Point Bonita.

Perched on a cliff more than 300 feet above the waves, this station produced a beacon visible for dozens of miles out in the Pacific—but only in fair weather. When low clouds and fog cloaked the coast, as they often do, the light was all but invisible out at sea. In the 1870s maritime officials sought to solve this problem by ordering construction of a new Point Bonita tower at a lower elevation. Ready for service in 1877, the hexagonal tower stood on a narrow ledge far down the cliff face.

Part of the ledge collapsed during the 1940s, leaving a yawning gap between the tower and the mainland. To provide access, the Coast Guard built a suspension bridge, which imaginative visitors may choose to see as a miniature version of the nearby Golden Gate Bridge. Together with their spectacular setting, the old tower and its remarkable bridge comprise one of the world's most beautiful light stations. ::

Point Clark Light

Location: Near Goderich, Ontario

Established: 1859

Tower height: 87 feet

Elevation of focal plane: 93 feet

Optic: Modern

Status: Active

Clinging to a cliff high above the Pacific, California's Point Bonita seems poised on the edge of destruction.

Point Clark Light
Bruce Roberts

Several massive limestone light towers were built in the Lake Huron and Georgian Bay region of Canada during the 1850s. Funded by the British Board of Trade, these magnificent structures are often referred to as "imperial towers." Many believe the finest of the imperials is the one at Point Clark, near Goderich, Ontario. Like several other such towers, it was built by contractor John Brown. Although it remains an active aid to navigation, the station also serves as a museum and historical attraction. ::

Point Iroquois Light

Location: Brimley, Michigan

Established: 1855

Tower height: 65 feet

Elevation of focal plane: 68 feet

Optic: Fresnel lens (removed)

Status: Deactivated in 1971

Point Iroquois Light
Bruce Roberts

Point Iroquois has a dark and bloody history. In 1862 a large Iroquois war party was ambushed and slaughtered here. However, the point subsequently earned a bright reputation as the site of a life-saving lighthouse that guided countless ships and sailors to safe harbor. Point Iroquois Light was once among the most important beacons on the lake, pointing the way to the Soo Locks at Sault Ste. Marie. Although Point Iroquois Light was deactivated in 1971, it is now part of the Hiawatha National Forest, and the beautifully restored brick tower and keeper's residence are home to a popular maritime museum. The station's original fourth-order Fresnel lens has been removed and is now on display in Washington DC at the Smithsonian Museum of Science and Technology. ::

Point Loma Light

Location: San Diego, California
Established: 1855
Tower height: 46 feet
Elevation of focal plane: 462 feet
Optic: Fresnel lens (third-order)
Status: Deactivated 1891

A legend holds that Point Loma was named for a beautiful Russian girl who survived a shipwreck on the southern California coast, only to be murdered by a local man whose attentions she had spurned. More likely the name derived from the Portuguese word for "light." Indeed, some claim the Spanish built fire beacons on the lofty point to guide their ships home from the open Pacific.

In the 1850s the Lighthouse Board sent contractor Francis Gibbons here to build the point's first official lighthouse, a small, Cape Cod–style residence with a tower rising through its roof. The design allowed the keeper to live, work, and store necessary materials all in the same building—a practical if not particularly comfortable arrangement.

Less practical was the station's 460-foot elevation, which situated the beacon above the fog banks that typically hug the coast. The tower's high light was all but invisible to mariners caught in the midst of low, thick fogs. In 1891 the original lighthouse was abandoned in favor of a steel-skeleton tower located at the foot of the cliffs. A central cylinder encloses a stairway leading to the lantern, where a third-order Fresnel lens continues to focus its light after more than a century. The older tower still stands, as well, and serves as a museum and attraction of Cabrillo National Monument. ::

A new skeleton-style tower (left) was built at Point Loma in 1891, but the original 1855 lighthouse (below) still stands.

Photos by Bruce Roberts

Point Pinos Light

Location: Pacific Grove, California

Established: 1855

Tower height: 43 feet

Elevation of focal plane: 89 feet

Optic: Fresnel lens (third-order)

Status: Active (automated in 1975)

Nearly 40 miles wide and extraordinarily deep, Monterey Bay forms a substantial dent in the central California coast. At Point Pinos, on the bay's southern lip, stands the state's oldest operating lighthouse. A Cape Cod–style residence with a central tower, the structure is typical of West Coast lighthouses built during the 1850s, many of them by contractor Francis Gibbons.

Now surrounded by a breathtakingly scenic municipal golf course, Point Pinos Light remains in operation but doubles as a museum operated by a local historical society. The station's historical interest is considerable. In the past it attracted frequent visits from notables such as John Steinbeck and Robert Louis Stevenson. Like Santa Barbara Light far to the south, the Point Pinos beacon was tended for many years by a determined woman. Emily Fish took the Point Pinos job after her socially connected San Francisco husband died, leaving her penniless. It is said Fish lived and entertained in fine style at the lighthouse. ::

Bruce Roberts

The historic Point Pinos Light (upper) is a familiar sight to residents and tourists on the Monterey Peninsula, a popular California resort area. On the other hand, the Point Retreat Light (lower) in Alaska is likely to be seen only by passengers on passing cruise ships and ferries or determined lighthouse buffs who charter boats in nearby Juneau. The Point Reyes Light (opposite page) north of San Francisco now helps attract visitors to a wild and scenic national seashore.

Bob and Sandra Shanklin

Point Retreat Light

Location: West of Juneau, Alaska

Established: 1904

Tower height: 25 feet

Elevation of focal plane: 63 feet

Optic: Modern (solar-powered)

Status: Active (automated in 1973)

Point Retreat Light is one of Alaska's most important sentinels. It marks the convergence of several key shipping channels that link Juneau with other cities in the Alaska panhandle. Ferries and freighters moving along the Inside Passage toward Alaska's capital city must round the north end of Admiralty Island, and the Point Retreat beacon sees them safely on their way. However, while the light itself remains essential to navigation, the station structures do not. After the light was automated in 1973, the Coast Guard had little use for the keeper's residence and other buildings here, and they were allowed to deteriorate. The Alaska Lighthouse Association in Juneau is now restoring the station for use as a maritime museum. ::

Point Reyes Light

Location: Point Reyes, California
Established: 1870
Tower height: 35 feet
Elevation of focal plane: 294 feet
Optic: Fresnel lens (first-order)
Status: Deactivated in 1975

The Point Reyes Light tower is only 35 feet tall, but during its active years, mariners considered it a little giant. Like many other West Coast light stations, this one got a substantial boost from its lofty site. Built atop a high ledge, the squat, cast-iron tower placed the focal plane of its first-order light nearly 300 feet above the Pacific. The extra elevation enabled it to reach vessels while they were still 20 miles or more from the coast. Mariners certainly welcomed the warning, since rocky Point Reyes had a reputation—one it has retained to this day—for smashing the hulls of ships. The clipper *Sea Nymph* and at least a half dozen other large vessels were lost here during the 1860s alone.

Keepers considered Point Reyes a dismal duty station. Most of the time station crews at the isolated site had only pelicans and seagulls for company. Fog shrouded the point for weeks at a stretch, and the constant droning of the station's foghorn could drive anyone to distraction. To tend the light, the keeper had to climb down a staircase of several hundred steps and then back up again, usually several times a night. In stormy weather gale-force winds howled across the cliff face, and the climb to the light was most safely made on hands and knees.

The Point Reyes station was deactivated in 1975 and replaced by an automated beacon in a separate structure, probably to the considerable relief of the Coast Guard crewmen assigned there at the time. The old lighthouse now serves as a tourist attraction of the Point Reyes National Seashore. The station's enormous first-order Fresnel lens with its sixteen bull's-eyes remains in the tower and is a big hit among visitors. ::

Bruce Roberts

Seen from the landward side, the Point Sur Light calls not just to mariners but also to motorists on California's remarkably scenic Big Sur Highway. In 1935 keepers here witnessed a bizarre tragedy when the giant helium dirigible *Macon* was ripped open by a storm, crashed into the Pacific, and sank just a few miles from Point Sur.

Bruce Roberts

Point Sur Light

Location: Near Big Sur, California

Established: 1889

Tower height: 48 feet

Elevation of focal plane: 273 feet

Optic: Aeromarine beacon

Status: Active (automated in 1972)

Since 1889 Point Sur Light has shone seaward from the brow of an enormous sandstone hump, which would be an island were it not for a narrow peninsula of sand. It took two years of backbreaking labor, construction of a special railroad, and more than $100,000 to build the station, but the effort was worthwhile. The waters off Big Sur rank among the most dangerous on the planet, but vessels approaching this coast from the north or the open ocean are now warned well in advance of the danger.

The station consists of a granite tower, an attached keeper's dwelling, and a number of support buildings all placed near the summit of the point. For many years a first-order Fresnel lens focused this important light, but in 1976 it was replaced by a rotating aeromarine beacon. The original classic prismatic lens is now on display at the Museum of Monterey, about 20 miles north of the lighthouse. ::

Point Vicente Light

Location: Los Angeles, California

Established: 1926

Tower height: 67 feet

Elevation of focal plane: 185 feet

Optic: Fresnel lens (third-order)

Status: Active (automated in 1973)

If Hollywood set designers were to build a lighthouse, it might very well look like this one. As

Only a couple of dozen miles from Hollywood, the gorgeous Point Vicente Lighthouse has turned up in more than its share of films.

Bruce Roberts

a matter of fact, more than a few film crews have used Point Vicente Light, with its graceful palms and clean white tower, as a backdrop for romantic movie scenes. The crosshatched windows of the lantern room lend a touch of the exotic, as does the station's ghostly reputation. A lady phantom is said to walk the grounds on foggy nights. The Point Vicente beacon is all business, however. Vessels moving along the coast south of Los Angeles rely on it to keep them at a safe distance from the Palos Verdes cliffs. ::

Point Wilson Light

Bruce Roberts

Point Wilson Light

Location: Near Port Townsend, Washington

Established: 1879

Tower height: 48 feet

Elevation of focal plane: 51 feet

Optic: Fresnel lens (fourth-order)

Status: Active (automated in 1979)

A bewildering maze of inlets and channels links the interior of Washington State with the Strait of Juan de Fuca and the Pacific Ocean. Point Wilson Light is one of several key navigational markers that guide vessels through these often narrow passages. Located near Port Townsend on the eastern side of the Olympic Peninsula, it marks the entrance to Washington's heavily trafficked Puget Sound.

Lighthouses in the Movies

Lighthouses have played starring roles or, at least, made cameo appearances in quite a number of Hollywood hits. The Gay Head Lighthouse on Martha's Vineyard showed up in the 1975 blockbuster *Jaws,* while more recently, Maine's Portland Head Light got a bit part in the critically acclaimed *Snow Falling on Cedars.* In 1992 a pair of California lighthouses got into the movies—Point Arena alongside Mel Gibson in *Forever Young* and Pigeon Point Light in the Richard Gere and Kim Basinger psychological thriller *Final Analysis.*

The year 1980 was big for lighthouse movies. *The Fog,* filmed appropriately enough at perpetually foggy Point Reyes Light northwest of San Francisco, told the story of the victims of a terrible century-old crime who emerged from the sea to exact ghastly retribution on the little seaside town where it had all happened. A bit less grisly was the 1980 film *Somewhere in Time,* with Christopher Reeve and Jane Seymour, which offered moviegoers a romantic view of Michigan's Round Island Light. The movie generated considerable interest in the decaying lighthouse, and it was eventually restored—in part with funds contributed by those who had seen the movie.

Lighthouses continue to play key roles in movies and, no doubt, will do so well into the future. Some recent additions to the lighthouse movie genre include the slapstick *Meet the Parents* (2000) with Robert DeNiro and Ben Stiller; the mysterious *Half Light* (2005) with Demi Moore; *The Light House* (2006), a nightmarish Canadian offering; and the rather dreamy *Lightkeepers* (2009) with Richard Dreyfuss and Blythe Danner.

Michigan's Round Island Lighthouse played an important role in the 1980s movie romance *Somewhere in Time.*
Bruce Roberts

Originally the lantern rested on the roof of the keeper's residence, but in 1914 a tower to house the light was built a short distance from the original structure.

In recent years, the Point Wilson tower and other nearby historic structures have been severely threatened by shore erosion. Engineers have concluded that the only way to save the lighthouse will be to move it to a safer location away from the crumbling cliffs. Once the move is complete, the lighthouse will become an attraction of Washington's Fort Worden State Park. ::

Point Aux Barques Light

Bruce Roberts

Pointe Aux Barques Light

Location: Port Austin, Michigan

Established: 1848

Tower height: 89 feet

Elevation of focal plane: 93 feet

Optic: Aeromarine beacon

Status: Active (automated in 1957)

Still in operation after more than one and a half centuries, the historic Pointe Aux Barques sentinel (top right) marks the southern approach to Saginaw Bay. The canoes of fur traders once gathered here in considerable numbers, prompting the French to give the place its name, which means "place of little boats." The existing conical brick tower dates to 1857; it replaced an earlier lighthouse considered inadequate by sailors who depended on it for guidance. A pair of museums now make their home here. One celebrates the lighthouse and its history, while the other is devoted to an underwater preserve. ::

Pointe Saint-Martin Light

Location: Biarritz, France

Established: 1834

Tower height: 154 feet

Elevation of focal plane: 240 feet

Optic: Fresnel lens

Status: Active (automated in 1980)

Pointe Saint-Martin Light

Henry Gonzales

The soaring red-brick Ponce de Leon tower is a beacon not just for ships, but also for tourists and historians. This fully restored light station houses one of the finest lighthouse museums in America.

Bruce Roberts

The simple elegance of its design combined with a gracious setting make this one of the most beautiful lighthouses in the world. The lofty, white conical tower (preceding page) marks the harbor of Biarritz on the coast near the border of France and Spain. Its beacon guides mariners through the Bay of Biscay and is visible from an impressive distance of up to 26 nautical miles, the light signal flashing twice every ten seconds. ::

Ponce de Leon Inlet Light

Location: Ponce Inlet, Florida
Established: 1887
Tower height: 175 feet
Elevation of focal plane: 164 feet
Optic: Fresnel lens (third-order)
Status: Active (automated in 1955)

An attempt in the 1830s to establish a light station at Ponce de Leon Inlet—then known as Mosquito Inlet—south of Cape Canaveral proved ill-fated. Having submitted a rock-bottom bid of $7,494 for the project, Winslow Lewis built a 45-foot brick tower in 1835 and fitted it with a lamp-and-reflector optic of his own design. Apparently, the quality of the structure matched its price, for the lighthouse did not weather a storm that struck the area only weeks after it was completed. Before repairs could be undertaken, a war party of Seminoles attacked the tower, doing so much additional damage that the station was abandoned.

More than a half century passed before the government tried once again to mark the inlet. This time the attempt was successful, and by 1887 a first-order light beamed seaward from atop the station's 175-foot brick tower. A 12-foot-thick concrete foundation more than 40 feet wide supports the tower's considerable mass. Such solid construction has enabled this structure to withstand countless storms as well as a mighty earthquake that shook the southeastern coast of the United States in 1886.

The Coast Guard deactivated Ponce de Leon Inlet Light in 1972 but returned it to service ten years later after a newer light tower at nearby Smyrna Dunes proved inadequate. Now equipped with an aeromarine optic, the old tower displays a flashing light with a range of about 17 miles. The Coast Guard still maintains the beacon, but the tower, residences, and other station property are owned by the town of Ponce de Leon Inlet and operated as a lighthouse museum—one of the best and most informative in America. A key attraction of the museum is its collection of sparkling lighthouse optics, including the station's original third-order Fresnel lens and a first-order lens that once shone in nearby Cape Canaveral Light. ::

Port Isabel Light

Location: Port Isabel, Texas

Established: 1852

Tower height: 57 feet

Elevation of focal plane: 82 feet

Optic: Fresnel lens (removed)

Status: Deactivated in 1905

During the Mexican War, General Zachary Taylor used Port Isabel as an army camp and staging area for his march southward to Monterrey. Taylor had won his battles against the Mexicans and been elected president of the United States by 1850, when Point Isabel was chosen as the site for a key south Texas light station. Completed in 1852, the station guided mariners faithfully until the Civil War darkened its lantern. On May 13, 1865, the last battle of the war—ironically, a Confederate victory—was fought at Palmitto Ranch, practically in the shadow of the brick tower.

Following the war, the station was repaired and its light restored. During the 1880s a local property owner filed a lawsuit claiming the US government had no title to the land on which the lighthouse stood. The government lost the suit and

The Port Isabel Lighthouse in Texas was built during the decade before the Civil War. That fratricidal conflict raged all around the light station at Port Isabel where the final battle of the war was fought and, ironically, won by the Confederates.

Bruce Roberts

ended up having to buy back its light station for approximately $5,000.

Deactivated in 1905, the Port Isabel Lighthouse stood empty and abandoned for decades—far longer, in fact, than it served as an active aid to navigation. In recent years, however, a new purpose has been found for the station. Lovingly restored, it serves as the focus of an ongoing campaign to promote tourism and community spirit in the town of Port Isabel, Texas. ::

Portland Bill Light

Portland Bill Light

Location: Near Weymouth, England
Established: 1716
Tower height: 134 feet
Elevation of focal plane: 141 feet
Optic: Fresnel lens (first-order)
Status: Active (automated in 1996)

Biting into the sea like the beak of some great stony bird, Portland Bill off England's southern coast creates swirling currents so powerful that vessels caught up in them may never break free again. To guide mariners through these hazardous waters, Trinity House authorized establishment of two beacons known as the Upper & Lower Portland Bill Lights. Built by a private consortium about 1716, separate Upper & Lower Portland Bill towers were fitted with enclosed lanterns and lit with coal fires. Unfortunately, these beacons did not prove particularly useful to mariners, partly because they were poorly maintained. On many occasions, the operators did not even bother to light the fires.

In the 1750s Trinity House terminated the private lease and took possession of the towers. In 1789, the Portland Bill Lighthouses became the first in England to be equipped with oil-burning Argand lamps. The bright lights produced by these innovative devices were further enhanced by highly polished reflectors. Eventually, the lamps and reflectors were replaced by even more efficient Fresnel lenses.

The Upper & Lower towers were rebuilt by Trinity House in 1869 and then replaced by a completely new lighthouse shortly after 1900. Its light signal is still focused by a first-order Fresnel lens, and the station continues to guide mariners safely past Portland Bill. Although they are no longer lighted, the 1869 towers still stand. The lower tower is used as a wildlife observatory. ::

Portland Head Light

Location: Near Portland, Maine

Established: 1791

Tower height: 80 feet

Elevation of focal plane: 101 feet

Optic: Aeromarine beacon

Status: Active (automated in 1989)

Some consider Portland Head Light the most beautiful lighthouse in America, and they may very well be right. Rising from a spectacular headland a few miles east of Portland, Maine, the old stone tower and rambling, red-roofed keeper's residence at Portland Head make great subjects for artists and photographers who arrive by the busload nearly every afternoon during the summer.

Students of history also flock here because Portland Head's past is as remarkable as its scenery. Construction of the fieldstone Portland Head tower was the first major project shouldered by the US federal government. Not long after taking office in 1789, President George Washington urged Congress to make lighthouse construction a priority. The Commonwealth of Massachusetts had already begun work on Portland Head Light, but, saddled by debts left over from the Revolutionary War, it soon ran out of money. To get the project moving again, Washington turned to Congress,

No less scenic than it is historic, the eighteenth-century Portland Head Lighthouse (above) in Maine attracts droves of summertime photographers. Perched on a similarly spectacular rocky cliff, Portland Bill Light (opposite page) has its warm-weather admirers as well. Both stations date to the eighteenth century.

Bruce Roberts

For many years Portland Head used a cannon as a fog signal.

but he managed to squeeze out of it a tight-fisted appropriation of only $1,500. The builders saved money on materials by gathering stones in nearby fields and hauling them to the construction site with the help of oxen. Despite repeated delays caused by storms and short funding, the tower was ready for service by January 1791.

Originally a little more than 70 feet tall, the tower was raised to its current height in 1885. Beginning in 1851 a Fresnel lens focused the Portland Head beacon; a modern automated optic

was installed in 1989. Flashing white every four seconds, the beacon can be seen for a distance of up to 24 nautical miles.

The station's first keeper, Joseph Greenleaf, tended the light until 1796. A long list of keepers followed in Greenleaf's footsteps, but none of them held the post of keeper longer than Joshua Strout. He came to Portland Head in 1869 and remained for thirty-five years, raising a large family in the station's wood-frame residence. Joseph Strout replaced his father as keeper in 1904 and served until 1928. ::

Portsmouth Harbor Light

Location: Portsmouth, New Hampshire
Established: 1771
Tower height: 48 feet
Elevation of focal plane: 52 feet
Optic: Fresnel lens (fourth-order)
Status: Active (automated in 1960)

Portsmouth Harbor Light is one of the oldest navigational beacons in North America, established five years before the signing of the Declaration of Independence. Not surprisingly, over its more than two centuries of service, the station has changed substantially, and the existing lighthouse is very unlike the one that stood during the eighteenth century. As a matter of fact, during the station's early years, it had no tower at all. Mariners arriving at Portsmouth were forced to rely on the meager guidance of a lantern hung from a pole near the harbor entrance.

Construction of an 80-foot octagonal wooden tower at Fort Constitution in 1784 gave Portsmouth its first conventional lighthouse. Damaged by the concussion of cannon fire at the fort, this tower was replaced by another octagonal structure in 1804. Located a relatively safe distance from the fort's powerful guns, the new tower lasted until 1877, when the existing cast-iron cylinder tower was put in its place. The fixed green beam

The existing cast-iron Portsmouth Harbor tower dates to the 1870s.

from this lighthouse, visible for about 12 miles, still guides vessels today.

Historical records show visits by many important persons to the Portsmouth Lighthouse over the years, among them General Lafayette, Daniel Webster, Henry David Thoreau, and President George Washington. It is said an early Portsmouth Harbor Light keeper was fired because Washington was dissatisfied with the appearance of the station. ∷

The old Presque Isle tower (above) is said to have a resident ghost. Interestingly, some believe the 1870 Presque Isle Light (below) is haunted as well.

Bruce Roberts

Presque Isle Light (Old)

Location: Presque Isle, Michigan

Established: 1840

Tower height: 38 feet

Elevation of focal plane: 36 feet

Optic: Fresnel lens (removed)

Status: Deactivated in 1870)

The original Presque Isle Lighthouse served mariners for little more than thirty years before it was replaced by a much taller and more effective tower nearby. However, the old stone structure still stands and has become a popular summertime tourist destination. A big part of its attraction lies in the resident ghost said to haunt the lantern and to shine a phantom beacon out over the lake waters in times of need. ∷

Presque Isle Light

Location: Presque Isle, Michigan

Established: 1871

Tower height: 109 feet

Elevation of focal plane: 113 feet

Optic: Fresnel lens (third-order)

Status: Active (automated in 1970)

In 1871 the Lighthouse Board ordered construction of a tall brick tower and adjacent keeper's residence at Presque Isle on Michigan's Lake Huron. The new station took over the duties of an earlier lighthouse, which had marked this stretch of lakeshore since

New Presque Isle

Bruce Roberts

1840. Although still an active maritime beacon, the station features an attractive museum in its two-story keeper's dwelling. ::

Psathoura Alonnisos Light

Location: Alonnisos, Greece
Established: 1895
Tower height: 58 feet
Elevation of focal plane: 135 feet
Optic: Aeromarine beacon (solar-powered)
Status: Active

Psathoura Alonnisos Light
Courtesy Harbour Lights

No doubt ancient Greek mariners navigated with the help of seamarks and, perhaps, lighted beacons as well, but few could have been as effective as the Psathoura Alonnisos lighthouse. For more than a century its powerful light has guided vessels through the northern reaches of the Aegean Sea. Its flashing light signal, now produced by a modern aeromarine beacon, can be spotted from up to 17 miles away. Electricity for the beacon is drawn from batteries recharged by solar panels. This and other Greek light stations are maintained by the Hellenic Lighthouse Service.

Although not particularly tall, the cylindrical Psathoura Alonnisos tower is striking. The masonry structure was built with brown or ruddy stones of many different sizes and shapes, leaving it with an appearance suggestive of an ancient ruin. The offshore area near the tower is now a preserve for Mediterranean seals. ::

Punta Mogote Light

Location: Mar del Plata, Argentina
Established: 1891
Tower height: 107 feet
Elevation of focal plane: 180 feet
Optic: Fresnel lens
Status: Active

One of many navigational stations operated by Argentina's Servicio de Hidrografía Naval, the Punta Mogote lighthouse dates to 1891. Painted with red and white bands, the tower marks an important

stretch of coast off Buenos Aires and is a familiar sight to seamen headed for Argentina's capital city. At night the station guides mariners with a bright white flash displayed every ten seconds. ::

Race Rock Light

Location: Near Fishers Island, New York
Established: 1879
Tower height: 45 feet
Elevation of focal plane: 67 feet
Optic: Aeromarine beacon
Status: Active (automated in 1978)

Race Rock Light is an outstanding example of engineering and construction executed under great difficulties. The station stands on an artificial island near the northeastern end of Long Island Sound. Building a light tower on Race Rock, an underwater ledge subjected to strong currents, was once thought impossible. However, a feasible plan was developed during the 1870s by engineer F. Hopkinson Smith, who later won fame as an author of lighthouse stories and as the architect who designed the foundation for the Statue of Liberty.

Constructing Race Rock's 10,000-ton underwater stone foundation took five years and cost nearly $250,000—an astronomical sum at the time. An additional $30,000 and three years were needed to complete the lighthouse, which began operation in 1879. Many would say the structure was well worth its considerable price as it has no doubt saved countless ships and lives during its one-and-a-quarter centuries of continuous operation.

The station consists of a square granite tower and attached keeper's residence. For nearly a century, the isolated residence was occupied full-time, but it has been vacant since the station was automated in 1978. The station's light continues to warn mariners with alternate red and white lights visible from as far as 14 miles away. Once focused by a fourth-order Fresnel lens, the light signal is now produced by an aeromarine beacon. ::

Punta Mogote Light
(opposite page bottom)
Courtesy Lighthouse Digest

Race Rock Light (right)
Bob and Sandra Shanklin

Now an ocean research station, the Race Rocks Lighthouse guards a dangerous outcropping of rocks near Victoria, British Columbia. Instead of rocks, miles of sandy shallows are the primary threat to shipping off Scotland's Rattray Head (opposite page lower).

Courtesy *Lighthouse Digest*

Race Rocks Light

Location: Sooke, British Columbia

Established: 1860

Tower height: 105 feet

Elevation of focal plane: 118 feet

Optic: Aeromarine beacon

Status: Active (automated in 1977)

Rising like great, stony whales from the waters off the southern tip of Vancouver Island, the Race Rocks rank among the most dangerous obstacles along the Pacific coast of North America. Recognizing the considerable threat they posed to shipping, Canadian maritime officials ordered construction of a lighthouse here in 1860. Stones for the tower were quarried and cut to size in Scotland then shipped halfway around the world to the construction site. There they were assembled, block by massive block, and the station was ready for duty just a few weeks after the Fisgard Light at nearby Esquimalt Harbor began to shine.

The Race Rocks Light began operation on December 22, 1860. Had the beacon been in service just a few days earlier, it might have saved the *Nanette,* a three-masted freighter lost on the rocks, along with a valuable cargo. Fortunately, the vessel's entire crew made it safely ashore, thanks to the timely assistance from the keeper of the not-yet-operational lighthouse.

Often cloaked in fog, the Race Rocks continued to claim ships even after the beacon became active. Among the vessels that foundered here were the *Nichola Biddle* in 1867, *Swordfish* in 1877, *Rosedale* in 1882, *Tess* in 1896, *Prince Victor* in 1901, and the ferry *Sechelt,* lost in 1911 along with fifty passengers. Most of these tragedies were attributed to the inadequacies of the station's foghorn, which was plagued for decades by a mysterious "silent zone" that seemed to block the otherwise deafening sound signal. Apparently the rocks and the great stone tower itself deflected the sound in such a way that it could not be heard, sometimes even from a short distance. Eventually, the problem was solved by moving the foghorn to a separate structure some distance from the tower.

Among the last in North America to lose its full-time keepers, the station was automated in 1997. Today the residence and other station buildings are used as an ocean research center. ⁘

Rattray Head Light

Location: Rattray, Scotland
Established: 1895
Tower height: 112 feet
Elevation of focal plane: 112 feet
Optic: Fresnel lens
Status: Active (automated in 1982)

Sandcastles wash away at high tide, but not this one. Northern Lighthouse Board engineer David Stevenson built Scotland's Rattray Head Light on a beach, but he gave it a fortress-like base to protect it from the tides. The massive base doubled as a fog-signal building and was able to accommodate a sizable late-nineteenth-century steam-driven compressor. The station still guides mariners with both light and sound signals. The flashing beacon can be seen for up to 24 nautical miles. ::

Rattray Head Light
Courtesy *Lighthouse Digest*

Rawley Point Light

Location: Twin Rivers, Wisconsin
Established: 1853
Tower height: 111 feet
Elevation of focal plane: 113 feet
Optic: Aeromarine beacon
Status: Active (automated in 1979)

The white steel tower of Rawley Point Light has warned mariners away from the deadly shoals off Wisconsin's Twin Rivers for more than a century, but the stately structure began its career as a World's Fair exhibit. A highlight of the 1893 Chicago Columbian Exposition, it was later dismantled and moved to Rawley Point, where it took the place of an earlier brick tower. Like many steel-skeleton towers, this one has an enclosed central cylinder containing a staircase for access to the lantern room. The ornate double gallery at the top, somewhat suggestive of a multilayer wedding cake, is an artifact of the tower's early career as a world's fair crowd pleaser. ::

Rawley Point Light
Bruce Roberts

Rock of Ages Light

Location: Near Isle Royale, Michigan

Established: 1908

Tower height: 117 feet

Elevation of focal plane: 130 feet

Optic: Modern

Status: Active (automated in 1978)

Keepers and their assistants once lived for months at a stretch inside the narrow steel tower of the Rock of Ages Light. They usually had little or no contact with the mainland and received mail and supplies only when lighthouse tenders made their sporadic visits. The sacrifices made by the lonely Rock of Ages keepers were necessary, for the light they tended marked one of the most dangerous obstacles in all the Great Lakes. Unfortunately, the station's powerful light was unable to save the

Rock of Ages Light

Bruce Roberts

freighter *George Cox*, lost on a nearby reef in 1933. Pulled from the wreck by the Rock of Ages crew, more than a hundred survivors huddled inside the tower until a ship arrived to take them ashore. Today the beacon is fully automated and requires only occasional visits by Coast Guard personnel. The station's original second-order Fresnel lens is now on display at the Isle Royal National Park information center in Windigo. ::

Rockland Breakwater Light

Location: Rockland, Maine

Established: 1902

Tower height: 25 feet

Elevation of focal plane: 39 feet

Optic: Modern

Status: Active (automated in 1964)

Because of their exposed location and vulnerability to the elements, breakwater lighthouses were seldom made of wood. However, a particularly fine example of a wooden breakwater lighthouse can be found in Rockland, Maine, once a bustling port where enormous quantities of construction stone were loaded onto freighters.

In 1888 the Lighthouse Board built an extensive breakwater at Rockland to protect vessels lying at anchor in the harbor from high waves rolling in off the ocean. In 1902 the breakwater was extended to a length of more than a mile, with a lighthouse at its outer end to guide mariners around the formidable man-made obstacle. The square, 25-foot wooden tower and attached two-story wooden dwelling sat atop a solid platform of squared-off granite blocks, a brick fog-signal building nearby.

The station has been partially restored through the efforts of a local lighthouse organization and remains in operation. Its modern optic (a replacement for the original fourth-order Fresnel lens) flashes white once every five seconds. The foghorn alerts vessels with blasts every fifteen seconds. ::

A number of strategies have been devised to protect lighthouses from the elements. A massive iron-and-concrete caisson lifts the Rock of Ages tower (opposite page) above damaging waves and winter ice on Lake Superior. A hefty stone platform shields the Rockland Breakwater Lighthouse (above) from ocean swells.

Bruce Roberts

Saddleback Ledge Light

Location: Isle au Haut Bay near Vinalhaven, Maine

Established: 1839

Tower height: 42 feet

Elevation of focal plane: 52 feet

Optic: Modern

Status: Active (automated in 1954)

Legendary for its isolation and exposure to storms, Saddleback Ledge Light clings to a barren rock about halfway between the islands of Isle au Haut and Vinalhaven. Despite its precarious location, the station and its cone-shaped stone tower have proven remarkably durable. Designed by noted nineteenth-century architect Alexander Parris, the tower has stood up to the very worst the Atlantic could throw at it since 1839.

For more than a century, keepers lived on the ledge to maintain the station's vital fog signal and beacon, which for many years was focused by a fourth-order Fresnel lens. Usually, the keeping crew was housed in cramped quarters inside the tower itself. Crewmembers must have been hardy individuals with considerable tolerance for isolation, for they were often marooned here for months at a time. The station's last keepers left the ledge in 1954, when its light was finally automated. ::

Saddleback Ledge Light

Bruce Roberts

Sambro Island Light

Location: Halifax, Nova Scotia

Established: 1760

Tower height: 80 feet

Elevation of focal plane: 135 feet

Optic: Aeromarine beacon

Status: Active (automated in 1988)

Although it was built in 1760 and is widely recognized as the oldest continuously operational lighthouse in North America, Sambro Island Light does not look its age. Painted with showy red and white bands, the old octagonal stone tower has a deceptively modern appearance. The station's age is of far less importance to mariners than its ability to guide them into Halifax Harbor, a task it handles with twenty-first-century efficiency.

The old tower owes its existence to a 1758 vote of the Nova Scotia General Assembly, which set aside £1,000 for its construction. The assembly raised the money by levying a tax on imported liquors, and two years after the vote was taken, the station was complete. Since that time it has guided a veritable parade of notables to Halifax, among them the famed explorer James Cook. Even while the tower was still under construction, General James Wolfe made use of it to guide his British war fleet to Halifax. Wolfe lost his life in 1759 while leading a successful assault on French-held Quebec. The station's original lens can be seen at the Maritime Museum of the Atlantic in Haifax, Nova Scotia. **::**

Sand Hills Light

Location: Near Eagle River, Michigan

Established: 1919

Tower height: 70 feet

Elevation of focal plane: 91 feet

Optic: Fresnel lens (removed)

Status: Deactivated in 1954

Sand Hills Light

Bruce Roberts

Sambro Island Light

Bob and Sandra Shanklin

An imposing brick building with a square tower rising from its roof, Michigan's Sand Hills Lighthouse served as an active light station for only about thirty-five years. The station was established in

1919 and deactivated during the 1950s. Afterward, the abandoned structure stood empty for decades, suffering greatly from weather and neglect. Its walls remained solid, however, and in the 1990s a local businessman was able to refurbish it for use as a bed-and-breakfast. The inn offers a view of Lake Superior as well as a taste of life in a Great Lakes lighthouse. ::

Sand Island Light

Location: Near Mobile, Alabama
Established: 1838
Tower height: 131 feet
Elevation of focal plane: 132 feet
Optic: Fresnel lens (removed)
Status: Deactivated in 1971

Under assault on all sides by the waters of the Gulf of Mexico, Alabama's Sand Island Light is one of the world's most threatened historic structures. It may very well have collapsed before you read this

Sand Island Light
Bruce Roberts

or might even fall while you hold this book in your hands. Abandoned more than four decades ago by the Coast Guard, the old tower had few friends until the late 1990s, when a local preservation group was formed to seek a way to save it. The struggle to save the historic structure continues as the tower is threatened anew each hurricane season.

Completed in 1872, the 131-foot structure took the place of earlier towers built in 1838 and 1859. The construction crew that built the big tower endured major storms and a yellow fever epidemic during their time on the job. Hard times continued after the structure was in service: A 1906 hurricane washed away the keeper's dwelling along with the keeper and his wife. ::

Sand Key Light

Location: Near Key West, Florida
Established: 1827
Tower height: 120 feet
Elevation of focal plane: 105 feet
Optic: Modern (solar-powered)
Status: Active (automated in 1941)

Its sands exposed only at low tide, Sand Key itself barely exists, but the big iron-skeleton lighthouse built here in 1853 by George Meade still stands. An earlier brick lighthouse built in 1827 vanished—along with all of Sand Key's dry land—in the mighty October 1846 hurricane. The same storm carried away the station's keeper, two members of his family, and a friend who happened to be visiting at the time.

The extraordinary durability of the existing tower is due to its iron-skeleton design. Since its walls are mostly open, gale-force winds can pass through harmlessly. A forest of stoutly braced iron legs, each of them anchored by screw piles, holds the lantern aloft. The station's flashing beacon is now solar powered and visible for about 13 nautical miles. ::

Sand Key Light
Bruce Roberts

merchants to increase commerce, the octagonal rubblestone tower is the oldest existing lighthouse in the United States. (Although Boston Harbor Light was established in 1716, its tower did not survive the Revolutionary War and was completely rebuilt in 1783.) The Sandy Hook tower was built by expert stonemason Isaac Conro. Like Boston's tower, Conro's lighthouse took considerable abuse from both British and Continental forces during the Revolutionary War, but it remained intact when the conflict ceased.

Originally known as New York Lighthouse, the station eventually became the object of a legal tug-of-war between New York and New Jersey. The squabble was settled once and for all in 1789, when the US federal government took possession of the station buildings and property.

When the Lighthouse Board inspectors examined all US lighthouses in 1852, they found this one to be in particularly good shape. Their report reads: "The tower of Sandy Hook . . . constructed in 1764, under royal charter . . . is now in a good state of preservation. Neither leaks nor cracks were observed in it." However, the board took a dim view of the station's lamp-and-reflector optic and replaced it in 1857 with a third-order Fresnel lens. That same lens still focuses the Sandy Hook beacon, visible for about 15 miles at sea.

Sandy Hook Light

Location: Near Highlands, New Jersey

Established: 1764

Tower height: 85 feet

Elevation of focal plane: 88 feet

Optic: Fresnel lens (third-order)

Status: Active (automated in 1965)

For nearly two and a half centuries, vessels bound for the bustling wharves along the Hudson River have looked to New Jersey's Sandy Hook Light for guidance. Built in 1764 by New York City

Sandy Hook • New Jersey

Courtesy Harbour Lights

Destroyed by Earthquake and Tsunami

Among the earliest navigational beacons on the West Coast, the Santa Barbara Light guided vessels through the Santa Barbara Channel from 1856 until 1925, when the station was destroyed by an earthquake. Like many early lighthouses built in the region in the 1850s, Santa Barbara Light consisted of a modest dwelling with a central tower rising through its roof. The station displayed a fixed red light, later changed to fixed white.

The Santa Barbara Lighthouse was home to one of America's longest-serving keepers, Julia F. Williams, who tended the light for more than forty years. She came to California with her husband, Albert, during the Gold Rush era. Albert was appointed keeper at Santa Barbara in 1856, but Julia Williams soon took over her husband's duties. In addition to keeping the light faithfully until 1905, she raised three boys and two girls at the station.

The end for Santa Barbara Light began with a rumble early on the morning of June 29, 1925. Fortunately, the earthquake's initial jolt threw the young keeper and his family out of bed, and they were able to escape before the building collapsed. When the shaking stopped, nothing remained of the historic structure but a pile of broken masonry and shattered lens prisms.

Also felled by an earthquake was Alaska's Unimak Island Lighthouse, but in this case, the agent of destruction was not the shaking itself but rather the powerful tsunami it generated. Having replaced an earlier structure only a few years before, the blocky, Art Deco–style lighthouse was still relatively new on April 1, 1946, when the ground began to tremble. Apparently the reinforced concrete building survived the initial shock of the quake, but not the mighty tidal wave that hit less than a half hour later. Striking at the speed of a jet airplane, the wave crushed the station, killing all five of its Coast Guard crewmen.

Like the Santa Barbara Lighthouse below, the Scotch Cap Light station (above) in Alaska succumbed to natural disaster. A tidal wave swept it away along with its entire crew in 1946.
Bob and Sandra Shanklin

Victim of a 1920s earthquake, the Santa Barbara Lighthouse no longer exists. The keeper and his family escaped before the building collapsed.
Photo Courtesy *Lighthouse Digest*

Shown as it appeared during the nineteenth century, the Sandy Hook Lighthouse (left) in northern New Jersey has changed little over the centuries. It is America's oldest still-standing light tower. The Seguin Island Light (below) also is no youngster. It was completed in 1795 while George Washington was still president.

Now part of the Gateway National Recreation Area, Sandy Hook Light underwent a $600,000 restoration in 2000. The National Park Service maintains station structures, but the US Coast Guard remains responsible for the light. ::

Seguin Island Light

Location: Near Georgetown, Maine
Established: 1795
Tower height: 53 feet
Elevation of focal plane: 180 feet
Optic: Fresnel lens (first-order)
Status: Active (automated in 1985)

One of several important light stations established during the presidency of George Washington, Seguin Island Light stands on the seaward side of a rugged island near the mouth of Maine's Kennebec River. The original wooden tower was destroyed by a storm in 1819. The existing granite structure dates to 1857, as does the station's first-order Fresnel lens. Although the tower's height is relatively modest, the elevation of the site gives it a significant boost, placing the focal plane of the light a lofty 180 feet above sea level. Often the flashing beacon can be seen for more than 18 miles.

Over the years, Seguin Island Light had more than forty keepers, the first a Revolutionary War soldier named John Polersky. It is said that the hard work and terrible weather ruined Polersky's health, and he died after only a few years on the job. In fact, few keepers could long endure the isolation and harsh conditions they faced on Seguin Island. John Salter proved hardy enough to remain at the station from 1825 until 1839, while Frank Bracey remained on duty from 1926 until 1945, but the average tenure for keepers was little more than four years. ::

Bruce Roberts

This photograph shows Alaska's Sentinel Island as it looked more than half a century ago, when the light station here still had full-time keepers and supplies were brought in by tender from Ketchikan. Unloaded at the dock on the right, food, fuel, and other materials were carried over an elevated walkway and up the hill to the lighthouse.

US Coast Guard

Sentinel Island Light

Location: Near Juneau, Alaska

Established: 1902

Tower height: 51 feet

Elevation of focal plane: 86 feet

Optic: Modern (solar-powered)

Status: Active (automated in 1966)

For more than a century, the Sentinel Island beacon has guided vessels moving in and out of Juneau, Alaska's capital city. The station was established during the Alaskan and Klondike Gold Rush years at the turn of the twentieth century, but the current reinforced concrete tower dates to 1935. The stark, modernist style of the main structure is typical of Alaska's existing lighthouses, most of which were built when Art Deco architecture was in vogue. Like a number of American light stations in Alaska and elsewhere, this one is now leased to a local organization dedicated to preserving it. The Coast Guard maintains the light, which is produced by a solar-powered Vega optic. ::

Seul Choix Point Light

Location: Gulliver, Michigan

Established: 1895

Tower height: 78 feet

Elevation of focal plane: 80 feet

Optic: Aeromarine beacon

Status: Active (automated in 1972)

French explorers recognized the harbor beyond Seul Choix Point as one of the few safe anchorages along the northern shore of Lake Michigan. Hence, their name for the site—which translates as "only choice." Seul Choix Point Light has been guiding vessels to this harbor of last refuge for more than

The living ocean looks especially lively as it lays siege to Scotland's Skerryvore Lighthouse (below). Designed by Alan Stevenson, the tower has been described as a "perfect structure." It has at least been good enough to withstand 170 years of pounding by waves. The summertime view of Michigan's Seul Choix tower (above) is perfectly lovely.

Bruce Roberts

a century. The brick tower and adjacent keeper's residence date to 1895. Both are now managed by a local historical society that operates them as a museum during the summer. ::

Skerryvore Light

Location: Off the west coast of Scotland

Established: 1844

Tower height: 157 feet

Elevation of focal plane: 151 feet

Optic: Fresnel lens

Status: Active (automated 1994)

Claimed to be a nearly perfect structure, the gently tapered Skerryvore Light tower was the masterpiece of prolific lighthouse designer Alan Stevenson. Although built nearly 170 years ago, the gray granite pillar remains to this day the tallest light tower in the British Isles. It marks a scatter of wave-swept rocks that have claimed many vessels. The interior of the tower is far from spacious, and chambers are reached by means of ladders rising through narrow vertical passageways. Despite the close quarters, keepers lived and worked here full time for more than a century. Getting to and from the station was no simple matter and impossible during gales. A major Atlantic storm could trap keepers here for days if not weeks at a time. ::

Skerryvore Light

Copyright Jean Guichard

Split Rock Light

Location: Two Harbors, Minnesota

Established: 1910

Tower height: 44 feet

Elevation of focal plane: 168 feet

Optic: Fresnel lens (third-order bivalve)

Status: Deactivated in 1969

Considered by many the most beautiful lighthouse on the Great Lakes, the yellow brick Split Rock tower crowns a craggy granite cliff a few miles

northwest of Two Harbors, Minnesota. Built by immigrant laborers in 1910, the tower guided ore freighters along the northwestern shore of Lake Superior for more than a half century. Split Rock Light now serves as a museum and historic attraction. Visitors who come here are treated to an unparalleled view of Lake Superior, as well as a close-up inspection of an early-twentieth-century lighthouse kept in excellent condition. ::

Split Rock Light (above) and St. Augustine Light (below)

Photos by Bruce Roberts

St. Augustine Light

Location: St. Augustine, Florida
Established: 1823
Tower height: 165 feet
Elevation of focal plane: 161 feet
Optic: Fresnel lens (first-order)
Status: Active (automated in 1955)

The Spanish may have maintained a navigational beacon at St. Augustine as early as the sixteenth century, but no one knows for certain. Federal customs officials found a modest tower here after the United States took possession of Florida in 1821. Remodeled and reinforced, the 30-foot structure became Florida's first official lighthouse. Thirty-four years later, the tower was raised to 52 feet and fitted with a fourth-order Fresnel lens. Like most Southern lighthouses, the St. Augustine lanterns were kept dark during the Civil War.

Following the war, the Lighthouse Board adopted a policy of marking the flat, often featureless Southern coastline with exceptionally tall towers. Consequently, a 165-foot brick tower was built at St. Augustine and equipped with a first-order Fresnel lens. The tower, adjacent keeper's residence, and storage structures were completed in 1874 and cost the government $105,000. The money was well spent: The station's huge lens still helps guide vessels with its fixed white beacon, visible up to 19 miles at sea. The lighthouse tower has another current use—its distinctive black and white stripes spiraling up into the sky make an impressive landmark. A museum in

the keeper's residence contains lighthouse exhibits and shipwreck artifacts. Energetic visitors are allowed to climb the sixteen-story tower. ::

St. Catherine's Light

Location: Isle of Wight, England
Established: 1323
Tower height: 285 feet
Elevation of focal plane: 435 feet
Optic: Fresnel lens (second-order)
Status: Active (automated in 1997)

One of the oldest navigational beacons in the British Isles or, for that matter, the world, St. Catherine's Light dates to the fourteenth century. When Walter de Godeton built the original tower in 1323, the Hundred Years War between England and France had only just begun. The medieval tower has vanished, although the ruins of St. Catherine's Oratory, a chapel built here at about the same time, still stand.

Today the St. Catherine's beacon shines from atop a bright white octagonal structure, which is itself more than 160 years old. Produced by a second-order Fresnel lens, the light signal marks the southern tip of the Isle of Wight with a flashing beacon visible for up to 30 nautical miles. During World War II, the German Luftwaffe bombed the station, killing three keepers. ::

St. David's Light

Location: St. David's Island, Bermuda
Established: 1879
Tower height: 55 feet
Elevation of focal plane: 208 feet
Optic: Fresnel lens (second-order)
Status: Active (automated in 1964)

While the Gibbs Hill Lighthouse guards the western end of Bermuda, the island's eastern side is marked by a brightly painted red and white tower on St. David's Island. Completed in November

St. Catherine's Light
Courtesy *Lighthouse Digest*

St. David's Light
Henry Gonzales

The St. Joseph Pier Lights in Michigan are so attractive they've been celebrated on a US Postal Service stamp. The stark white tower at St. Simons is no less impressive. (opposite page, left)

Bruce Roberts

1879, the octagonal masonry structure was fitted with a second-order Fresnel lens. Although the tower is only 55 feet tall from the ground to its lantern room, the elevation of its site places the focal plane of the light more than 200 feet above the Atlantic. ::

St. Joseph Pier Lights

Location: St. Joseph, Michigan

Established: 1907

Tower heights: 57 feet (inner tower), 35 feet (outer tower)

Elevation of focal planes: 53 feet (inner tower), 31 feet (outer tower)

Optics: Fresnel lens (inner tower); modern (outer tower)

Status: Active

Counted among the most beautiful and distinctive light towers in America, Michigan's St. Joseph Pier Lights have been featured on a US postage stamp. Like other Great Lakes pier lights, these serve as range beacons for vessels approaching the harbor. The lights appear in vertical alignment when seen from the middle of the safe channel. Both towers are cast-iron structures. The inner one stands on top of a square fog-signal building. ::

St. Simons Island Light

Location: St. Simons Island, Georgia

Established: 1810

Tower height: 104 feet

Elevation of focal plane: 106 feet

Optic: Fresnel lens (third-order)

Status: Active (automated in 1953)

A 75-foot tower of brick and coquina, a soft stone made up of compressed oyster shells and coral, marked Georgia's St. Simons Island as early as 1810. To prevent fires, the station's lamps were suspended in the lantern room with chains. All but destroyed by Confederate troops in 1862, the tower and other station structures were rebuilt following the Civil War. The existing brick tower and adjacent

St. Simons Island Light

Bruce Roberts

almost a mile into the sea. At its far end, a tall, white stone cylinder rises boldly from the rock. This is Start Point Light, and it has been guiding mariners in and out of Start Bay since 1838. The tower owes its gothic appearance, much like that of a castle turret, to engineer James Walker, who is better known for building Bishop Rock Light.

During the 1830s Scotland's Alan Stevenson made certain important improvements to the Fresnel lens, and Trinity House first used a Stevenson-style optic at Start Point. Revolved by clockwork machinery, the lens produced two signals, one fixed and the other flashing. The primary beacon still alerts mariners with three quick flashes every ten seconds and is visible for a distance of 25 nautical miles. ::

Victorian-style keeper's residence were completed in 1872. The third-order Fresnel lens placed in the tower at that time remains in use today, focusing a beacon visible for up to 22 nautical miles. The keeper's residence houses a fascinating museum.

A bizarre tragedy struck the station in 1880 when keeper Fred Osborne was shot and killed by his assistant, apparently in self-defense. Some say that Osborne's ghost still haunts the tower. ::

Start Point Light

Location: South Devon, England

Established: 1836

Tower height: 92 feet

Elevation of focal plane: 203 feet

Optic: Fresnel lens (third-order)

Status: Active (automated in 1993)

Along the south side of Start Bay near Dartmouth an exposed and mostly barren peninsula extends

The lofty Start Point Lighthouse likely looked much like this 100 years ago.

Library of Congress

Sturgeon Bay Ship Canal Light

Bruce Roberts

Sturgeon Bay Ship Canal Light

Location: Sturgeon Bay, Wisconsin

Established: 1903

Tower height: 98 feet

Elevation of focal plane: 107 feet

Optic: Fresnel lens (third-order)

Status: Active

Held erect by latticework buttresses, the Sturgeon Bay Ship Canal Light's tower was considered experimental when completed in 1899. The structure must surely have exceeded the expectations of its builders: It has stood up to more than a century of Wisconsin blizzards and Lake Michigan storms. The light continues to guide vessels into the Sturgeon Bay Canal, which offers a shortcut for vessels moving between Lake Michigan and Green Bay. A secondary beacon at the end of a nearby pier accompanies this primary light. ::

Sturgeon Point Light

Location: Alcona, Michigan

Established: 1869

Tower height: 71 feet

Elevation of focal plane: 69 feet

Optic: Fresnel lens (third-order)

Status: Active (automated in 1939)

Following the Civil War, repeated shipping disasters in the waters off Michigan's Sturgeon Point led to construction of this Lake Huron lighthouse. The station's beacon warned vessels away from a nearby reef, but even after it began operation in 1869, the hazardous waters here continued to claim ships and lives. Among the notable wrecks were the wooden steamer *Marine City* (burned in 1880), the schooner *Venus* (lost in 1887), the schooner *Ispeming* (lost in

Sturgeon Point Light

Bruce Roberts

Suances Light
Henry Gonzales

1903), and the freighter *Clifton* (lost in 1924). The original Fresnel lens remains in use more than 140 years after it was installed. Sometimes described as a "lake lens," it is slightly larger and more powerful than a standard third-order Fresnel optic. ::

Suances Light

Location: Cantabrian coast of Spain
Established: 1863
Tower height: 30 feet
Elevation of focal plane: 115 feet
Optic: Reflecting
Status: Active

Although quite modest in height, the Suances tower gets a sufficient boost from the rugged cliffs of northern Spain to place the focal plane of its light more than 100 feet above the waves. The station's revolving optic features reflectors capable

of producing a beacon visible for more than 20 miles at sea. Protected from the weather by a terracotta roof, the station residence is still occupied by keepers. ::

Table Cape Light

Location: Near Wynyard, Australia (Tasmania)
Established: 1884
Tower height: 82 feet
Elevation of focal plane: 591 feet
Optic: Fresnel lens (second-order)
Status: Active (automated in 1923)

Built during the nineteenth century to guide timber freighters crossing to Tasmania from the Australian mainland, Table Cape Light was constructed with bricks that had first served as ballast in ships. The lighthouse stands on a flat-topped eminence not far from a sheer cliff dropping several hundred feet to the sea. The nearly 600-foot elevation of its focal plane makes this one of the loftiest navigational lights in the world. Not surprisingly, the flashing beacon has an impressive range, and it can be seen from the decks of vessels more than 30 miles away. ::

Australia can boast a considerable number of nineteenth century lighthouses, among them the Table Cape tower (above) in Tasmania. Courtesy *Lighthouse Digest*

Thomas Point Shoal Light

Location: Near Annapolis, Maryland
Established: 1825
Tower height: 43 feet
Elevation of focal plane: 43 feet
Optic: Modern (solar-powered)
Status: Active (automated in 1986)

Dozens, perhaps hundreds, of cottage-style, screw-pile lighthouses once marked the protected waterways of the southern United States. Of these, only Thomas Point Shoal Light remains in operation at its original site. Perched on iron legs solidly anchored with screw piles to Chesapeake Bay's muddy bottom, the hexagonal lighthouse stands guard over a troublesome navigational obstacle near the middle of the great bay. Tons of stone protect the building from winter ice floes, the nemesis of this and other Chesapeake lighthouses.

The existing open-water structure was built in 1875 and took the place of an onshore lighthouse long considered inadequate by mariners. For more than a century, keepers lived and worked in the station's cramped quarters with only a small launch providing access to shore. ::

Pictured in an old photograph (left), Thomas Point Shoal is the last active screw-pile lighthouse on the Chesapeake Bay. National Archives

Tibbetts Point Light

Location: Cape Vincent, New York

Established: 1827

Tower height: 58 feet

Elevation of focal plane: 69 feet

Optic: Fresnel lens (fourth-order)

Status: Active (automated in 1981)

Located at the far northeastern end of Lake Ontario near the entrance of the St. Lawrence River, Tibbetts Point Light remains a vital aid to navigation. Like many old light stations, however, this one now serves a variety of purposes: museum, youth hostel, and popular summertime destination for lighthouse lovers and photographers. History buffs also find plenty to interest them at Tibbetts Point. For instance, Mohawk war parties once used nearby islands as a gathering place.

The lighthouse, too, claims a long history. The existing brick-and-stucco tower dates to 1854, when it replaced a stone structure that had stood for nearly a generation. The station once depended on whale-oil lamps, but these eventually gave way to oil or kerosene and then to electric bulbs. The station's 150-year-old Fresnel lens is still in use. ::

Tibbetts Point Light

Bruce Roberts

Tower of Hercules Light

Location: La Coruña, Spain

Established: AD 100

Tower height: 161 feet

Elevation of focal plane: 348 feet

Optic: Modern

Status: Active

Considered to be the oldest operational lighthouse in the world, the Tower of Hercules has guided mariners for nearly 2,000 years. Its place in legend is almost as prominent as its status as a maritime marker. According to myth, the hulking stone tower was built by Hercules himself over the bones of a giant he had vanquished in battle. More likely, the tower was erected by order of the Roman emperor

Tower of Hercules Light

Henry Gonzales

Trajan during the second century. An engraved Latin inscription at the foot of the tower mentions an architect who lived during the reign of Trajan. The inscription translates: "Dedicated to Marte Augustus, Cayo Servio Lupo, architect of Aeminium in Lusitania." Regardless of who built it, there can be no doubt of the tower's great age and early use by navigators. Ancient manuscripts mention the tower, and early historians refer to its use by the formidable Roman navy.

Over the centuries, the tower suffered from attacks by Vikings, from cannon fire by Francis Drake's warships, and perhaps most of all, from neglect. By the late sixteenth century little remained of it but tumbled ruins. Repeated efforts to restore the tower and place it back in service as a lighthouse came to naught until 1785, when the Maritime Consulate of Spain's King Charles III undertook a complete reconstruction. It took five years to shore up the walls, armor them with a fresh covering of granite, and place a modern lantern on top.

Since 1790, the Tower of Hercules, also known as La Coruña Light, has served continuously as a navigational beacon. Its light once fueled by olive oil, the lantern room now features a modern optic. The light signal flashes four times each minute and has a range of 23 nautical miles. ::

Tybee Island Light

Location: Tybee Island, Georgia
Established: 1791
Tower height: 154 feet
Elevation of focal plane: 144 feet
Optic: Fresnel lens (first-order)
Status: Active (automated in 1972)

Although officially established in 1791, when the US federal government was only about two years old, Tybee Island Light was a latecomer in providing navigational aid to mariners off the shores of Tybee. The island's history as a key seamark dates all the way back to the days of Georgia's settlement as a colony.

Tybee Island Light
Bruce Roberts

Georgia's founding father, James Oglethorpe, had a wooden navigational tower built here in 1736, and a lighted tower is said to have stood here as early as 1742. Several subsequent structures of either wood or brick helped mark the island and the nearby entrance to the Savannah River before the station became federal property.

In 1788 the state of Georgia began construction of a massive brick tower on Tybee Island. Completed under federal authority in 1791, it stood about 100 feet tall and was lit with spermaceti candles. A lamp-and-reflector system replaced the candles during the early nineteenth century, and in 1857 a second-order Fresnel lens was installed.

Like many navigational stations in the southern United States, Tybee Island Light suffered considerably during the Civil War. In 1861, retreating Confederate troops destroyed the tower stairway, and Union occupation forces did further damage. By the war's end, the station lay in ruins. A raging cholera epidemic delayed repairs, and restoration was not completed until 1867. However, the work was done well and resulted in a far more impressive Tybee Island light station. Construction crews managed to incorporate the base of the original tower into their massive new structure, which rose more than 150 feet. Fitted with a first-order Fresnel lens able to send its signal nearly 20 miles out to sea, the tower continues to aid mariners today. Now under lease to a local historical society, the tower received major restoration in the 1990s. ::

Umpqua River Light

Location: Near Reedsport, Oregon
Established: 1856
Tower height: 61 feet
Elevation of focal plane: 165 feet
Optic: Fresnel lens (first-order)
Status: Active (automated in 1966)

Built in 1856, during the initial wave of lighthouse construction in the American West, the original Umpqua River lighthouse stood for only a few years before storm-driven tides swept it away. More than thirty years passed before the Lighthouse Board once more focused attention on the central Oregon coast. In 1894 light stations were established here and at Heceta Head, about 40 miles north. The two stations are similar in several respects. The nearly identical brick-and-stucco towers are located on elevated sites, enabling their powerful flashing beacons to reach vessels at considerable distances. Both stations were automated during the 1960s,

Umpqua River Light
Bruce Roberts

but even so, they still make use of their magnificent first-order Fresnel lenses. ::

West Quoddy Head Light

Location: Near Lubec, Maine
Established: 1808
Tower height: 49 feet
Elevation of focal plane: 83 feet
Optic: Fresnel lens (third-order)
Status: Active (automated in 1988)

Lighthouses nearly always sit on prominent points of land or at the mouths of important harbors—places easy to find on a map or navigational chart. However,

West Quoddy Head Light
Bruce Roberts

West Quoddy Head Light
Bruce Roberts

few light towers are more strategically located than this one on Maine's West Quoddy Head. West Quoddy Head is the easternmost point in the United States—its lighthouse is the first structure on US soil to be warmed by the morning sun.

Poised near the edge of a 40-foot cliff overlooking the turbulent Bay of Fundy, the distinctive red-and-white-striped tower points the way to Lubec Channel, a key navigational passage. Just across the narrows is East Quoddy Head on Campobello Island, where a Canadian lighthouse marks the opposite side of the channel entrance. Fishing boats and freighters headed for Lubec, Eastport, and Calais depend on these lights to help them find the channel and avoid dangerous rocks near the shore.

Established in 1808 during the administration of President Thomas Jefferson, the West Quoddy Head light station has served mariners for nearly two centuries. The original rubblestone tower stood until 1858, when it was demolished and replaced by a 49-foot brick tower. The third-order Fresnel lens installed at that time remains in operation, guiding mariners with a flashing light visible more than 18 nautical miles away.

Early West Quoddy Head keepers used bells, steam whistles, and even a cannon to alert fogbound sailors. Now the station's foghorn, located in a separate brick building a short distance from the tower, has an electric eye that senses when the air is moisture-laden. The station buildings and property are now part of Quoddy Head State Park. The former keeper's residence, now the park welcome center, sits near a trail that leads visitors through a stretch of real arctic tundra, a testament to the bleak conditions faced by generations of West Quoddy Head keepers. ::

Westkapelle High Light

Location: Westkapelle, Netherlands
Established: 1815
Tower height: 179 feet
Elevation of focal plane: 161 feet
Optic: Fresnel
Status: Active

Westkapelle High Light
Courtesy *Lighthouse Digest*

One of the world's most unusual navigational aids, Westkapelle High Light consists of a lantern perched on top of an ornate church tower. Located in Zeeland Province on the south coast of the Netherlands, it serves as a "high" or rear range light. The front range tower stands at water's edge on a nearby beach. These beacons are maintained by the Netherlands Ministry of Traffic, Public Works, and Water Management. ::

Whitefish Point Light

Location: Paradise, Michigan
Established: 1848
Tower height: 76 feet
Elevation of focal plane: 80 feet
Optic: Aeromarine beacon
Status: Active

Few lighthouses can claim a more strategic location than the one at Whitefish Point on Michigan's Upper Peninsula. Positioned at the far eastern end of Lake Superior, it marks the entrance to Whitefish Bay and points the way to the locks at Sault Ste. Marie. Vessels caught in one of Lake Superior's notorious autumn storms often use this beacon to help them reach the relatively calm waters of the bay.

The US government acknowledged the importance of Whitefish Point by building Lake Superior's first true lighthouse here in 1848. Eventually, its masonry tower gave way to the existing steel-skeleton structure, which must have seemed ultramodern when it was erected in 1861. The tower's open walls offer little resistance to storm winds, allowing them to pass through without doing damage. As a result, this tower, built at the beginning of the Civil War, still serves mariners.

One group of mariners the beacon could not manage to assist were those aboard the ill-fated *Edmund Fitzgerald,* lost in a blizzard off Whitefish Point in 1975. The *Fitzgerald* did not get close enough to see the light before it broke apart and sank. Ironically, on this tragic day the *Fitzgerald*

Whitefish Point Light
Bruce Roberts

captain could not have seen the light anyway— it had been knocked out of action by the raging storm. Fittingly, Whitefish Point is now home to one of the nation's best maritime attractions, the Great Lakes Shipwreck Museum. ::

Wind Point Light
Bruce Roberts

Wind Point Light

Location: Racine, Wisconsin

Established: 1880

Tower height: 108 feet

Elevation of focal plane: 111 feet

Optic: Aeromarine beacon

Status: Active (automated in 1964)

It took nearly three years to build the tall brick light tower that still marks the harbor entrance at Racine, Wisconsin. Completed in 1880, it replaced an earlier light station never considered entirely satisfactory. During its early years, the station displayed an unusual double beacon produced by a pair of Fresnel optics, one a third-order lens and the other a fifth-order lens. Today the Village of Wind Point manages the station's structures as a historic attraction, while the Coast Guard maintains the automated light. ::

Wolf Trap Light

Location: Near Mathews, Virginia

Established: 1870

Tower height: 52 feet

Elevation of focal plane: 52 feet

Optic: Modern (solar-powered)

Status: Active (automated in 1971)

In 1691 the British warship HMS *Wolfe* ran aground on a notorious shoal near the Virginia shore of the Chesapeake Bay. By unloading the vessel's heavy guns and stores, the crew managed to refloat and save the *Wolfe,* but the shoal was ever after known as the Wolf Trap. Despite the considerable threat it posed to shipping, the shoal was not marked with a light until 1870, when a cottage-style, screw-pile lighthouse was built here. Like many similar Chesapeake Bay screw-pile structures, this one was swept away by winter ice. The existing lighthouse dates to 1893. Set atop a massive cast-iron and concrete caisson, the bright red structure is all but impervious to storms and ice. The light flashes every fifteen seconds. ::

The 1870s cottage-style structure (above) that once marked the treacherous Wolf Trap Shoal in the Chesapeake Bay was eventually knocked off its screw piles by floating ice. In 1893 it was replaced by a more stable caisson lighthouse that still marks the shoal today.

National Archives

APPENDIX

The following organizations are good sources of additional information for anyone interested in lighthouse preservation or in doing further lighthouse research.

National and International Lighthouse Organizations

American Lighthouse Foundation

PO Box 565

Rockland, ME 04841

www.lighthousefoundation.org

Among the nation's most influential lighthouse organizations, the American Lighthouse Foundation is dedicated to the preservation of historic lighthouses throughout America and the world. The foundation spreads the word when historic lighthouses are in trouble and whenever possible contributes money and support for restoration and maintenance. The group, originally known as the New England Lighthouse Foundation, came together in 1994 and since that time has helped save numerous endangered lighthouses, including the Little River lighthouse in Maine and Race Point Light near Provincetown, Massachusetts.

Association of Lighthouse Keepers

www.alk.org.uk

The association website provides a forum for everyone interested in lighthouses. Filled with photography and information on lighthouses around the world, the association journal is called *The Lamp*. Membership is open to everyone.

Australian Lighthouse Association

PO Box 4734

Knox City, VIC 3152

Australia

www.lighthouse.net.au

This association has made its voice heard in the debate over the future of Australian lighthouses.

It maintains an extensive database and helps bring Australia's lighthouse heritage to the attention of the world.

Dutch Lighthouse Association

Frans la Poutre, De Kuiperij 13

7437 CW Bathman

The Netherlands

www.vuurtorens.org

The association's website is in Dutch only but contains information on and photographs of lighthouses in The Netherlands.

Lighthouse Digest Magazine

Foghorn Publishing

PO Box 250

East Machias, ME 04630

The world's most widely distributed monthly lighthouse magazine promotes lighthouse preservation and maintains a "Doomsday List" of threatened lighthouse structures.

National Lighthouse Museum

One Lighthouse Plaza

PO Box 10296

Staten Island, NY 10301-0296

www.lighthousemuseum.org

This exciting national museum is a treasure trove of information on lighthouses throughout America. Located on the site of the old Staten Island Lighthouse Depot, the museum contains America's largest and most comprehensive collection of lighthouse artifacts.

Nova Scotia Lighthouse Preservation Society

c/o Maritime Museum of the Atlantic

1675 Lower Water St.

Halifax, Nova Scotia B3J 1S3

Canada

www.nslps.org

United States Life-Saving Service Heritage Association

PO Box 213

Hull, ME 02045

www.uslife-savingservice.org

The Association helps preserve the history and relics related to the US Lifesaving Service.

United States Lighthouse Society

9005 Point No Point Rd.

Hansville, WA 98340

www.uslhs.org

One of the largest and oldest lighthouse organizations in the world, the society publishes *The Keepers Log* and promotes lighthouse preservation through its various chapters.

World Lighthouse Society

The Anchorage

Craignure, Isle of Mull

Scotland, PA65 6AY

www.worldlighthouses.org

This relatively new organization is attracting a broad membership of individuals interested in preservation of lighthouses around the world.

Local and Regional Lighthouse Organizations

* Recommended lighthouse museum

Absecon Lighthouse*

31 S. Rhode Island Ave.

Atlantic City, NJ 08401

www.abseconlighthouse.org

Beavertail Lighthouse Museum Association*

PO Box 83

Jamestown, RI 02835

www.beavertaillight.org

Bird Island Light Preservation Society

2 Spring St.

Marion, MA 02738

Cape May Lighthouse*

Mid-Atlantic Center for the Arts

1048 Washington St.

PO Box 340

Cape May, NJ 08204

www.capemaymac.org

Chesapeake Bay Maritime Museum, Inc.

PO Box 636

St. Michaels, MD 21663

www.cbmm.org

Chesapeake Chapter United States Lighthouse Society

PO Box 1270

Annandale, VA 22003

www.cheslights.org

This highly active group promotes lighthouse preservation throughout the Chesapeake Bay region.

Currituck Beach Lighthouse

1101 Corolla Village Rd.

PO Box 58

Corolla, NC 27927

www.currituckbeachlight.com

Delaware River & Bay Lighthouse Foundation

PO Box 708

Lewes, DE 19958

www.delawarebaylights.org

Dutch Island Lighthouse Society

PO Box 435

Saunderstown, RI 02874

www.dutchislandlighthouse.org

East Brother Lighthouse, Inc.

117 Park Place

Point Richmond, CA 94801

www.ebls.org

This group operates a very attractive lighthouse bed-and-breakfast at East Brother Light in San Francisco Bay.

Fairport Harbor Marine Museum and Lighthouse★

129 Second St.

Fairport Harbor, OH 44077

www.fairportharbor.org

Florida Lighthouse Association

PO Box 1667

St. Petersburg, FL 33731

www.floridalighthouses.org

Friends of Flying Santa, Inc.

PO Box 80047

Stoneham, MA 02180

www.flyingsanta.com

The Friends fund Christmas flights to New England lighthouses. The flights were begun in the 1920s by Captain William Wincapaw, a pilot who delivered Christmas packages to families living at remote light stations.

Friends of Seguin Island, Inc.

72 Front St.

Bath, ME 04530

www.seguinisland.org

Great Lakes Lighthouse Keepers Association

206 Lake St.

PO Box 219

Mackinaw City, MI 49701

www.gllka.com

One of the most active and effective lighthouse organizations in America, the Association was incorporated in 1983 to preserve lighthouses and lighthouse history; an important association goal is working with young people to "develop a new generation of preservationists."

Great Lakes Shipwreck Historical Society & Museum

18335 N. Whitefish Point Rd.

Paradise, MI 49768

Although its primary focus is shipwrecks, the society operates a fine museum at Whitefish Point on the Michigan Upper Peninsula. The museum features the historic and architecturally unique Whitefish Point Light.

Horton Point Lighthouse and Nautical Museum★

Southold Historical Society

Prince Building, 54325 Main Rd.

PO Box 1

Southhold, NY 11971

www.southoldhistoricalsociety.org

Inland Seas Maritime Museum★

480 Main St.

Vermillion, OH 44089

www.inlandseas.org

This excellent maritime museum offers perspective on the Great Lakes and their lighthouses.

Juneau Lighthouse Association

PO Box 22163

Juneau, AK 99802

www.5fingerlighthouse.com

The nonprofit association is dedicated to the preservation of Alaska's Five Finger Light.

Maine Lighthouse Museum

1 Park Dr.

PO Box F

Rockland, ME 04841

www.mainelighthousemuseum.com

One of the finest lighthouse museums in America, it features an extraordinary collection of Fresnel lenses and other lighthouse equipment.

Montauk Lighthouse Museum★

PO Box 112

Montauk, NY 11954

(631) 685-2544

www.montauklighthouse.com

Morris Island Project

Save the Light, Inc.

PO Box 106

Folly Beach, SC 29439

www.savethelight.org

With government assistance, preservationists at Save the Lighthouse hope to restore the historic Morris Island (Charleston) Light.

Nauset Light Preservation Society

PO Box 941

Eastham, MA 02642

www.nausetlight.org

Outer Banks

Lighthouse Society

PO Box 1005

Morehead City, NC 28557

www.outer-banks.com/lighthouse-society

One of the most active lighthouse groups in America, the society supports lighthouse preservation efforts in North Carolina and throughout America. The society raised public awareness of the plight of the Cape Hatteras Light before its widely publicized move in 1999.

Point Arena Lighthouse and Museum★

PO Box 11

45500 Lighthouse Rd.

Point Arena, CA 95468

www.pointarenalighthouse.com

Ponce de Leon Inlet Lighthouse Museum★

4931 S. Peninsula Dr.

Ponce Inlet, FL 32127

www.ponceinlet.org

One of the best lighthouse museums in the United States or the world, it features a fine array of Fresnel lenses.

Portland Head Light Museum★

1000 Shore Rd.

Cape Elizabeth, ME 04107

www.portlandheadlight.com

This museum focuses on history and relics related to the scenic Portland Head Light.

Project Gurnet & Bug Lights, Inc.

PO Box 2167

Duxbury, MA 02331

www.buglight.org

Rose Island Lighthouse Foundation

PO Box 1419

Newport, RI 02840

www.roseislandlighthouse.org

The foundation operates an attractive bed-and-breakfast at the offshore Rose Island Light.

Sand Island Preservation Group, Inc.

6148 Old Pascagoula Rd.

Theodore, AL 36582

www.sandislandlighthouse.com

This organization is struggling to save one of America's most endangered light towers, Sand Island Light in Mobile Bay.

Sodus Bay Lighthouse Museum★

7066 N. Ontario St.

Sodus Point, NY 14555

www.soduspointlighthouse.org

St. Augustine Lighthouse Museum★

81 Lighthouse Ave.

St. Augustine, FL 32080

www.staugustinelighthouse.com

This museum ranks among America's finest and most popular lighthouse destinations.

Westport Maritime Museum★

2201 Westhaven Dr.

PO Box 1074

Westport, WA 98595

www.westportwa.com/museum

The museum houses the old Destruction Island Fresnel lens and offers tours of the Grays Harbor lighthouse.

INDEX

ABOUT THE AUTHOR

Ray Jones is the author of more than forty books on an extraordinarily wide range of topics including American history, architecture, carpentry, paleontology, and golf. He is the world's most widely published expert on historic lighthouses and has written more than twenty volumes on that topic alone. His award-winning first edition of *Lighthouse Encyclopedia* is considered the definitive treatment of the subject. Ray has also authored or coauthored several highly successful companion books for PBS including *Niagara Falls: An Intimate Portrait, Windows to the Sea, The War of 1812: Guide to Battlefields and Historic Sites,* and *Legendary Lighthouses.*